LAMENTATIONS *IN THE COOL OF THE EVENING*

---WORDS OF THE PROPHET

Red Jordan Arobateau

**LAMENTATIONS
IN THE COOL OF THE EVENING
--Words Of The Prophet.
Copyright c. 2007 by Red Jordan Arobateau.
All rights reserved.**

First combined edition. 2nd editing.

Any resemblance to any person living or dead is purely coincidental.

ISBN: 978-0-6151-6611-7

Published by RED JORDAN PRESS
484 Lake Park Ave. PMB 228
Oakland, CA 94610
USA

A writer's art is a tool for justice.

-- PASSAGE Volume 1

When Adam and Eve ate of the Tree of the Knowledge of good and evil the Creator strolled back to the garden and saw them— they had covered themselves in fig leaves— because they suddenly had the idea that they were naked, and were ashamed, so Creator knew they had eaten the fruit S/He had instructed them not to touch. And Creator sure was mad. Mad! But holding Her peace She went away… Then came back in the cool of the evening to take vengeance.

--WORKS, 2007

Contents:

I. **Lamentations**
II. **Infinite Love**
III. **Handbook for the Daughters Of Courage**
IV. **Midrash/Commentary**
V. **Works**

Editors note: — LAMENTATIONS IN THE COOL OF THE EVENING is a compellation of the first 5 books of JOURNEY, the daily journal/diary of Master Author Red Jordan Arobateau. In the beginning there was not a title for JOURNEY. Since I've put these 5 books of JOURNEY together in one binding I wanted to give the first one a name like the others, hence Lamentations. This first section was used in pieces throughout my Unity of Utopia Sci-Fi series.

How does the city sit solitary that was full of people!
How is she become as a widow! She that was great among the nations, and princess among the provinces, how is she become tributary!

She weepth sore in the night, and her tears are on her cheeks: among all her lovers she has none to comfort her: all her friends have dealt treacherously with her, they are become her enemies.

--Jeremiah 1 1-2

LAMENTATIONS
Journey 1

Editors note; the following section was used in EMPIRE!

1.
The beginning of JOURNEY, so here it is like PASSAGE, with quotes from everything from the Maoist International Newsletter to the Holy Bible.... I am biting out great chunks of life, and the Bancroft and my fans & buyers are purchasing little pieces of it. A sample, 1" thick, on my desk for preparation: **E-MAILS CONCERNING RED'S PLAY PORTRAITS FROM A GHETTOIZED POPULATION, FROM THE CASTING CALLS TO THE FINAL END, 2006**. Going to arrange them in chronological order, bind them and sell to the Bancroft. A copy goes to Jasmin too who wants to see them-- her schedule was too busy to read when they passed by her at the time-- then that is done. Can't publish that on the public market tho, real names in it. Oh, also have stolen a kiss from Rosa Salazar---not on her mouth of course! As she quickly snaps her head away out of reach of my lips when I try. The kiss lands wet, SMACK, on her neck.

What a great gift God has given me! What a magical book PASSAGE is, what an eternal scent wafts in from its pages! Maybe this Journal of days-- this JOURNEY is what's gonna put me over-- into the limelight of public discovery---and into fate. "Red will be read," as the Madame of a quaint fetish brothel once stated, proudly at her mastery of puns, (see Madame V. in her 'ho house in the Outlaw Chronicle Series).

Saw a fellow traveler yesterday-- a bum from whom I turn my head at first glace assuming to be an intrusive insane panhandling pest, but as walked by with a quick step noticed on the sidewalk at his feet an oversize attaché case covered with duct tape & streaked with color, --- and a tell tale folio bulging with painted-on paper of an artist! Another special being of God, another 'set aside' out of the common realm and work-a-day-world. Suffering quite obviously.

I realize now God has filled the sails of my desires with inspiration-- it was my great love to see things in a super interested way and jot it down in verse on paper or a quick sketch in a drawing book--- provided by my Good Father who bought me art & writing supplies on his daily wages as a working man (a desk job, buyer in an office run by Jewish people). Likewise this starving watercolorist on a bench, he is gifted—as well as afflicted. He must persist thru the adversity! And also I am here to inform you that the great artist does not really desire fame—but for their works to survive—if that takes fame, to push their art out of the impermanent shadows of obscurity and invisibility into the blazing light of day within some spotlight, so be it! A great commotion might be needed!

There is a wise saying; 'if de bird gets too big s/he breaks de perch and all de other birds falls down!' Meaning if this bird gets too full-of-itself, puffed up ego, etc., and I don't want to be like that, nor to harm anyone by my works left behind me! *Wise saying just invented by the artist.

Had placed an 8-foot by 4 curb-found mirror in his studio which gazed at him. In it were reflections of surfaces of self. Now it has been replaced by canvass upon which, from out of the well-depths of his soul will come imagery captured in color. To see what he can draw out of that.

I will begin painting soon! (Sat. Sept 24, 2006 Autumn Equinox.)

***

My document might be considered subversive by agents of our current government! Does it say somewhere in the US Constitution that treason means *disloyalty to the nation itself, but not necessarily to a current body governing our nation?* Again, this thing about patriotism and what's going on in leadership occupying the White House today! Because I am a patriot, but loath, hate & detest almost every single thing this stolen-presidency puppet has done! Anyway I must speak politics—a dry subject usually, except in times like this when it's become inflammatory because America's wounds, ills, grievances, & world-trespasses have begun to bleed and ooze pus so badly over our universe! I must speak truths observant to a social scene! Any great work of life is to prepare the children, the next generation, for what will come-- so they will feel safe, secure within the danger, and hence their security and survival will be optimal.

To end the evil wherever it is.

To comfort crying people.
To protect.

Dear Children, my readers to come, (cum) our world is composed of flowing waters, oceans, land masses, mountains; there is a starry sky above, there is gravity, and there is God. Yes, a Creator. ---Who is just all part of the thing, and we might as well accept it now, for our journey will be easier with Her (Him) available, and in a hairs breath of a prayers reach--concerning all matters: IE; the pervert (a good pervert)* and her/his lover having finally found themselves in bed together after a long persistent courtship; the pervert having finally convinced her-him what an exceptional lover he/she is, has gotten the trade to bed! —But finds after 2 laborious hours using every technique said lover has failed to have an orgasm. The wise pervert raises up his/her head to the heavens and utters a silent prayer-- for Creator to intervene in this sad, tedious fiasco and grant the lover an orgasm! Upon which returning industriously to the task of fleshly manipulation (use your imagination Children) about five minutes later, the lover comes and comes indeed! Copiously! So you see our Creator is ever at hand, present in all situations, ready and willing to come (cum) to the aid of those who ASK! She is aware of all our politics, our sexuality, our very lives breath!

*There are good perverts, and evil doing ones, who are described, but not endorsed nor applauded in my texts--in fact the opposite, they are placed very low upon the human scale of value; those who do damage willingly or unwillingly mindlessly or mindfully to any other life forms, human, or animal or the environment. Especially concerning during sex.

So as illustrated already, JOURNEY is a full-scale wild-ranging beast.

This torrent of words!

JOURNEY will just be that, with no attempt at weaving a plot thru the thing. Tho several are certain to appear… It also is a continuation/outgrowth of the finite AUTUMN CHANGES after which came PASSAGE, which also had an end. –They all departed from my prior 40-year herstory of fiction.

You know if I decide to continue JOURNEY into still another dispensation---ending the journal part like I did PASSAGE--- with another series (which essentially moved from the Unofficial Semi-Autobiography of Red Jordan Arobateau, into PASSAGE) an account; views and observations of daily changes, passages towards reconfiguring myself again as a fine-artist, out of the 40 year drudge of novel writing, short stories, back into oil paintings; I will call it Passion. PASSION.

Every humanbeing leaves a trail of detris, excrement's. Emotional stuff, things they say, mistakes they make, which has to be cut off & discarded. Stuff which doesn't endure so there's a stream of rubbish behind their life as well along with their good works that more or less stand the test of time. One life goal? There's a sort of criticism, an elimination of stuff no longer necessary, stripping the self bare to go foreword in spirit, not be flesh-bound.

JOURNEY! Passion!

Now onto something still topical…

Sexy TS muy simpatico Mami Rosa has showed Red, illustratedo, on her fine curvy body with pinches of golden tan fingers tipped with long red fingernails accented against her soft yellowish-white flesh how she pulled and tugged at the skin of her male chest repeatedly, first beginning as a 14 year old girl, to encourage the extra skin growth necessary for the 'de implants of las tetas falsas' which she would not be able to afford for another decade, then, how she likewise just pulled & tugged at her scrotum-- got it so it hung down half way down her thighs, towards her knees, this preformed over another 20 years --so necessary for the construction of the new labia lips of her vagina which she now has!

A deep, dark, mysterious, pungent, many-layered hole to fuck. Mami has one!

Her panties: She wore the type, lacy, satin, bikini style, which were easily pushed aside by finger tips of golden tan fingers reveling her new pussy to me. Opening her legs in her desk chair at office in the storage room of the Sex Shoppe of her employment she spread her labia lips (once hairy scrotal tissue). "Best pussy I've ever seen yet …

On anybody!" Transman Red exclaimed delightedly, licking his lips and clapping his hands.

His mad impulse was to lick her pussy! Get right down there on his knees on the storage room floor but restrained himself. He knew he could strap on his cock & give it to her good—any size she wanted---- & told her so. But was denied entry.

The new transsexual woman must learn the rules of living female, to become fully integrated into the normal social world of gender successfully.... But most especially as a New Woman whose not able to pass successfully. She's not going to be able to get answers even to ordinary questions. She is not listened to. When she speaks she is ignored. She is ridiculed. She is ignored *at best*. She is ill-treated.

Again, like the starving artist, we must persist! Remember, all the peoples of the world are Gods! All belong to God-- first because She created them. Also secondly, because some of us have committed ourselves to Her.

Why I have become a literary activist, and take this awful risk of unpopularity, of tomatoes, eggs thrown? I have nothing else to do with my life! That's why! This malformed society has taken from me everything people hold dear, starting with my mother at an early age taken by segregation, incest, systemic abuse of women, (not by my dad), and by schizophrenia. My mother, a beautiful, intelligent, Colored woman (that's 3 strikes against her in a row) Missing In Action.

Repeat as I said before about me being a bewildered citizen who belongs ton a nation which the rest of the world denounces in fiery rhetoric night & day all spread across the tabloids, podiums of earth… and increasingly in actuality burning the effigy of America and its ridiculous U$ President dummy doused in gasoline & lit with matches from a dozen hands similar to fragging of US America soldiers of their own higher ups in the military in another unpopular war—in some peoples memory--- Viet Nam. Upon my daily journey find it easy to search at a glance passing, news rack coin-return slots for a forgotten quarter or dime; can't help but see headlines big black bold print these foreign diplomats criticizing our U$ policy. They really say what it is. Information of how we have propped up our economy by going over to other nations and grabbing stuff from them—stuff which belongs to THEM, not to U$!!

> When I was young, times there was no food. —When living at dads house our refrigerator was always well stocked—but I still might not eat due to my mental illness, so I would go out solely on inspirations wings.

Lets talk about transsexuality, homosexuality, being an artist, a political activist—all of it! Let me tell you what it is—a driving imperative. You know how tumultuous sex can be? Longings, desires, lusts, some thwarted, others over-indulged. Especially in the beginning teenage years the unfamiliar coursings of being on the threshold of adulthood after having had a brief decade of simply learning the lessons of childhood—you know how tumultuous sex can be? Then imagine what its like for sex, double-crossed as it is for us transsexuals, being on the interior a woman, finally presenting as one, but still having male lusts, a frantic scrambling to find & situate oneself in this society like a survivor on a raft of mishap, set adrift... sometimes an individual who has lived almost from their first day as 'Quaint Irene', an odd character amidst the milling norm, their dissatisfaction being both inward from the sexual misfiring angst, plus growing greater outwardly due to them ill fitting inside the established social frame. Finally the dream vision lays close ahead, hormone therapy, surgery, transition itself! But upon completing their Sex Change find life is far from perfect, maybe at that point some begin to go slightly insane.

I look at the effeminate male; the naturally-occurring mannish woman; we are such a delicate construct- different from the norm, pushing gender boundaries further--not completely by our own decisions, but what biology has bestowed upon us from before our birth. An impoverished street trans woman forced back into boy clothes, her wig (too ratty) combed out with vigorous strokes, yet in her bald shaved head, an effeminate flounce of hands, Alors, she bes wo-man! Shining thru! Two lesbians in leather & starched bluejeans. Very masculine vibrations---of both the smaller femme and the larger butch, dressed identical--- not just their chaps/vests and short haircuts, but their mannerisms, the voice tone, the lack of 'feminance and something else different too... we are such a delicate complexity, a mental hard-drive programming of computer or clock-work intricacy by which God has made us! And locked back somewhere in the archives of genetic history, is our key!

Visited the East Bay today, to the Bancroft's temporary location while the library on campus is undergoing a drastic retrofit, which will last 3 years. Hope it survives all the shaken' & quaken' yet to arrive! Am delivering the stuff mentioned—via a metal roll cart, there's so much.... My creations. Out the window of the BART train look at a nostalgic sight ... Our old grim stone cement walled hotel. Freeways cuts air at distance so that just a slice of it is visible, grey cornice that fronts on Oakland's 14th street on Jefferson, 2 blocks below Broadway ... Life was there was hard. Warm bodies, her & me in bed; a sagging hotel mattress with old cigarette burns------had only the dream of my art, her of her dance & so little security at my minimum wage jobs. Now have a permanent income & have established much in this new studio in a good neighborhood—yet am alone. Back then had 2 warm bodies, a dream, few scruffy possessions, and the misty future.... Oh. Want to thank you Husky and Mew--- for both of you accompanying me as long as you could hold on. That meant each going into illness & pain, before we made the decision to release you. Thank you for holding me in your love. Your grasp on this earth was very strong (16, 17 years apiece). What will I feel at the hour of my death?

>*Hail Mary full of Grace,*
>*God is with you,*
>*Blessed are you among women.*
>*Blessed is the fruit of your womb, Jesus.*

Did I get a few of the things I wanted? Have I achieved my rights? Friends whom I've made, will they hold my soul between their human hands? Will they miss me after I am released from this earth?

Well, these days California is being sunny, but not too hot. A whiff in the air of long-ago times. Sun drenched summers, barbeque picnics, soda pop, watermelon, '50's hit music soul station remember, can taste it in my mind. For an instant stirring in the air it's just like home. Those time won't come back again. I existed in a totally black life then thru the 1940's. '50's. Then beginning 1960 began to escape into the racially mixed artist areas of Hyde Park, Near North Side, Greenwich Village.

Down in the TL there's grime, dirt, and as curtains of a street-front rented room are fluttering in a breeze I see the same sofabed pushed aside against a wall like I did to make more painting space. I well remember the poor days, everlasting and onstretching, with pencil and paper, easel and brushes, typewriter ribbons and stamps to mail out a hundred solicitations which all received NO, but am proud of my work, have overcome and actually get a few sales per month!

Where the dream lives, the people prosper. At least in their hearts.

I should not hear one single clink of a tin can in my garbage can, because am now now turning all the empties into flowerpots. That's right. Using a great gold mine, two bins of found earth in humongous planters wheeled home in the dead of night after a terrific windstorm dislodged them from a fancy deluxe hotel lobby. Cuttings from friend's plants. (Rosa Salazar.) Surreptitious 'home-birth deliveries' of minor shoots. Seeds of stuff. Potatoes purchased from the supermarket set in water to root.

Me and Doctor Sam discuss our respective vocations over coffee at STARFUCKS after a Chinese food dinner on Polk Street, & browsing in a going-out of business bookstore (where purchased retrospects of Picasso, O'Keefe and Masaccio-- for $5.70!). We speak of in-the-closet polticos who veto gay marriage bills. But I will not criticize politicians, lawyers who lead double lives---evading prying eyes of their clientele and constituents. I have chosen a life work that has the least restraints imposed upon it from without--- how else can a creative spirit truly be just that? Artistes are notoriously iconoclasts, scandalous, doing stuff, which embarrasses their families and gets them run out of town.

My God, I am going to quote this---its taken from an anarchist pamphlet published in Andalusia, I found it in that book about Picasso by John Berger ('65, Pantheon Press) who lifted it originally from a quote in Spanish Labyrinth by Gerald Brenan (Cambridge University Press 1945). By an unnamed radical, 1900'rds:

> **On this planet there is infinite accumulations of riches, which, without monopoly, are enough to assure the happiness of all human beings. We-- all of us have the right to well-being and when Anarchy comes in, we shall every one of us take from the common store whatever we need: (men), without distinction, will be happy: love will be the only law in social relations!**

So can you believe the Anarchists of the distant past, a century ago were speaking the same language as us today? — That of revolution!

Terra Viva! Young punks of Mexico City are starting gardens on top of cleared-out garbage dumps. Their feverish call is for punks to plant this permavegitation around the world! The People must abandon the errant ways of plasticized civilization and go foreword into a higher degree of civilized integration of nature back into life, once again. Just like in the beginning, when we lived exclusively on the land, dwelled in tribes, and were closer to God. Closer to The Garden. A radical re-integration of nature, science, progress, into societies advanced civilizations, and lifestyle. With regard for Sea Turtles, Elephants, and all living beings. Instead of murder, genocide, and brutality wrecked against the lower life forms. Whose revenge against us has been mad cow disease, obesity & a few other strange virus's.

Terra Viva! punks look the same as punks worldwide with wild pink/lime-green/chartruse/blu/violet hair; piercings, tattoos, sawed off slacks, safety-pinned clothes. They are young, fierce, idealistic.

***

Well, must tell my ongoing fantasy ever since that day a few weeks past when finishing up PASSAGE, as noted had found fortuitously upon 2 separate days, looking into abandon cartons of books put out on the street first Il Nuovo Dizionario Inglese Garzanti (an Italian-American dictionary) AND, next, a travel book written in 1965 about Venice! So, its been Venice in wake-dreams ever since.... (Hence the Masaccio). Perusing Italy travel books at Borders Free Reading Room. If I win big at Indian gaming, $12,000 or more, we're on our way! I'll pay for L., Jasmin, and me, Semi-Non Professor Turnip and Dr. Sam. Would pay a friend of Dalora's to watch our brood of animals and plants, and be gone 1 month! Of course Sam couldn't stay that long being a doctor and everybody else would loose their jobs... *Oh well...* Venice has many streets which are actually canals and not solid at all (except if they freeze over to ice in winter)... how romantic. It has a low crime rate, because it's too difficult for thieves to escape! There's a canal or bridge blocking nearly every turn! Maybe there are sail-by shootings, don't know, but a drive-by shooter couldn't get further then a couple of blocks on a paved street before they'd have to leap out of their car to cross some footbridge or jump into a canal and swim for dear life!

Streets of heaven are paved with gold so they say—for my whole lifetime 60 years I've heard that refrain—which means that the material, the cheapest the most ill-considered, that is valued the least, is what the Saints use to walk on Up There—where as here on earth, Gold is all we think about! If earth streets were made of it, folks would be out frantically cracking apart the roads with jackhammers, striking it with pick axes, digging frantically with shovels, prying chunks of gold out of the street with their fingernails till their fingers wore off into stumps of blood and they still wouldn't stop! —I go on and on!

Dear Children I hope these books are something all of you can use— use not simply in the manner which was suggested that poor recluse Henry Darger might have indulged himself in his own private art collection, (self illustrated by drawing, painting, and collage of magazine cutouts of the human figure found by scavenging trashbins at night); but also to uplift and to inspire you, and to illustrate agape--- world love-- for all creatures from the sea turtles to the butterfly to the mother orangutan who looks down with love at her newborn baby orangutan cradled in her arms, caressing it's orange fur. To imbue the hardened hearts of the children of this world with greater love. To put you in touch with spirituality as a constant reminder.

God has given each one of Her/His creatures a voice. A throat. A sound, issuing out of a mouth. All animals have a voice. Here is mine:
>Grey fluff feathers
>merging shimmery haze.
>Sleek of wing,
>Pink feet,

one, hobbles briskly;
two crippled, gnarled nubs.
Pigeons dine at curbside
Chinese rice,
spilled out of a white carton
decorated with red dragons.
Stuff your beaks!
Stuff your beaks!
Stuff them full my Birds!
Of your lucky largess
in gratitude!

On the corner of Post & Polk; midway down the block world-famous Divas, spawn of the now-gone tavern the Motherload, home of tranny hookers, transwoman shows, and general fun hangout for a sector of our trans/queer demimonde; some artistic diva has tied a long purple scarf which blows in the breeze to summon in the trans-starved wayfarer, to call back all sistas lost at sea. For a sea change. *Read: Calling tricks. Just got out of jail. To have a drink among friends.* As the small stocky Transman stomped wearly up the incline, his heavy sack of art upon his back he thought thus: 'Oh again wish there was more love between us brothers and you sisters.' Well, isn't that the way of this human race anyway? Dividedness is a certain commonality among our species.

Well saw Rosa Salazar today on a short pitstop at the Sex Shoppe. She was busy with her catalogues, her bespeckled face stuck inside lace & bondage. Couldn't bother to talk. Recoiled at my touch upon her bare golden tan shoulder. Again I will abandon the pursuit of this crazy, beautiful, temperamental tranny girl. It's a lost cause. She don't think of me as a man, just a Transman. She wants raw dick on the hoof! AND, get this! She don't want that dick inside her new pussy, no! Mami wants it up her original pussy—her ass hole! That manpussy she's been fucken' with for 35 years! She takes 8 or 9 juicy inches of cock! Why 'in de asse?' Because it pounds her prostrate gland, which she greedily relishes! The male prostate gland, its theorized has a corresponding site within the biological born female body—but inside the vagina. The "G" Spot. Stimulation of this leads to female ejaculation as well as orgasm. However, Mami's new pussy sadly does not come equipped with this spot, so, the old Prostate will just have to do!

Red's little flirtation with the buxom senorita has little hope of ever flowering into a romance worthy of being novel-length…

Although her hard work in life and diligent self-betterment had availed her of a vagaplasty; XXXX still had a big dick; she carried it right between her ears, in her head. Male thinking. No, this is not another character of whom I'm speaking, but yes it's our beautiful Mami Rosa with whom you are familiar! Sex change women are not always de facto woman-identified, nor feminists. And many, if not most remain in an all-male world as much as possible. Preferring male-born individuals for companions, lovers, and compatriots. If they really wanted to be like women they'd try to be around them. But something about a true 'fish' they internally find repelling. Problem is, some of their male lovers are no longer accessible—as the key to those old boyfriends hearts and beds is for the woman to possess a biological dick between her legs he can grope or fantasize about while giving her pussy butt a good pounding with his own dick. Also, their poorer sisters who cannot afford SRS may be so intimidated by the presence of their friend, The Queen, who now sits upon her Throne of gender perfection, that they can't stand to be around her! Find it too threatening! So the bewildered new woman may suffer loss of old friendships as well. The objective of the antiquated Harry Benjamin Standards Of Care was that such new females should go out into the world fearlessly as women, assuming a totally new identity in some new city where no one knows them and blend into the scenery there among normals, which mostly doesn't happen. Many girls (and boys) still wind up eventually being attached to the trans demi-mode in some way.

Speaking of men, emotions and differences, must know about men, men cannot cry. Women accuse men of holding back tears, to gain power by not showing their emotions as if it was totally voluntary occurrence.

Men on testosterone can't cry. Do you know how hard it is to really keep from crying? Men don't 'fight back the tears'—that is something which is visible (a bit of water in the corner of an eye, a watery look, a gritted expression)--- the tears just aren't there! My greatest release was to be able to cry when sad, depressed, in despair, when in sympathy for someone else's problems! What a cleansing of soul! Once on testosterone I noticed my ability to cry vanished within a month or less. Me who use to break down and cry several times per day, or every other day! Fully. Deeply. Heart wrenchingly.

***

'Wal, let me tell yuh! Speaking of painful inclines and huge sacks of art … I rather have my life be a gradual incline and no decline whatsoever—except in old age physicality which is inevitable--- but not my spirit, my art, nor my popularity, nor my love, nor my friendships, nor my prayers to the Creator! Hope they increase with fire! By the way…I really don't know God, I know God is good and God is great and people struggle a lifetime to know God, but I don't really know more then that... I pray, I pray often for what is right for me, for better things to come of my life and then I'm waiting for an answer. Just like everyone.

Wiggle your toes in appreciation of God!
For She is great!

Yuh know, looking back at some of this stuff just written, see all the foolish daydreams, which will soon melt away, into the mist… Like Venice… Well, just as long as my higher values don't die! My great inspirations!

Gonna come a time when God is gonna come for us and take back our immortal soul with Her, or Him back to heaven. Its Gods soul who S/He gives to us, and one day She takes it back. Its gonna happen to all of us. People don't talk about that in the political field but they should because its just as much a fact of life as water, earth, wind and fire. The soul--and its ascent after this life on earth is done. Then we enter into a new dimension. Che Guverra got assassinated--at the moment of his death his soul soared beyond radical politics and was reclaimed by Creator. Mao Tse-tung, the great Chinese leader who liberated women, and brought education to the masses while liberating the poorest peasants from under rulers economic yoke… All of them had to die and all of them have souls & spirits which don't expire with the body but which travel on--so this needs to be mentioned from time to time in political circles as well as holy temples and mystic religious places. It's the final end of the human phase of our souls dispensation.

For the second time this week; 3rd in 5 weeks, have done an interview for a reporter re: FTM transition. Bolstered my ego. Also it gave me an opportunity to wander into the past with memories ordinarily would not have had. The 2nd interview, radio, for KQED got my voice live answering direct questions about personal transition how it affected me; relationships etc. The first was fellow Transman M.'s film; similar, more centered around the nature of our trans community and how it has evolved. During the 3rd, a reporter gathering data for a proposed article to the Bay Guardian asked who were the first transsexuals I remember seeing before taking the plunge myself and this really got my mental wheels spinning because had to push memory further and further back, realizing each successive memory actually wasn't the first, and, the one before it hadn't truly been the actual first sighting, etc…and the list grew greater the further back I probed my memory… the shocking FTM on hormones who was explained to me in private by his ex-girlfriend; about the procedure he'd done….guys who subsequently left the lesbian community and started new lives—so this started me thinking.... back even further then that. Don't forget all this time thru the 50's, 60's, 70's, 80's, I'd been dwelling in ignorance, in the allusion I was a butch dike. Fini! End of the line! When actually I'd been impersonating a man all that time. Some of us not yet realized transsexuals were more passable into gay society or lesbian, and there we perched, in our dis-ease. So let me tell you the way it was 'back in the day' in the gay clubs there would always be this strange fringe element lurking slightly apart and not among the crowds of gay women & men, all the non-gay hangers-on. Cootchie-cootchie mans, sneaky voyeurs, middleaged tricks, etc. Plus there was these ultra radical freaks who went to the very few social havens they knew, the clubs of their 'cousins' the gays. These strange creatures only meeting place was a gangster run tavern, alleys, slum or special bohemian streets, or afterhours dive. They'd be so far gone weird we normal gays shuddered at the sight of them! We mocked, jeered, pointed our fingers at them behind their backs, as if they couldn't hear us! Half women's apparel, half men's; lopsided wigs, ill-fitting men's suits but not doing this as a lesbian or a gay, but actually trying to BE the sex they sadly weren't born. Realize now these monsters were transsexuals set out of time with no place.

There's an on-going list of them in many of my old books. (See STORIES FROM THE DANCE OF LIFE Vol. 3, the end piece. Also some of the novels from that time like HO STROLL'S depiction of the black gay club Soulville.

* * *

Day Comes To Ten Thousand Studio Rooms
Poetry by Red Jordan Arobateau

Day comes to ten thousand studio rooms.

The bell, which rings summoning humans, cries out.
BBBRRRRRRRRINNNNNNNHHHG!
The enormous cat is dislodged from place
under his armpit, amid the blankets & sheets.

He brushed his head like you would shine a shoe,
 and out he went.

Upon another days journey over this blue planet.

The tip of San Francisco, Chinatown, is surrounded by
 water; blue. @ X of Sacramento/Mason can see down
 both streets in both directions to lands end, —water,
curve of the peninsula where the city sits. Look down
 the 2 separate streets to the water! Water! Blue!
While walking up Sacramento to the top, Huntington
 Park, stop @ Tortoises fountain. See the spooky
carousal children at play in bronze circa 1942,
 a year before his birth.

& he goes round about the town
upon various and sundry errands
of by now forgotten meaning.

A pigeon spins whirling, one wing upraised. Shows
its soft white body down; it spins two erratic
circles in succession, POP!
Sheds a feather. Fluffs up,
then upon two pink/red feet
proceeds upon its way.

A feather for her hat!

She murmurs softly:
Drink greedily my birds!
Drink greedily the water
I've poured out for you
 into the crevices.
Let your throats warble!
Drink great gulps
 of life!

"I'm sick"
cries a homeless man covered by a blue blanket
laying in the street.
"I'M SICK."
He means look at me somebody!
Can somebody help me?
Take away the pain!

>   *It was a magical time,*
>   *& so uncertain.....*

Jours sans. (Days without.) No matter! Despite
poverty, loneliness, and non-success follow Creator
Children—it is Her way, which is best! Even if it be
living humbly and simply in a trailer park. (Nowhere to
rent, no where to dance, no where to paint, no where
to write, no where to live in San Francisco.) Rather
then a mansion on the hill built off somebody else's
mistakes. Live with your conscious clear!
Free in Her Arms!

Like radical author Jessica Mitford (not a single
biography; only one book in print today).
I will write/paint my expressions & they will BE until
the shroud of time covers them up.

***

Photocopy another page.
At end of day with the janitor.
Closing up at Trans Space. Downstairs, outside, night
has fallen; the pavement is sparkling with some
infinitesimal tiny specks of silver rock so the street
has glitter---fitting for a clientele of divas (many of
them fallen stars themselves).

Night comes again to ten thousand studio rooms.

***

Setting the stage for his masturbations he typed the following on his minor computer (to be printed out later on the major one):

She was stretched out on a dais, clothes in disarray revealing her nakedness. His penis was hard and hot and slips easily into her tight vagina, plunging up to his balls. He moaned. Great was his enjoyment of her. He had pulled out her enormous breasts from under her brazier, under her half-open disarrayed silk blouse. He licked and stroked her titties nursing greedily on her taut nipples. He rose over her now pumping his turgid organ inside her pussy as she lay beneath him, open, receiving his fucking. He rose and fell over her stroking and moaning, petting and sucking her big luscious breasts.

This is pornography and a welcome addition to JOURNEY. This sex act can be simulated by Transmen everywhere and is every day during their acts of copulation. But let us not dwell on the least of the bodily functions! Let us drop the subject and move on to more uplifted topics! (This sudden 'dropping of the subject' is reminiscent of the lover who, even during the moments of ecstasy as his hips are pumping involuntarily, chest heaving breath, still manages somehow, by wildly thrashing, to throw off the paraphernalia of his stimulation towards that height! ---The falsies! Tears off his frilly nightgown! Kicks off his golden backless strapless high heel pumps with contortions of his hairy muscular legs! So that he might instantly revert once again to a somber masculinity-- after the fun is done! How necessary this is so that he might fully enjoy the remainder of the ecstatic orgasmic crest, as a man once again, his true self!) So! What follows the smut? A Christian Homily? A didactic political diatribe? No, since this is a sort of my diary, what follows is somewhat personal.... A brief revelation—who is it I dare not name! S/he has surfaced in my dreams! Three times so far! Heshe is sinister; gazing half behind the mirror in kitchen, larger, sturdier in nondescript clothes covering him, obscuring her, twisting a moustache of one who is sinister or mysterious; who posses a plot for self purpose which may well be used against others to achieve what s/he wants. S/he offers a cash dollarbill of some increment, -- but it is printed green and perfect only on one side, the other is blank! Portending that he-she will pretend to give, but will only take! A vision of the Florida Keys on a map and money. The key to him/her is money and little else. Whatever other truly decent emotions feelings s/he possesses, money is key.

Later on this subject. I've begun to pray against it already!

***

God is great and God is good, and before the rise of advanced civilizations who left records chiseled into stone; dead languages scribed on papyrus scrolls; organized communities, city states with priests, shamans; there existed small tribal groups of early humanbeings who worshiped God without formalized religion, without language, nor words even, who raised their heads to the sky and hearts up within them, and hands outstretched to something above-- they called upon this Being who had created them (tho they didn't know it) this Being who made their heavens and their earth from the beginning. These early humans are with Creator right now in Paradise! They weren't numbered in any particular book of records, took no sacred oaths of allegiance, they did not plead the Blood of the Lamb--a very sophisticated concept of redemption of sin--nor did they call upon Diana, Allah, Buddha, Adonai, Jesus, Muhammad, Vishnu, Great Mother, Goddess or God by any other name, these early ones without language or words or religious creed. All this established protocol, which we need so much has evolved over 78,000 years. There was no special numbered group who would make it to heaven, no chosen peoples back then. God was God then, God is God now. God worked Her dramatic unfolding of the human pageant, the miraculous unfolding of heavens and earth. And we need just praise Her by any means or names, and forget about just who is 'getting into heaven' and who isn't! Or what name must be invoked! Or what tradition honored! One belief done in faith, love, devotion, and prayer is the same as the next! And remember those gurus, priests, ministers, mullahs, those clerics whose pompous titles evolved out of the masses of common peoples blind belief, those appointed religious leaders sometimes, they're having gaining a high position in that spiritual institution has little or nothing to do with having faith at all but what text one memorizes and how one maneuvers themselves among their peers towards the avenues of power. Some great unfeeling men who are essentially atheists have reigned from the papacy I'm sure, as well as sacrosanct thrones of many many other religious dispensations; passing down edicts, rules, restrictions upon the heads of the common believers often to their detriment, but above all for their social control.

Today one can see works of a great diversity of religions where cosmopolitanism has spread them to all corners of this globe. Wherever cities and towns are inhabited by many diverse types and cultures and practices of people, so that a person in need of speaking to Creator, just might conveniently duck into any passing place of worship they pass, kneel down (in fact, or in mind-- while sitting sedately on a church pew or chair) or knell on a floor mat, depending on which brand of holy place it is and cast up their requests to the Divine Being in any possible way, language, or formal practice as they are in during that time! And God will answer for God is a miracle worker!

**Great is My loneliness
for My lost sheep.**

Creator gives us these words, so we will be not clueless on the erratic path stumbled thru wildly like the grace-less, uneducated ignorant masses wielding a caveman club; ignorance. Furthermore regarding another sin (while we are on the subject) greed—plain & simple not all our ills can be blamed on advancing Korporate Mega-Kapitlaism. (That overworked point) It's only human nature. It's in all of us... Greed, Ignorance, & the aforementioned Lust! Furthermore there is the everpresent sin of prostitution to material wealth; the obsession for possessing stuff! That line between sanity, too real & raw, and insane infatuation with material objects. Fine satin dresses vs. the progress of the spirit. Journey to the soul thru all the layers of crap!

>A triangular piece of pizza,
>yellow, red, beige
>captured under a garbage can lid.
>Liberate it dear children!
>Toss it to the sidewalk!
>Dine birds! Dine!
>Feast on the engorgement of the human race
>overstuffing itself
>in their hungry sorrows.
>Dine!
>Then fly!
>Fly on your newfound strength!

Like Darger, Van Gogh, Proust, I'm ready to open up my treasure of unknown art to the world! Where will come the break thru? The illumination? The discoverer? From what direction does the messenger ride?

God gives a person a headstart that's all talent is, —or genius. Anybody who works hard enough is gonna at least become an OK artist. Geniuses are special constructs. But most anybody can produce something of merit if they dedicate themselves wholeheartedly to the task!

There it is almost done, liberated from obscurity all 22 volumes of ancient & forgotten lore written in my '30's; encapsulated into the Juvenilia Series. However a blow of adversity is struck! Now the policy against my use of the Trans Space copy machine has escalated! The door to the location of the machine is locked. The staff person who unlocks the door for me must stand guard counting EACH COPY spitting out of the machine—insuring it does not exceed 15!

AGGGGGURRAHHH! Thank God my Re Photocopy project is almost **Done!** Only 4 more books to go, but all of them double length—originally in 2 volumes each. However a new catastrophe awaits! Next day wearily the Transman Mounts the stairs to the infamous 2nd floor Trans Center, to be greeted by a photocopy CODE! Which means from now on all his copies will be **counted mechanically by the machine!** The high-quantity press is done! Fini! Thank Goddess he finished most of it beforehand! Now as far as making any money off this Re-Photocopying project, it may take decades! So it's always a labor of love, not profit, must say in my defense! For I might peddle only 2 books per year!

Transman Red glanced thru the ancient pages of the old stuff, a puzzling look upon his sweaty yellow face. Stuff he did at crucial times of change or upheaval in his life seem raw & pure and not as manufactured. I.e. books written immediately around his Sex Change; (STREET OF DREAMS, DOING IT FOR THE MISTRESS, AUTUMN CHANGES) circa 1998; HOW'S MARS---my first trip alone to New York seeking a gay world, 1963. Must say, am having a blast reading thru these ancient books—my Juvenilia!

2.
Attended shul tonight—Friday services—for the first time in awhile, and truly felt close to Creator. Enjoyed the service, and find am beginning to be able to stutter thru a few of the Hebrew hymns by memory. The food was appreciated afterwards, as was the hospitality. Realize I've missed this place, and intend to come back more frequently. Oh by the way, I forgot to add Rabbi, to my list of ministers, mullahs, priests, gurus, etc., while denouncing them all in the last pages! Equal opportunity! At library got an excellent book about the Donner Pass Party by a man called Stewart. A book for its author to be proud of. A book is a friend! Am just hanging in there for now, over this long 3 day 'Columbus Day' holiday—with precious little to do with self, and thus alone. Not fun. Must work to stay positive and not give way to the blues. Need a girlfriend!

> *All the hope that remained was*
> *faint clouds of smoke*
> *from chimneys in the distant horizon.*

'Thank goodness for my birds who are chortling upon me now', he thought, even as he wrote it. 'And for Little...' (huge) ... 'Mr. Fluffy, curled up in the bathroom sink sleeping, awaiting release from cat-jail when the feathered pets are returned to the safety of their home...' (cage) ... 'which they truly love.' Everybody loves a happy home. All Gods creatures. Oh, an astounding happening at shule, a Jewish member has returned from a trip to Israel where he/she witnessed the destruction along the Gaza strip and was so moved that he wound up marching in a Palestinian Liberation parade in protest to Zionism! S/he proclaimed her beliefs from the bema (pulpit, Christians) to a hushed and raptly attentive congregation. Heavy stuff. Transman Red sat in a pew stroking his beard, gazing pensively as he/she told his story to us. Closing with the sukat parable---you know, the one about building a fragile house, which easily blows away, but not worrying about this because this is how our lives are here on this earth! Fragile, and the things we struggle for so long so easily blown away ... However, this does not necessarily mean powerlessness, not at all...

It's surprising how many such fragile things can have such a strong even stronger effect then things attempted by force. Not by muscle or might. On the affluent upper Fillmore Street a grey head woman nods politely at me—knows me from my volunteering at the abandon dog clinic--- now I can't be seen hollering BITCHES and MUTHAFUCKAS! at the top of my lungs to somebody at the bus stop who makes me mad. She might witness it! My father, too, was the first great reason. I lived up to his expectations, which was very basic. Don't just don't fall and get in trouble! (Meaning jail or drugs or something awful.) His wish was not 'be a great genius or university professor or a person of social affluence'—some impossible goal. A testimony about my Dad.

PS. As much as possible Dad tried to follow his heavenly beliefs...

***

Ever since their masculine beginnings, man-dikes have secretly looked at other butches & compared themselves in ranking on the masculine scale. Am I as much a man as her? Do I dress harder?

Am I as stockily built? Is my chest flattened out enough? --Like hers? --Relentlessly, and cruelly comparing themselves. Gee look at that butch! She stood up and won the fight! --- While I ran away from it! Men do this. So when all begin to see the irrefutable, non-ignorable results of others transitioning-- which won't be ignored-- what new men are doing with their bodies it made any red-blooded butch eat their hearts out in tortured envy. Realizing dimly, for maybe the first time that we could do it too. Their strong, sinuous physiques, their fledgling beards, gruff voices, how easy they jockeyed with each other in public places—like wild teenage boys fired by their new found nuts-- with impunity, before the eyes of straight lookers on, who expect this behavior of boys—something we'd only been before allowed to do safely in private gatherings. Of course we ate our hearts out with envy until we couldn't take it & finally stepped on board the testosterone wagon… The ultimate perversion is when we go deep against into our own inner standard of what is right for us; when we bow, conforming to a scowling society who would, if able decide for us our own rules of lust!

***

The larger the baggage the smaller the soul. Steamer trunks & luggage & bags & baggage preoccupation. The bible says God will send you there. God will equip you. Take only food and clothing for two days change upon your journey. God will furnish the rest. Ironic, if at the later part of my life I ascend into a more spiritual plane; write about Saintly stuff openly, instead of disguising it, or tacking it on in back pages of already written novels, 'Sermons' I'd wrote giving you my philosophy like a pinch of salt to flavor the stew of stuff—pornography, plot, fabulous dialogue, etc, --- what if it becomes the primary thing? Well this world is waiting for help at every turn! It needs a spiritual viewpoint whenever possible, and people will indeed listen, just for a moment you'll have their ear!

***

& there it was, the moon rising from outer space beyond the earths crust; moon, majestic, ominous, threatening, stormy, it rose swiftly illustrating the slow turning of the world. A homeless woman secures her blankets in a tree while she's out forging for food--- in the garbage cans-- while richer tourists vacation in $100 per day hotel rooms which come with free continental breakfasts. We need a political jab or two to keep the world on its toes, moving in humane directions, but also practical guidelines for self-defense of person, home & nation. So I'll make a another rant right here—but this one disguised in a poetic coat.

> A funland carnival
> of affluence;
> 4 sailors in uniform black/white
> amid 100 tourists.
> 2 army commanders show off stars/stripes;
> are a class apart; they appraise
> the fine establishments;
> "I hear that place's an excellent restaurant."
> This is the military,
> which enforces the affluence.
> I see the mighty arches they make.
>
> *The truth is not here.*
> *---That is all locked, deep*
> *inside the monastery of contemplation.*

The rich men's club on Sacramento and Mason gazes at Tortoise Fountain Park from half lidded eyes.
All brains, wealth up inside that old rock fortress. Homeless sleep in the park outside.
Grace Cathedrals tenants toss
intermediate prayers across to
Heaven where we will go someday.

> *The city sinks down again*
> *on both sides of this green square.*
>
> 2 things remember children,
> resist! You resist and run
> with all possible strength
> towards victory!
> SMASH THE MACHINE!
> Struggle always.
> Follow your heavenly beliefs!

***

Transman stopped a moment from a fixed routine to contemplate his artistic position. It was uncertain. Unlike years of dedication to a purpose unchanging but for titles he wrote & increasing maturation of style. He had broken off novel writing 2 years back, solely devoted his energies to the different journals & plays, laboring over typewriter/computer while his birds clucked/chortled upon his shoulders burning the midnight oil. The Re-Photocopy Series was all but done. He truly was at a crossroads! This is what he'd actually written in the Authors Foreword upon the last of those books, BOOGIE NIGHTS:

> ***Think of his-her early decision at the crossroads of life, weather to pursue art; writing & painting, upstairs in those gutted-out rooms, or to cross over some invisible divide, going instead up a more secure well-paved path of a Civil Servant, and it's affects on my lack of fortunes today—but, now possessing a wealth of art! Think of the time of choices, and of risk, of expending energy towards some uncertain future! Well, this series-reprinting machine is winding down, and once again finds the artist at his hour of decision—to settle back down into painting once again along with continuing to write? To pickup brush, tubes of oil, red, yellow, green, blue? Holding a blank canvass, ready, the easel is waiting!***

It was now he realized he'd have to pick up the brush & oils once more---while he was still able---if he was going to do it at all! Also it occurred to him those 2 promised plays were yet undone... Maybe if I think about Venice again, water canals, gondolas, boats, foreign aromas, dining with friends in small cafes on platters of spicy Venetian food, picking up pallet, smock, brushes, colors, and being a fine arts oil painter it will all come true!

Today Acorn bookstore on Polk Strassa is finally closing—after an extension of one week from the date they planned. Got a Frans Hals folio for 65 cents. Italian tenor emotes a dramatic aria piped into this vast, emptied space. The shelves all gone, but for a few, which loom, leaning against a wall waiting to be transported out by the highest bidder. And books are stacked everywhere over the floor.

Must confess for the last year or so a gnawing pang has nagged me from back corners of my mind, that having abandon the genre of the novel, (last endeavor being STAGE DOOR, circa 2003)--- a fiction form, & putting in its place the more easy-to-do journal/diary, that I'm cheating myself, and the public, cutting short my abilities, plus limiting my range of expression…. Well this AUTUMN CHANGES stuff is easier to do! I attempted to interject a brief whisper of a novel into PASSAGE with that Rondo stuff which was excellent, spine tingling! A Murder Mystery! Containing the beautiful transsexual Rosa Salazar. And now, it's back! Come back strong! The yen! In fact a novel is beginning to churn, ruminate, asserting itself into my daily work routine! However, now am also planning to return to oil painting as well! How in hell can I possibly switch from journal to novel and oil painting, (not to mention finishing up the two infernal plays) plus the stresses of daily necessity to procure food, scrape up rent monies, plus try to have a social life! So as not to be so godforsaken lonely! How can my tenuous artistic elasticity & stamina possibly take on the discipline of:

1. Art
2. The structure & planning a novel takes.
3. Venting my daily observations, which have now become so necessary to me in a Journal?

Maybe I will write a novel—combined with a Journal—a novel/journal! Taking all the liberty in the world! A domain where verse can be inserted, dreams recorded, my everyday political rants printed out, ---- combined with my forte—fiction! All under one binding & title! It will flow much easier! Then rushing back & forth from book to book! Thank Creator that I have now switched to computer, much easier to use then oldfashion typewriter; its speeded up.

I've been writing a long long time but at some point I also became a publication company, don't quite remember what date, but its reflected on my earliest chapbooks of poetry COME TO THE BLACK MARKET, that early '70's genre …… I am leaving these words behind Dear Children so that you might understand more about my times, and be able to catalogue my art… Remember, we are all food for some other being. Green plants grow to become food to lower animals. Lower animals for greater. Humans are food for subsequent generations--their own daughters & sons feed off of them.... You provide my dinner Dear Children, for dollars, dimes, nickels & pennies by purchasing my books. And I am food .... I am food for you.

Miscellaneous notes from EMPIRE!:
Red had written: '*I know it is hard for people, my loneliness is temporal, theirs, lifelong. Deformed, mentally ill.*' He had written so much about the homeless—a state he was perpetually teetering on just a few hundred dollars away per month from being cast into its pit. And about being alone, and isolated. About being disfranchised, and outcasted.

> *The churches of my faith are shut against us.*
> *The cathedrals are darkened.*
> *Gone stone cold.*
> *Large oaken doors shut.*
> *& the shul is dancing in Dolores street.*
> *Someone whirling with a Torah*
> *clutched in her hands*
> *They dance!*
> *In the joy of Creator*
> *and community.*

According to Prophet Red: 'Everybody, every creature, every soul of God has a place. Where they are in is their place. Some by de facto it's the only place they are able to go. Others have chosen; but chose to be among the fallen because they must abase themselves, loose themselves. Some build great towers by industry, cleverness, & fortitude, amass gold, and prosper in the sight of others. But at some point everybody will look up from this place in finality. Maybe not until their final end. All, questioning why they are here. What they have become. What they have done with their lives.'

> So it had come about that Star1.vax was beginning to change… As the Prophet had said, 'I'm ready for destiny. Today is the first day of my life.' So now too Star1.vax believed as well this was the time of reckoning for him.

From EMPIRE! ---2007.

3.
Am just preparing the cast emails from my dead play. **E-MAILS CONCERNING RED'S PLAY PORTRAITS FROM A GHETTOIZED POPULATION, FROM THE CASTING CALLS TO THE FINAL END, DEC 2005 TO JULY 2006** for archiving at the Bancroft. Talk about drama! The crème de la crème of drama! This is some juicy stuff! --correspondence between a dozen or so persons. Wonder if the Bancroft will pay me $50 for it! Samples:

>--I am writing to inform you all that we finally have a full cast. As you all know we will be welcoming a number of new cast members into our family. Because of this we will have to start working from the top of the play once more.
>
>---She's full of it! I could smell her elitist attitude from a mile away...that's why she got a small role.
>
>--In the interest of professionalism and mutual respect refrain from ranting, accusations, and comparisons among cast members! In general the average adult does not respond well to this type of communication.
>
>--I need to explain my blow-up the other night. If you are not guilty of any of the things I mention, I'm obviously not talking about you!
>
>--Sorry about my attitude! I am not quitting the play, I never quit anything in my life and I will be damned if this is the first!
>
>--Another one bites the dust ladies and gents Unfortunately we have lost Boy/Girl.
>
>--I'm sorry to do this but I am just not at a place in my life right now where I can be a productive member of this cast. Believe me, this was a hard decision for me to make. I'm quitting.
>
>--I am hereby announcing to you that I am no longer a member of the cast.

--At this point I am requesting everyone who is going to quit the play to reply to this group email, so that you can tell everyone. Please don't waste the cast's time by calling in Thursday or the day before the run.

---There will be rehearsal tonight as we planned. Don't worry. I have a solution for everything. ----Red.

Oh what a joke! Ha Ha Ha Ha! —Red thought in hindsight. It was later evening, after his rounds of errands and socializing to the best of his ability outside, he was back home fussing over a paper-laden desk. Well am assembling the latest packet. (For the Bancroft.) To be ready to accompany the first volume of my new novel-journal* EMPIRE! as soon as am able to close it. William Faulkner wrote this to Roger S. his publisher asking for a $250 advance: "It's either this or put the novel aside and go whoring again with short stories." Hence my whorings for the Bancroft for this trick ($100) & a few other collectors at $15, $20, $25.* Quick cash to help pay the rent.

* Journoval...?
*A whore will tell you the small-money little customer gets the same thing the big spender does.

He went to visit the abandoned dogs once more:

    I've come to mop up the blood
of emotional wounds.
The all-but invisible cuts
that erupt surprisingly.
In barks and wolfs and a fang or claw
 marks on my arm---they are afraid
from how they were mistreated
 in puppyhood.
Come to comfort you furry friend.
 To pray you find a happy home.
I hold you in my embrace.

        ***

Once past Golden Gate and Hyde Street the crazy drug infested insanity starts. Stern & serene governmental buildings; museum, grey stone, the older edifices & modern, steel & glass streamlined are replaced by squat low ugly tenements and cheep small-room hotels. A visible population of hags, winos & jittering dopefiends who stay outdoors and crack dance their monthly welfare stipend away in the disco of the alleys in a single night.

Jittery hypes go cross the street flowing with traffic against the red light. Walk out in the middle between honking speeding cars, in a hurry to the needle exchange program. A hag babbles, rummaging at the corner gutter. It's a good thing ho's kain't fly--; cause that bitch would be everywhere! Traffic must halt! or run her over. And above all the whitestone cathedral gazes down O'Farrell Street in inspired stone.

The inhabitants respond to the rough demands of the street, which made life so untenable here. --- Policy is if you can't take care of yourself the smiles turn to frowns.

An exotic dancer, bare legs; in black tight satin dress steps on her way to strip joint employment. "DRESS LIKE ME! DRESS LIKE ME! YOU AIN'T NO DIFFERENT THEN ME!" Howls she, defensively back at loitering men hassling her while walking from her car to work at the strip club carrying a costume bag. Its 4 pm.

> A lamentation song howls
> thru the night
> Softly & soothing.
> Jungle rhythms
> everconstant
> as a heartbeat.

Naturally the next day finds him at Trans Space. These girls, these girls. Money is their language. They banter on & on about superficial stuff—yet all want love! It is their basic heart-dream. Too bad they seldom get it.

We are very close-knit group---transsexuals—its such a small world all trannys know each other in any particular city if they participate in T-events at all, and aren't afraid to be recognized. Not stealth nor self-isolating. So we identify with each other, us men. Are even acquainted with our transgender sisters--the mtfs-- but we do inhabit 2 separate spheres. Apart from the occasional romance between ftm/mtf, few penetrate the veil thru into the sisters' real lives. Sadly, occasionally when one does get thru all their feminine allure, false eyelashes, the high-pitched voiced banter and real truly gets to know these new women one might be tempted to exclaim, under all that they're still men! ---There in the problem lies. It's not male behavior, but its not female behavior either. Oh well, won't abandon my fine idea of more love between us.

In this big post-millennium, pre-apocalypse big city one hears conservations like: "I'm not sure what her rent is, *but*…." Because greedy landlord moguls have made gold their God. We are all worshipers of strange & various fruits in our own way. Witness the vain Transwoman/Transman! Here is a brother Transman in love with his new self, moustache, bulging biceps, slim hips, male bulk, who can't distance his vision from the mirror too long…. Small minded people and very selfish. Consuming their focus measuring how many centimeters their dick grew that week. There's other things in life guy!

Well, Dear JOURNEY (title of my journal) am killing lonesome time by going to library, getting on line & books checked out, studying about the Donner party. It was a testament to human endurance & human will.

Whoops! Forgot to mention, was it October 15? —When finally put black typefont to white paper and began to write that science fiction novel! My newest project since finishing up PASSAGE. New creation and tending the garden of my old stuff—which means selling books/art prints in person, checking online sales outlets etc. Also archiving. My salvage of those 22 abandon, dusty file cabinet-bound-books has been running smoothly. Must mention that in front of each title of my Re-Photocopy series is a newly composed Authors Foreword, but they are not synopsis or little book reviews that describe the contents of the work, as one would assume. No. Just what thoughts each triggered when I held the book up in my hands & examined it for the first time. (Some, after 30 years.) Am pleased that it's almost over—results; a master copy cut for each, plus 2 copies, one off to the Bancroft at a reasonable price ($20-35), one to sell at higher price to any public interested whereupon to earn the cash to afford copying fees for any subsequent volumes--- given that this free-copying probably won't last forever and won't be able to do it here. Almost all of them are now done—minus 4...

Black hat upon his head, the stoic poet marched single-mindedly to Trans Space, up the stairs lugging his heavy backpack. Transman Red is in for a sad surprise upon gaining the door to the photocopy room. **AGGGGGGGGGGGGGGUURRRGH!** His Re-Photocopy program has run aground! It has been stricken! Fate, the great despoiler of fortunes has struck again! No more copies left on his 'account' and the director doesn't return for a week to correct the error! He'll keep going however! Pay for it himself! At infernal Kinko's Kurrupt Korprate Kopy center. That money comes out of food & rent however...

> He was strong in his radical coat
> of arms.
> walked on beaches
> of the universe.
> He fancied pigeons.
> And made his fate as he was.
> Not pretending to be someone else.
> Raconteur, idealist; hardworker.
> A truly marvelous person.

People may accuse me of having a big ego, tooting my own horn, this is not precisely the truth. It is The Work I am tooting a horn about! This body of art to which I've given my energies, my time, most of my entire life in fact! Having the same desire as any parent to see that their child goes out into the world and finds her/his place! So I want my works to go out—out of myself, out of my personal possession, out of my filecabinet & book shelves into this world and there find their rightful and deserved position—whither it be great or small, that is Gods decision! However mass-popular, or arcane this writer/artist becomes let it become a fact that he received his justified due!

History shows people in a different light then what they were. How history will view me; I hope I will have not been seen as idiot full of sound & fury at best; at worst malignant. My desire about the whole matter, ultimately I guess it's to leave this world a better place then when I found it --in some small/great measure.

Some people look at passionate artists and claim the only true passion is the love for Christ (read Mohammed, Buddha, etc.) Some people look at great leaders as if they were anointed. Revere them, deify them. And who's to say many aren't anointed? And who is to say a good work is not a true love? You don't have to preach the Gospel to be anointed you could be doing Creators work and so be blessed. I know I was led to art, gifted by it…. And by Who if not some great, wise and infinite Force?

Right Wing Religious Fundamentalist Bigot Asshole: *The end days are coming will you be taken up with God or will you be left behind!*

Red: *Well I'd want to stay around awhile then! I'd stay behind because so many people need help. I'd be helping people.*

God: **That's a Christian.**

Speaking of leaders what amazes me most, and is most disheartening, is not what a few stupid, crazy & insane men up in the White House can do, but that so much of the rest of our nation went along with it, voted for him for a 2nd term!

> See the American city
> garbage cans overflowing.
> So much wealth.
> So much waste.

Often in these times with this terrible headline news (of atrocities in the Middle East wars, feminine in Africa) I wonder: God, if it was worth it to create this human race. Answer from a wise religious leader: Yes! Because so many people have done precisely what God has said to, they have proved love and care for their own children, their own family and their own people thru undying effort, and have had sympathy, compassion & done good works for those not of their own. Untold billions of people down thru the ages have done precisely this.

> The grave lays open
> like it has lost its occupant.
> Risen on resurrection day.

I think of the beautiful *'Hay-yah, Hay-yah, Hay-yah, Hay'* ritual religious song of the Native American Indians. I been to shul tonight, and plan to attend Eucharist at Grace Cathedral one of these Sundays soon. Think a person can worship Creator in all faiths. —And still be worshiping the same Great Being Who made us all!

Transman Red had gone to Jewish temple, to Native American spiritual ceremonies. Buddhist meditations. Other Eastern Religious sects. Danced with Sufi's. And sat in dozens & dozens of different churches which fall under the Christian classification. He'd been accepted into this tribe of folks and that-- made to feel welcome--but since he had not been born into that particular tribe always had this little uneasy feeling in the back of his mind that he didn't really belong. He'd been like an orphan for a long long while and appreciated any hospitality.

Is Armageddon really here? Doomsday come now? Who will do the fatal deed? **Then the shot that killed all of human civilizations was fired—the shot before the end…**

> *--It is so hard & so much grief.*
> --Follow the stars Red.
> *Follow the stars*
> they will guide you back home.
> Follow the stars,
> that's all I can tell you now.
> The stars will point the way.
>
> 4.

On the other side of the world
there is a fishing village built into the cliff side
of the sea wall.
People must scramble up &
 down steep cliffs
for all their needs.
Casting their nets for fish.
Drawing water from wells.
Cooking.
Building shelter.
Birthing babies.
God it's so poor.
& so hard.
It is so poor & so cruel
 for so many.

The rich are getting richer.
We know. The poor people know.

Jesus, Mohammad, Elijah, Buddha, The Great Mother, all walked thru this world with the greatest simplicity. Michael J. Fox the stricken movie star appears on Television, a jittering spastic puppet diminished by the disease Multiple Scoliosis. I use to hate Michael J. Fox. To me he was a privileged twerp. Now I don't hate him. I see his compromised body shaking before the cameras pleading for stem cell research to continue- research, which will benefit untold millions of other human beings to follow. Mother Teresa wore just 2 habits, it was the only clothes she had. Her nuns lived in simplicity, eating meagerly, dwelling almost without possessions of any kind. Washing and bathing in cold water—not heated-- in order to share in some measure the adversity of the poor & disfranchised of this world. I don't hate her. I don't reject her. It's because of the degree of suffering. I'm sick of people who have so much!

These folks, these folks. They want masters. They want kings. They get war, poverty, starvation. They don't want that, but that's what they get when they won't think for themselves! And this is what we're getting right here in America, greatest nation on earth! Greatest ever seen! We're voting for the wrong leaders for the wrong reasons---and flushing a nation down the toilet!

As you rise higher in the body of Christ/Mohammad/ Moses/The Eternal/Great Mother/) some of the old stuff must fall away. Self! Self. ----The putting aside of self—that is The Way. The Path gurus speak of.

To use the higher path first throw away mirrors---- then the higher way opens to us.

> The nuns prepare my way for me.
> With a humble bow.
> Attired in severe black/white habits,
> They take my full-length mirror;
> lay it lengthwise on the ground
> so I can walk over it.
> Thus my Journey begins.

The poor artist must live the monastic life of a saint in self-deprivation. Accept physical hunger deriving from a hunger to know the Divine.

You must hold to the Way. Yes, isn't The Path putting aside of self? So that one might see more clearly? This self & all its desires, needs & fears.

Noticed I'd gone to church, prayed a prayer that day, went to shul that evening and continued the same prayer that I began that morning in church. It's the same God, the same faith & the same prayers---just in a different language.

Church, shul, mediations---I've had difficulties with all of them.

But make no mistake you believers! God has extended Gods-self into every single nation, every people, in every single time and place and by many different Names!

The Lord(ess) God most High has thrown a wangdangle on me. God of all Creation I'm moved to tears! Fighting faucets of water back as we exit Grace Cathedral into the black night; in a clear sight (for there are no tall buildings) there over the park square, way, way above, set in a dark black blue sky;

a blaring flaming and furious moon! MOON!

God is always outdoing Gods self! A huge 30-foot diameter circular stained glass window cemented in stone shone like a precious jewel set on the face of Grace Cathedral, lifts its breast up to the moon in heavenly offering!

An unusual stratus of clouds formed to look like an underline for emphasis under this full moon, or a reversed eyebrow beneath an eye.

God is sending signs & wonders in the heavens!

A day later in a different part of the city I continue my astronomy. Veils & veils of white/grey clouds above the moon (but none of them upon it) being now like an eyebrow in its proper place.

No more copies at Trans Center. The new director has forbad it. —In her again-changing-of-the-mind. It's a good damn thing I did what I did while I could!

Have come full circle back. Returning to the printing of 7 copies of each new work as I did 30 years ago in 1978. From now on. At the height of free copying it was 16 (of PASSAGE). So my station is removed to Kostly Korporate Kinko's. As far as the restoration project, am now making the Re-Photocopy Series at one sheet (1 copy of 4 pages, back-to-back) per day of those ancient originals. The next day return to Korporate Kostly with the new master to make additional 2 copies. Because I said I'd do 3 copies each of 22 titles. Such a painstaking pace now! Like how in that movie with Morgan Freeman some white celebrity star dug, dug, dug, tunneling his way thru prison walls to freedom 2 spoonful of soil at a time over 20 years! Excruciating! Lucky ELECTRO SHOCK DOKTOR was almost done upon the largess. Too bad I had saved almost all of the double length books until the end.

In JOURNEY I, at 7 copies, continue my progress thru this world. This diary of days. The latest dresh* is this: I said I wanted to write/paint things of beauty—here is a quote pertaining to that very fact: *'it is only though symbols of beauty that our poor spirits can raise themselves from things temporal to things eternal."*
    Abbe Suger, De Administratione, circa 1126.

*--Hebrew; a commentary.

    ***

Editors addition--- from EMPIRE! In which Mablev473.vax honors her class with one of the Prophets poems:

> *I will tell you the tribe to which you belong.*
> I think what is happening there
> is much more horrible then people know.
> Half of a whole generation has lost
> the old teachings,
> the old ways.
> They have lost themselves.
> Where are the elders?
> If they would just stay among us!
> Where are the soldiers
> who would stand among us?
>
> Stay & do service my sisters
> & brothers.
> Lead them on the spiritual path.
> Tell them of the ancient ways.
> Do service.
>
> Answer them.
> Answer their questions.
> Fill the young peoples hearts
> with hope.
> *Make your people be My people,*
> says Creator.

5.

S/he prayed at nighttime. So tired, so exhausted, shuffled to bed, found himself uttering the words, which were: "Mother Jesus! Mother Jesus!" Stammered out of his mouth.

He/she prayed at eventide: 'For those both domestic and foreign who's fate has been to be murdered, maimed, destroyed by our nations military adventures.'

He milled around while in the common ground of the park--then went up up the cement steps of the mighty Cathedral.

This edifice is castlesque. Minds eye can see back to ancient eras, falcons who inhabited castles of the early and middle ages, living in rafters, who shat everywhere, even upon the heads of royalty; nobles & vassals alike and the hounds who bedded down with the soldiers in straw on the cold stone floors; falcons swooping down to receive their portion of bread and mead, the hounds baying up/down rocky stairwells; these ill lit unventilated fortresses where smoky firebrands lit corridors and smoked up the interior, and warmth was scanty, provided by sections of tree trunks burning in huge fireplaces taller then a human, and heat was retained by thick rich tapestry's indicative of unparallel wealth which had been captured, seized as some prize which adorned the walls.

Approaching this vast stone fortress of the Cathedral, he prayed upon each of its steps:

(A step.) 'For all those whose hearts is so heavy.'

(Another step.) 'For the innocents. The children in orphanages because of war and domestic spousal abuse. The animals tortured in slaughterhouses to feed us.'

(Now clutching onto bronze railing.) 'For the environment, to save our air, our water, so that all of us animals and humans can have a future goddamn it!'

S/he prayed at nighttime, that, when, upon his becoming rich, all his/her gifts to the church (synagogue, other religious centers) be well-blessed and deeply received.

(Last set of cement steps, speckled grey.) I approach the last step hobbling on one leg, just as the Cathedral bells begin to chime their last note. Its 6pm.

Entered the massive gold gilt doors, he prays: 'I bow deeply from the heart to the majesty of God.'

Congregates dressed in their funeral clothes, those walking corpses--- wearing smiles on their moribund faces. Smiles of the dead. Drinking up inspiration from the angelic choir at Grace Cathedral sung from gifted throats of the choir. Pure--- awestruck we listeners are being purified.

The Transman let his gaze drift upwards, up, up, to the loftiest part, those arches which uphold this great ceiling—then vision fell again, to observe the well-heeled crowd in which he was sitting.

Behold the church straining at its weakest point! Its breaking! From sheer wealth! There's too much money inside here! In the pockets, purses, checkbooks of this congregation! Too many houses are owned between them! More then their share! It is breaking down the church of Christ!

Thought that out of the congregants, 700, 800? No, over 1,000, that Sunday afternoon only the woman who sang the chorals had the voice of the very finest angel, and that he too was very gifted, prolific, spiritually sighted---that how few people out of this thousand were a specialist in their own field! To whom the other 999 must come to hear the angelic solo, read the fascinating novel, or receive benefit from the surgeon, master in her/his own domain.

***

Attended the two-spirits Harvest Day celebration. Native American GLBT. Ate fry bread, succotash, turkey. Partook of Native prayers. It's a way of life to which all are invited, Indian, white, black, Asian, all. In a changing world.

Colorado Indian musicians were striking the drums with fury. The drums are sounding danger! People must change their ways fast—for there's the inheritance of all blood spilt & hurt done to the red peoples. — The ancient chants speak truths. That a cycle is upon its returning swing—so listen, its of importance, these red prophets:

> We walk as warriors.
> In a powerful & spiritual manner.
> Walk in a sacred manner
> Walk in a sacred way.
> Walk as a warrior.

Yes people, —that cycle is returning. You ones who love Creator must do the right thing & set food back on the tables of the poor from which you or your ancestors once amassed their great wealth! Set foot on the right path least we be caught up in the flood, the far-reaching destruction which is sweeping over this world--- returned with a vengeance! Go in the right direction! The Path.

The terrible part of it all is—this is not a work of vendetta or vengeance by human hands, which is thus more easily combated by human minds, but a work of justice set into motion by Creator Herself. The God, the One who made us all.

> The emotions of human hearts grow hard.
> Times become so vicious, so cruel,
> that it becomes unbearable for the human soul.
>
> & that's where God steps in.

***

> God *is* good.
> All others are pieces of good.
> (If they're smart.)

God: Make your people be my people.

Red: Well OK... (Begrudgingly) If that's what You want...

God: No Red, that's what YOU want. I'm calling you back home you must hold to the Path!

***

En-route thru the TL this afternoon. Junkie hype—skinny, lounges against a building. Vamp. A Dracula cloaked in narcotic shroud, invisible but oozing out of her own aurora like death. Explosive insane stalk the Tenderloin babbling frothing hate. Grown up fast into adults stumbling druggies on the street are crazed unhappy children laughing over 3rd grade jokes

There's all these food places, little cheep eateries in the dive environs. Somebody has money & in junkie spirit of generosity takes everybody to eat. So the fires of human charity are not burned out utterly.

>*Their young life being so bad,*
>*such a cruel upbringing*
>*that they've lost part of themselves.*
>*Too much gouged out. --*
>*So they must have a blood sacrifice*
>*Only spilling of blood—human blood*
>*Will ease the torment.*
>*Their blood—*
>*Or someone else's.*

I see my other toothless could-have-been-self in one of the dwindling supply of cheap crack-ho hotels (the other residence hotels slowly continuing to fall before affluent yuppie gentrification) a soon-to–die not transitioned transbutch hustler, welfare chiseler sometime part-time phoneroom worker living on the lowest rung scrambling with half pint of whiskey in her hand.

A young Red, angrier back then because he didn't understand how things worked, even buying a cup of coffee from employee behind the counter without creating an argument with the proprietor.

Suddenly, as if in finality, the grimy streets themselves make the final pronouncement of their fate, as the further out of dead-center of the

TL you go the streets get cleaner; no stray newspapers, fewer wandering disheveled bums w/vacant stares staggering to nowhere or doomed dopefiends on intent purposes of criminal stratagems. It's all coming to an end! Being sanitized! Gentrified! It's outcasts removed!

Alcohol/drugs are not the worst offense the offense against the self, it is the giving-up of hope that is worst. These other tresspasses spring from that.

***

Look up 1930's painter on Internet—Thomas Hart Betran. Writer Painter. I must pick up the brush, pallet, & oil colors! Maybe this will let me into a very elite group that of other writer/painters---in heaven at least (so all could be there including past, present, future) all of us down the ages or right here on earth. Must start, or be without my glorious paintings forever.

You've seen them before, ersatz, poseur, failed, or procrastinating artists in whose 'studio' (4 walls only being used to live inside, tossing & turning on a rumbled bed) the same canvass stretchers sit unmoved from storage, unused brushes stuck by size in decorative vases gathering dust, and others, once too-briefly used sadly sit aside of the sink in a glass jar. Their fine sable hair stuck together in a non-rehabilateable qlucky glooy mess of by-now evaporated turpentine solvent once meant to dissolve oil paint and now the very adhesive which binds them in their death throes in an oily dried up Sargasso sea— if the artist ever regains her inspired balls she will have to go out & procure a passel of new tools.

When you're young you have all these desires, yearnings, that drive one out to explore the world, to search, to fulfill their inner longings. Full of energy. But as you get older this dissipates… For some it lasts quite a while, but eventually those longings do modify, cool. And it's a good thing, because those yearnings and desires torture a person to the death!

Oh by the way must add once more about AUTUMN CHANGES*—this is a total fabrication! Lies all lies told but thru using the voices of a conglomerate of other folks for instance the following case study....

Case study #450:
Some peoples live lives very difficult because they can't locate themselves on the sexual /gender chart. Sex & gender and how that is acted out in society and in bed. A case history comes to mind—most strange, that of Signore Serpeggiarevere Calvin Lezzardo Consigliore Di Poitou, a military officer of substantial degree and a high-ranking director (Consigliore) of the Committee Of Internal Affairs.

Signore Calvin was stocky, well built, masculine in demeanor and attire—but in a female range of height. Handsome, well-groomed, well-mannered male, circumspect, moderate in actions and in dress. Not remarkable whatsoever---except by one thing he did. Which was, he was seen in lesbian taverns of the late 1960's and all thru the decade of the 1970's that heyday, age old since the tenuous rise of woman's taverns back in the 1800'rds, when they finally began to wane due to the clean & sober movement which swept thru the dike community when lesbians stopped drinking, stopped going to bars; this not-too mysteriously coinciding with the opening up of many more avenues for them to go, not in a small part thanks to the Women's Liberation movement. Signore Calvin would come in to some women's-only bar—in uniform-- in his leisure hours after his duties as an official di Poitou and stand or take a barstool. Legally he could not be kept out since as a public place by the state code they must serve any customers who gave them no reason to be ejected. And as he never posed a threat (other then that, in the suspicious women's eyes, of his actually *being* there), over time he was just regarded as a fixture around the place---like a drably decorative column supporting the ceiling stuck off in the corner somewhere gathering dust. He would sit silently and stare at the crowd, but not obtrusively, watching the dancers, the revelers, and sip 3 or 4 alcoholic drinks during the course of an evening.

After the death of nearly all of the Lesbian Bars, which had come and gone by name, location, usually numbering about a half dozen in any given year, he was lost sight of. But a decade later the Signore, graying around the temples and having added an extra 40 pounds to his girth so that he now resembled a roly-poly soldier boy doll in dress uniform was observed in the following situations: #1. At the office of Dr.------ a notorious physician whose clientele was almost exclusive transsexual, a little on the shady side, who administered injections of female hormones for the desperate trans female population of those queer-unfriendly times and also testosterone to the intrepid sparse few FTMs who might make their way upstairs to his 3rd floor Tenderloin office. But under slightly dubious circumstances came these hormone treatments. First, they were sold at high prices to the desperate & marginalized transsexual clientele, *and*, the Physician was a renowned tranny chaser, trick, surreptitious tit & ass groper, & proved later to be a cross-dresser himself, who had secretly been titillating his fantasies on the parade of bedraggled showgirls in nylon hose who swished and sashayed up his grimy steps—which was the true purpose of his 'office' from the start. #2. Year 2000. On numerous occasions, after dark, in his car pulling up to the curb of Post near Larkin Street picking up a transsexual sex worker, the finer sort, passable, and dressed in diaphanous veils and silks of the highest quality which clung to her body and high pumps on shapely legs, this not a happenstance encounter but a call--date, prearranged. Finally, #3. Now, having arrived full circle, the Signore, was seen, by witnesses, frequenting a modern day transsexual clinic, the reason being a consultation on his own potential transition, to female!

*--The Authors Master Work, his Semi-Unofficial Diary.

***

Grace Cathedral also has rats. Some ugly big ones. —6" to 8 long. See a shadowy rat slithering out of a raised flowerbed, climb down the side of its stone retaining wall, scurry underneath the rain/sun weathered wooden benches with curved backs & disappear behind the perpetual water fountain. The two-legged rats are worse. Every religious institution of every faith on earth has them. Those in clerics costumes. Who have worked their way into the church and climb up thru the scaffold of its inner workings. Worse because they destroy My fabric. Says the Lord(ess). They eat away at My Body.

Now I am poor, I am busy picking up dropped coins off the streets of Babylon in its Last (falling) Days, dimes pennies nickels & dreaming meanwhile of giving millions to inter-faith institutions that help raise up the plight of women, children, and the poor.

Recall those days just before holidays how I felt like God was walking into my life. And Christ, literally. Tall, so beautiful, in the finest array of incalculably rich fabric so full of peace, radiating inner light. Felt the reverberations of God, so thick with substance unshakable.

Well I'll be honest about it, Creator had showed me, upon moving into my small studio, that it was in fact a cell and I was a nun-priest, a devotee, living nearby a Christian church where I could do service and be connected into the flock of the Most High, so that was 5 years ago, and tonight after Grace Cathedral (2nd time in my life there) am thinking, when the minister cried *follow!* Meaning the Christ is calling us to follow, which means giving up everything, monies, desires of self, etc, that I am in fact a nun-priest in the service of the Most High, by my own self's choice, and so here we are!

When I was a new Christian I towed the party line. All I knew were Christians in my church during that era—broke off from the other friends of different faiths long ago as a transient person may do over the progress of time. And believed then, as my church taught, the only way to heaven was thru the one Christ, now I believe many others of many other faiths who worship Creator in spirit and truth and love, and need and sorrow and even joy will see the Great Heaven open to them!

All this worship at various venues, am learning a smattering of Hebrew! To go with my poquito Spanish as learned from the lips of the lovely Rosa Salazar.

> The kind Mohammad came to me
> because I was weary & so worn out.
> He comforted me.
> *I am the same.* Same
> As the Christ. I Am
> Buddha. Mohammad. Christ.
> Our Great Mother.

Walking from the Animal Shelter where I heard great news! Two dogs I'd visited, prayed for have are going home! They've been adopted!

> *When a lost animal gets a home*
> *it's the most wonderful day in the world.*
> Greater then the Coronation
> of Kings & Queens,
> *with all their pomp, circumstance & gold.*
> *Because it's from the heart.*

Walking past the green hill park see homeless huddled there. It is truly justice that, given the painful climb to civilization's peeks & heights some lowly humanbeing carrying ragged backpacks/bedrolls would crawl on their hands & knees thru the city streets so grand & built up & richly heralded, towards a green park to hide themselves under leafy boughs of trees, bushes, taking a place on the damp soil, putting themselves back into the human race's early forest beginnings to survive mentally & economically among the sky scrapers and towers of this fierce empire.

God: Red have I created people to be like beasts?

Red: You created people to be people. Beasts to be beasts.

God has presented her/his case with the opening statement.

These well to do people who pass by, who have taken over SF turned it into a high rent capital of the U$A---- they won't be dancing they won't be singing! Those who have forgotten about their infringements upon this bitter world!

God I want to go everywhere and do everything, in Your heaven! I want to sit on the perches with the birds to be near them! I want to run with tigers! I want to go all over Your creation and see everyone and greet all animals and people with love, and dance with joy!

> It's a beautiful place.
> A marvelous place.

> Where animal families are restored,
> mother and child,
> and human families live in peace.

We are crossing some kind of great plane divided from heaven & separated out of chaos. We are passing from an opening end to a closing across a landscape full of rising & setting suns, moons. The Good Shepherd/ Mohammad/ Great Mother/Buddah leads the way and comforts us on our journey.

> *I am the alpha & omega*
> *I am with you until the end of days.*
> *--Jesus Christ, 2006 AD.*

'God my work is a lonely work.'

He was known as 'the Prophet who went by his own way.'

People laughed at him because he was different, but very soon they were to listen to him with an astute ear, nodding their heads in deep reflection.

'I'm such a mess.' Thought the Transman, but under the mighty arches of Grace Cathedral he saw the world in its pain—how much more of a mess! So much imaginable wealth held in the hands of a few, a few who seek to control the planet and seize power! So much misery of so many; untold masses of suffering others. This, richest nation on earth, —the most affluent time in history.

The bells of the Cathedral chimed their last note high in the cement tower like pronouncement sealed, judgment given.

Just one shake and I'll set it all straight! Says God.

Editors note; from EMPIRE!
He sold aluminum cans at the recycling center which $, he must promptly pop into the gorging mouth of KKK. (The printing center.) 'Sell all CD records & DVD's in my house; it would have been nice

to have classical music to paint too—but have done this because I want to tell it to you! And you and you and you! Here is my words: AGGGGHHHHHHHHHHHHHHHHHHHHHHHHHHHHHHH HHHHHHHHHHHHHHHHHHHHHHHHHHHHHHHHHHHH HHHHHHHHHHHHHHHHHHHHHHHHHHHHHHHhhhhhhhh Hhhhhhhhhhhhhhhhhhhhhhhhhhhhhhhhhhhhhhhhhhhhhh Hhhhhhhhhhhhhhhhhhhhhhhhhhhhhhhhh! Whoops! This is costing 10 cents at the Korporate Killer!

6.
The latest no copy policy of the new director has really hurt Transman. Who must spend precious coins on copies at KKK. (Korporate Kinkos Kopy center or some other shop.

The Arobateau treasury is in penury.

Up in the morning, hungry, no food in the pantry---forgot to go to food bank, so busy writing JOURNEY. My last will & testament of a struggling survivor in this cruel New Age of kapitalist feudalism, starving under rent control despite which landlords keep gouging out pieces of flesh, friends are Ellis-acted out of their homes; in general prices continue to rise, and old peoples pension (like mine) is substandard. There's money everywhere--you just don't see it. People dying for lack of money, people dying with money.

Walk to the library (9 blocks) not a single sou on the streets! Nor any aluminum containers but 2 beer cans. Didn't take them. Can't go around smelling like a brewery the rest of the evening. Maybe will shake down some treats out of my group at Muddy Waters coffee shop tonight.

> 'Journeys are very perilous' said Quip, 'especially outside the coach. Wheels come off, Horses take fright, coachmen drive too fast, coaches overturn.'

> Charles Dickens from a novel, 1829.

Times are tough. Assuage myself with thoughts of politics;

> *Now the clamor of war responds not only in the high places, but also in the remote corners of the realm. The people are*

> *filled with dismay. Fear creeps into the towns and villages. No place is safe, neither the Bourg as refuge nor the open country as a way of escape. Men know not weather it is safer to flee or to stay.*
>
> Mana Vita Sancti Hugonis; circa 1600rds.

And spirituality:

> The Savior is poor dressed in poor clothes, and walks on foot or rides on the back of a slow old mule--the Savior is poor so that s/he can speak to the common wo/man.
>
> Red Jordan Arobateau from JOURNEY, 2006.

There's a new song out whose refrain is 'Lets go to prison' with a telling photo of a bar of soap on the shower room floor. Is it about arrests for activism? Students arrested for protesting our fascist government? Or is it a drug song, about being busted for sales of Heroin, or Crack Cocaine?' If society isn't pro-active, and just simply punishing, vindicating, criminalizing those persons problematic, its children are going to glorify the very worst aspects of it, they will eroticize it, incorporate it into their being; they will go down, down, down to the bottom riding on pains coattails via drugs, alcohol abuse, violence, & other self-life murders.

Drive with Non-Professor Turnip; we pass the rough part of town, TL, see many who dwell there not because of poverty, but because of drugs/alcohol/ insanity and giving up—being like sieves thru which all resources pass. They can hold nothing. Some great sorrow has broken them early.

There had a strange thought. That my gift was given to me so I would find the right path. I was so damaged as a child—to the breaking point. ---I remember that, starting at ten. In my fantasies of murder. Glorifying of the hypodermic needle. And me hating and envisioning the breaking down of all structure. But in my art, knew I had a tool—my art sustained me long enough thru this life, gave me a purpose, gave me power, and gave me hope for the future, so that it sustained me long enough to heal. For half a century I existed on this. I lived on art like nourishment—until I reached a point that enough of the sad stuff had slowly filtered out of my mind & soul. Yes I found the right path. Took the higher road.

Very soon I will close this JOURNEY & hand it over to the children of the near-future. I hope the citizens of that unknown dispensation which awaits, just beyond the mists of God's real time will get a copy, that at least one or two of these few photocopies I could afford to make (bound in yellow card stock) will survive thru that tumultuous JOURNEY which entails wearing-away of material stuff, atrophy of a stock of too few volumes sold or distributed from their first beginning.

7.
192 steps up Mason Street from Pine to the hill's top on Broadway. 39 steps up to the grand, ornate Cathedral entrance, which is fine, thick old wood, with fixtures wrought in bronze.

It had been exactly a month. He headed up the hill. Another round full moon shone down! He approached the cement steps praying with vengeance!

(A step.) 'Oh Lord(ess) Have Mercy. Protect! Protect us!' (Friends, animals, innocents.)

(Another step.) 'Oh yeah, and protect me too.'

(Now aloud in a feverish plea!) "Save the animals God Almighty! Please! The pigeons in New York City! They're trapping and shipping the birds out to Jersey City to use as target practice!

> A bullet pierces the grey fluffy breast
> of the pigeon.
> May its soul ascend
> to the Great Mother
> of all homeless pigeons!
> May they live there in eternity
> in the house of our loving Creator,
> Amein.

Dear Children, Children of the future! I do not see how you can live your lives one more instant without turning those thoughts and feelings upwards to we know not what, but searching for the pure, the divine, the good and the saving One. Because we all run the race, and begin to know at some point we're going to drop out of that race—realizing this more strong and stronger as we go further and further. That it just remains a question of how long, how far we can travel, and upon what great impulse.

Every detail of our lives eclipses blocks of time---so its important not to dwell on anything but ones bare bones necessities. For me, the art to which I've been given and have expended on that, everything. Energy wise, time wise, all wise. It is my great impulse.

Wherever epochal dramas, journals, novels, poems…. one writes and presents to the world; written information, ink & quill-scribed bibles, Korans, torahs —the labors of monastic priests, --- stone tablets, papyrus scrolls; to modern day computer print-outs, time has a habit of taking out of context what it will; accentuating in bright lights what it may choose by popular demand, drowning the rest in obscurity. The paparazzi will appropriate its favorite messages. So the visionary runs the risk of their lofty passages being edited out & the other, common crap remaining, which ain't exactly what you'd meant to say! What will the future know about me? That Red was a spiritual person, a thinker? My guess he'll be noted for his excesses of eroticism. 'Certain Passages…'thus labeled a sex crazed horny horn dog.

Now, for my last exhortation, closing this first volume of JOURNEY, (the Daily Diary), about theology. To remind you that regarding our Holy Bible-- just what it says, it means. – "In My house there are many mansions." All kinds of diverse persons and groups and beliefs are in the huge, universal mansion of Creator! Thus you all are going to be up there dancing in joy!

Maybe I will be known as a prophet by future generations!

Poet! Scavenger!

I have an enviable freedom because of being my own publisher. I don't have no editor, no reviewers, no critiques, no distributor... so no one tells me anything. Are the results better writing? Would I get writers block like so many famous artists who suddenly have a 'public' to account to? If so, it's a little late—since Red Jordan Press catalogues over-80 separate books!

Salvador Dali was a consummate artist plus he knew how to market himself. When you become proficient in your genre then you're free to wander the world self-defining into a character. This 'character' helps peddle your product. *'I will go wandering....'*

State of Empire 2006:
Pressure on the large continental land masses causes them to actually sink too, as well as the sea level rising due to natural, epochal variances, plus global warming—human created, this an unnatural cause. Island nations are Disappearing. Islanders see the water level rise further and further inland. They report having first noticed the sea level had risen a while back, slowly, but recently greatly, and now it's up to their back doorsteps. Leaders of Island Nations are greatly alarmed for their people and are asking nearby continental nations which are safe being on higher ground, for sanctuary; some for thousand; others tens of thousands of their population. They shortly will be a people with no land.

Over the last 50 years land loss has accelerated to 50 miles per year. There is a slow collapse of the ecosystems of species of flora & fauna, that are now dying out at an alarming rate, predicting their likely extinction if some compassionate reversal of human behavior isn't forthcoming. The rising sea level gobbles up 2 acres of delta lands by the hour. Loss of all wetlands and swamps and marshes is a possibility. Soon coastlines may be submerged. Without wetlands the oceans are lapping at the foundation rock upon which the coastal cities are built, gnawing away at the landmass underneath which supports them. This predicts a land failure of many surrounding coastal regions, thus shrinking the landmass of continents, the complete eliminating whole cities, states and sea-level nations like Holland. —Dear Children, let's hope this is not a prognosis for the future!

The human experience is full of traps. Traps springing! The economic variety, and also crime and failure; those cut down in wars by early death. —Some traps are ones can foresee, some, one can't.

***

Little and poor and short he moved thru the night city streets relatively unscathed, because he looked mean enough to put up a fight and too poor to be worth anything.

He came out of Chinatown, where blocks of Chinese novelty markets are advertising sales, -- due to perpetually closing--- as a lure to customers. Past where the homeless are hunkered down in Laech Wellessa (Ivy) street, 3 shopping carts deep along the curb. Empire, San Francisco of the open hands. *"I don't want no Heroin. I don't fuck with Heroin..."* His Journey to the transsexual clinic to get hormones. Beside the water cooler a roach scuttles across the tile floor narrowly missing his foot.

Signs of the resistance have sprouted up everywhere, for times have gotten rougher everywhere tout la monde.

Eternal Impeachment!

Hence a re-call on both divine and governmental levels. Impeach: To bring a public official before the proper tribunal on a charge of wrongdoing. Meaning the faux president of those stolen elections, (U$A 2004, 2000). The bribed Supreme Court which suspended recount of the votes of that unjust and tampered election, and the governor of the state who ordered the Supreme Court to halt the recount. Meaning the Halliburton/& U$ Vice President cartel that went to war to make money and were loyal to that cause alone, --- even tho in so doing shortchanged the war effort by refusing to pay for adequate backup to keep total peace on the streets of Baghdad and its environs, thus, de facto murdered 400,000 Iraqi nationals, plus 3,500 U$ military service men & women—all on the sake of saving money! No money for communication systems between ground/air troops of our armed forces! No money for armor to plate the convoy vehicles bringing supplies in & out of Baghdad, no money to buy bulletproof vests for the infantry solders in the line of fire! (They had to buy their own if they wanted it. Or get their parents to send it to them from back in America.) I could go on and on! Yet 93 billion dollars every 3 months allotted to this war effort pick-pocketed out of the wallets & purses of American workers!

It would be foolish, foolish, foolish for me to idolize revolutionary warriors & preach actions, which could cost you your future--- acts I myself probably will never do. This in the style of a Mafioso don who puts out a 'contract' or commissions 'hits' (murder) upon his enemies to lower rank soldiers. In my case a flaming firebrand who puts out a contract on the entire ruling class, plus current fascist government in power. Even our own Emma Goldman idolized in previous writings who paid a man to commit a revolutionary assassination she herself could not/would not attempt. But likewise it would be a great error for me to dam up or label 'unthinkable', or 'unwise' what may prove to be the only avenue of action which may well be left to citizens of the future weather that be far or near, who by the happenstance of fate in conflux with the progressively downward spiraling standard of living and digress of liberty & independence, may leave that future generation at the absolute nadir of existence, having had every last human right stripped away from them, and no recourse as to change their miserable condition, except by violent, desperate acts. This awful digress having started with, at the beginning, overlords who had set the tone by controlling industry, tho they don't labor in it—the means of production according to Karl Marx--- and set bare survival wages for a norm, offering no workers benefits; to the impossibility of ownership of housing, even a room of ones own by the manipulations of rich land-stealing moguls. All these enemies of the people who eat 3/4 of the pie themselves, hoarding the rest for their families alone-- digressing from that point, to the last, those petty bosses latest come along, underlings who rush in on the coattails of their masters at a later date, who proceed to snatch up every crumb, leaving for the people, a totally empty plate.

On the other hand, for reflection here's a quote from Dorothy Day, circa 1915:

> "Life and struggle seem very tawdry in the twilight. This bleak countryside makes me feel that I should struggle for my soul instead of my political rights… I feel peculiarly small and lonely tonight."

So as far as what I'm preaching, leave it to yourselves, your conscious—and above all the times in which you live when reading these words—they will speak to you the correct path you must choose.

    Red Jordan Arobateau
    December 8, 2006
    5:36 AM Pacific Standard Time
    San Francisco, CA
    USA

Editors note; the following section was used in MAN GONE/STARVAX.

8.
What am I going to tell them when they come to me with bare feet & their hands open—having nothing? That their birth rights have been sold away by their stupid parents---that is my generation-- who has sided with the rich ones, supported mega wealthy oil polluters by driving gas guzzling cars, voted for corrupt & bigoted politicians & thus ruined our atmosphere & made enemies of all the weaker nations when they could have made friends? That even the poor ones, darker ones who suffer, dying trapped inside roach/rat ghettos, while their white counterparts struggle to survive in trailer parks inside vans with leaky rusted-out roofs and no wheels to go also sold their vote likewise to the rich who promised to feed their sons and daughters to the war machine, or forfeited their power by not voting at all? Each side has bigots against all the rest, whites hateful of darker races, darker races hateful of lighter, many of them caring not a bit about the inferior status of women, and all of them hateful of queers.

God has set the rules & your monkey parents disobeyed them for money and out of hate so first of all to begin with don't be like them!

Whatever happened to the idea of justice & mercy?

Let me repeat again the present system must be overturned now!

The workers must have a claim upon the products they make; and must no longer be penalized because they lacked capital to finance business/factory's from the start up. The same goes for housing!

(I guess I always wrote like I was about to be evicted—from one of those low cost rooming houses; always on the move—fast, so that my current novel would be substantial enough that an editor could finish it for me, tying up the stray ends as I lay dying.)

The Christian/Judaic mission must be taken to new heights—revolutionary acts.

Only by these acts of a Godly mission will God be moved! Acts paramount over academia and talk. If they have any meaning at all these acts must be termed revolutionary.

Now my dear Revolutionary Children, my precious anarchists dressed in black who smash the windows of Koporate Kapitalism, I must tell you something you don't want to hear. Listen. We are all going on a journey to the Most High. Remember this Dear Comrades. The Muslim people, the Wiccans, they are all going on a journey to the Most High. Those ones ½ torn out of the fabric of humanity—they are all going on a journey to the Most High. Change-Makers Karl Marx, Chairman Mao, Fidel Castro, Angela Davis and Emma Goldman are going/have gone on a journey to greet the Most High. And so are you and I.

Dear Children; don't be misled—it is only by struggle that a heaven on earth will be achieved. Natural progress of history will not attain these sympathetic goals—nor will its brilliant minds, its brightest analysts and best political theorists—nor will its military arms of great might. There is no Utopia, which comes about thru any of these means, sadly. Not thru its Karl Marx's, not thru its Thomas Jefferson's, not thru its Einstein's. It is thru our daily struggle in a Christ* like mind.
*Fill in your deity, Great Mother, Eloheim, Mohammad, et al.

Are we working for change—complete change? Or are we just shucking & jiving; going thru the motions of revolutionaries?

Next, I must digress to tell a second terrible truth—I must be a witness to greater evil (further beyond the Korporate Kapitalism and petty despots of this secular age. A beyond-death evil worse then all the heads of state ruling our current puppet world.

All are in the realm. Everybody in the realm has a number. If you are in God/Jesus/Great Mother/ Creator/ Mohammad/ Buddha (et al's) flock you, like the other ones, have a number, so you can be counted, but not all with a number are in God's flock. Some who are evil are extremely low numbers, frighteningly low numbers—that is large ones. The big numbers of incalculable digits. The numbers of saints are near the top. Higher, and smaller meaning numbers like 1, 2, 200, or 500, etc. As you see these are much smaller then the huge ones. And you can imagine numbers, which are so much longer. (For example, number 666,666,666,666,666,666,666,666.) Some religious theorists have suggested that a Hitler for instance would suffer 1 lifetime for every 1 soul he snuffed out, his number might be one thousand times the body count of his causation, that's utterly low down, (but there is no bottom to hell). Some individuals do evil because of being only concerned with self and to attain goals of self no matter what the cost, irregardless if it hurts others, but they aren't particularly super evil. Just ordinarily evil. The super evil, those with frighteningly low ranking numbers (larger numbers hence) are these who seek to establish empires, or mini domains on earth which will be guaranteed to their jurisdiction to the life thereafter (hell) in which they have a vested part, mapped out and deeded to them in advance in which their followers, captives, etc., will be stored and will work there and inhabit that place within their pre-arranged domain. Until some Saint, or the Most High Her/Himself comes to free them. -- God's got everybody's number—yuh better believe it!

Now, to sum that up, its already been said, we deal not with flesh but with principalities and powers.

OK, so what can we do?

An act we must begin is to found Communities of Spirit. I'm certainly not the first to talk about it!

All those worried about death, disease, social decay in its demonic workings on this earth, which are of this world and beyond have one easy solution. To lead a spiritual life. *And then to act on higher values.* That is one direct edict---a simple one; stay connected to some body of faith & belief, a church or synagogue, mosque, ashram, gathering of spirit such as Native American dance circle/drumming worships; to steadfastly participate in these uplifting spiritual values which spread the light, uplift the spirit and provide redemption of sin. We can't go wrong in partaking in these upsweeping spiritual values, *as we continue to work visibly for change within our communities.*

Also once you know it not an inherited gift so much as a daily exercise, one must stay focused on God and the things of Her because ultimately we get lost without the weekly service in some holy temple, that's what its all about. Keeping ourselves in constant joining with the Divine, opening and perpetuating a clear channel between you & Creator.

To take the vow of poverty is the most rudimentary way to counterbalance in some small measure the greed gobbling up this earth and all its accompanying warfare.

Peace children!

So speaking of works, this is the one I'm discovering. It is Building A Community of Spirit. There are many examples of these, among them the Catholic Workers Houses formed in the middle of the last century.

Now what is a spiritual community? I do not know! I've lived in communes with friends, housemates, which is similar just without a religious binding to hold us together... But one clue in the puzzle is to remember that each of us is an arm, leg; a finger, toe, on the body of the Almighty. So we are connected already. We are family.

Before I begin to talk about The Work, another brief note:
> The church should be like a family, the truth of God incarnate. Acting and being the Word, not just hearing about it briefly in a Sunday/Friday/Saturday sermon once or twice a month. Those church going inspirations, which fire us in bursts and fits throughout a lifetime are only instructions. How often do we follow the recipe? The higher church, the more advanced illustration of Gods word, would be a more thorough and human interactive church, in which the members are living the Word 90% of the time, not just 10% as the average Christian, Jew or Muslim, Native or Wiccian does today. The nuns and priests supposedly live their lives dedicated to serving God, in cloisters, monasteries, where the discovery and study of Creator is a lifelong occupation and a place where good works are done, like feeding the poor or teaching a church school for children. These safe houses would be similar. A place where people could put into action their religious faith without having to struggle just to begin the fight. A place whereby living collectively 90 % of time all resources don't have to go to meet a landlords demands, and other survival issues.

Now here are some thoughts on houses Dorothy Day style:

3 points would be observed. Spiritual Center. Poverty. Activism.

A religion-centered home, in which all participants actively prey, worship study the Bible, Koran, Torah, Women's Mysteries, Native Ceremonies, etc; hold regular services, including daily prayer/worship times.

A base by which the members can do charitable, or activist work, which often is not paid labor. When living collectively in safe houses only daily bills need be maintained which are cheaper then buying a house in which terrific mortgages are required. And by many different people living there, each with a small income, more time can be liberated from each person's schedule, so they are free to peruse their charity/action of choice.

In these houses stray dogs and cats saved from being gassed to death by animal control authorities may live out their lives protected, fed, and cared for. Each house will have its minimum/maximum of several dogs, and a small colony of cats. The house collective will do animal love, bonding and care.

In these houses only foods purchased meat-wise will be free-range cattle, poultry that is humanely slaughtered after a mature lifespan. Some houses may be vegan/vegetarian.

All who live in these dwellings will be members of this loose-bound collective and take the vow of semi-poverty. No grandiose lifestyles nor investment funds nor materialisms or consumerism allowed!

The utmost security will be practiced in these houses for the protection of its animals and its human populations. The charitable works involving sheltering non-collective strangers must be done by arraigning for housing, room, shelter *outside the safe house itself* in some rental facility for the poor. Cannot, must not run the risk of taking a stranger into the house thus inviting disaster! Must preserve self in order to fully and permanently be a resource that can help others.

We must buoy ourselves up in these houses of Creator, these temples of praise to Creator, and truly live the spiritual lifestyle, keep ourselves collectively strong to do battle against the buffet and foment of the embroiled world surrounding us, and to have a spiritual center, which holds fast.

Adjacent to these Houses of Spirit will be friends & associates who, by them not being able or willing to keep the aforementioned vows, yet nevertheless are drawn by Spirit to participate in the Work of these collectives will be considered, and may participate in many acts, functions and processes of the Spiritual Community.

> "Obviously the greater part of the thousands of heathens who first heard the Gospel of God made man, and accepted the new belief, understood no more than a fraction of what their conversion really meant and must lead to."

> Catherine of Siena, by Sigrid Undset, 1934.

Had to mention this quote, because it speaks to the strenuous path many pilgrims discover once they begin to seek the Most High and attempt to do Her Holy Works. Remember, proceed with caution. Here is a quote given to me, which appears in AUTUMN CHANGES:

> *God is a terrible truth.*

9.
Since the people still suffer an authority which has unjustly seized us and keeps a hold over us, and this authority has not gave way; gave us space to breath & be; and since our conditions have worsened; (no medical coverage now) despite how hard we work & thru no fault of our own, it becomes necessary to create an uprising equal to the need of our oppression.

We have frontiers upon which to make life better for the planet. The area of social justice. Science. Medicine. Outer space travel, & planetary cultivation. Oceanic exploration, & harvesting. Animal protection, & productivity. So many new agricultural tools! But how can these be used when corrupt power constantly intervenes with humane progress to grab profit out of it for themselves!

Don't forget we are participants in the work of God!

Section. (?) XXII: Violent Acts To Overthrow Empire. (To be used after radical acts of physical sabotage.). I must refer to JOURNEY Chapter 7. First, let me remind you, I wrote earlier, that violence isn't endorsed for violence sake, and how the whole nation of India was beneath the thumb of the British as a colony and how that yoke was entirely shrugged off by means of *passive resistance* by the leadership of Mahatma Gandhi. Also, so many people believe that any violent acts are against God our Creator. But now let me reference this alternative passage about when conditions have grown so severe and people have been reduced so low, and apathy is the current shape of being alive while any spirit of *true* life has gone long ago, generations ago, killed off by the successive poundings of those more powerful, thus there is no backbone left to fight with. A time when humanity has been reduced to the point it leaves no other way but for those still able, to resort to violence:

> It would be foolish, foolish, foolish for me to idolize revolutionary warriors & preach actions, which could cost you your future--- acts I myself probably will never do. This in the style of a Mafioso don who puts out a 'contract' or commissions 'hits' (murder) upon his enemies to lower rank soldiers. In my case a flaming firebrand who puts out a contract on the entire ruling class, plus the current fascist government in power. Even our own Emma Goldman idolized in previous writings who paid a man to commit a revolutionary assassination she herself could not/would not attempt. But likewise it would be a great error for me to dam up or label 'unthinkable', or 'unwise' what may prove to be the only avenue of action which may well be left to citizens of the future weather that future be far or near, who by the happenstance of fate in conflux with the progressively downward spiraling standard of living and digress of liberty & independence, may leave that future generation at the absolute nadir of existence, having had every last human right stripped away from them, and no recourse as to change their miserable condition, except by violent, desperate acts. This awful digress having started with, at the beginning, overlords who had set the tone by controlling industry, tho they don't labor in it—the means of production according to Karl Marx--- and set bare survival wages for a norm, so that one could never amass sufficient monies to begin a business. Offering no workers benefits; to the impossibility of ownership of housing, even a room of ones own by

the manipulations of rich land-stealing moguls. All these enemies of the people who eat 3/4 of the pie themselves, hoarding the rest for their families alone-- digressing from that point, to the last state, those petty bosses latest come along, underlings, who rush in on the coattails of their masters at a later date, who proceed to snatch up every crumb, leaving for the people, a totally empty plate.

Empire! 2006.

Let me emphasize a pivotal phrase. '*It would be a great error for me to dam up or label 'unthinkable', or 'unwise' what may prove to be the only avenue of action which may well be left to citizens of the future.*'

I must ask myself, do I want this on my conscious? Do you want it on your karma? I do not! On the other hand can one stand by helplessly and watch as innocent humanity, animals and our environment are swallowed up in a vicious cesspool of drug-addicted moguls who greedily stuff their wallets with absolutely no care for the future?

I don't want that on my conscious either! I don't want neglect, on my karma—that I did nothing! Averting my face from the atrocities! I do not!

Let us turn from the topic of violent resistance. It means struggle, even murder by assassination, and acts of physical sabotage against a monstrous construct. Today's current state of affairs is a monstrous construct rapidly approaching ones such as Hitler fascism was early in the Nazi empire circa 1934, such as slavery of black people was in our country 200 years ago, such as our own young America in the1700rds was under the British who then ruled us as one of their subservient colonies, such as the empire which was Rome, the Spanish Conquistadors bringing their iron shackles to enslave the Indians of Mexico; all empires which eventually meet with violent rebellions. And such as many compare to our growing snowballing problems in America today. Let us turn from this topic temporarily, since this is such a volatile issue and I, being only too human do not claim to have all the answers!

Who does have the answers? Wise people teach us that the answers lie first, and foremost within each human soul.

Let us talk briefly about The Path. This is a term taken from Buddhist Meditations. Many religious disciplines will demand, upon greater inspection and further following, that the seeker, give more of themselves to the Creator then they might have realized:
> ('Obviously the greater part of the thousands of heathens who first heard the Gospel of God made man, and accepted the new belief, understood no more than a fraction of what their conversion really meant and must lead to.')

Anyway the ordinary person, even the ordinary worshiper seated upon any pew or mat in any time or place will tell you in speaking about their ordinary lives and familiar situations; "You can't give your whole heart!" and there in lies the problem. As religious disciples seeking the Most High we eventually find we *are* called to give our whole heart—and more and more of this becomes apparent the further into Creator we wander by Her/His various Paths.

So discovering the length we will go to serve Creator, the depths of vows we will take, is an individual decision, done ideally, while in a 2-way discussion with Creator who leads us to the truth by Spirit. And thus what Acts or Works we do with our common lives or our common-becoming-Holy lives is also defined by us in concert with God. Whether we are to be nuns, cloistered, living in poverty; taking the vow of silence for 30 years, whether we are to be the widow who throws into the collection plate her last penny, weather we are to be on the barricades fists upraised fighting against corrupt authority, we must see for ourselves—follow The Path!

Believers in Christian faith speak of a daily, ongoing 'supernatural consolation' they receive from God. Meaning something physical or emotional they can actually feel within themselves. Yes, Creator touches us and will speak to us, if we fervently ask.

Sometimes God melts the borders of time, space, so the person can *see* whereas before they saw not. (Now we see thru a glass darkly, but then face to face.) And permeates thru these too-solid flesh walls by which we demand limits. This Revelation to us, this Truth imparted to us, is a Gift from God. (For there is no time, no past, and all are mixed into the future, and beyond these mists is the Dwelling place of Spirit. —it's all the same, past, present, future, these are only human limits, not even animal limits. For the animals of earth are in constant touch with heaven, & thereby with other animals who've gone beyond who are now rendered peaceful, laying down together with all sorts of animals.)

Seek the Creator, be aware of self, and you will find your mission, which is Creators intent for you!

Religions/Spiritual people must take a stand! Those of all faiths and denominations—without judgment cast at each other—because our world is at stake! The human race is going to suffer tremendously & shortly it will be in great need!

10.
I approach the temple of the Most High & what did I see? —This layered observation. Sunrise: when a shopkeeper arrives to work into the morning and walks into the cold stone doorway—there is the telltale layer of cardboard from the bed of a homeless person who was asleep there the night before.

2 Caucasian street men, scraggly, dirty clothes, howling; "THEY FUCKEN' PEPPER SPRAY ME IN THE FACE! FUCKEN' COPS!" "Yeah, yeah, yeah!" The other snarls in agreement; his leg shoots up into the air, his heavy boot kicks a red fire emergency signal post, so it vibrates in shock. (Is this where false alarms come from?)

"You want to get beat? I been beat I been put into the hospital!"

Signs of a terrific thrashing on his face blue-black swelling; cuts on his forehead, furrowed, browned broken skin puffed up 3 times normal size in broken patches. And the expression on his face is sour & sad.

The walk thru the TL continues with a white building manager hollering at a black street bum; "Why you throw garbage over my fence! Don't ever throw garbage over my fence again!" While a security guard stands scowling at the man. Black Man On The Run!

The once poverty-stricken TL is getting more upscale, and now people do care about their property. Times change. Poor people are put further and further out. They never did act right nor have much. Well, the fact that they never had a claim on any part of the master plan is a contributing factor to them not seeming to respect person, nor property.

More human misery when he gained Market Street in time to see a female vagrant being busted; picked up, thrown into the back of police squad car. A single male cop nearly 7 feet tall swings her huge rolling suitcase, just confiscated, into back of the squad car's open trunk. Peer thru the glass into the squads back window— it's a cage, bars across on all sides with a woman, white, stringy hair, clothing of a very poor street dweller, who howls; hands cuffed behind her back she rises and falls in the back seat in mental anguish. She's off to jail or the Looney Bin.

Sunset: A homeless man making his bed, prepares the spot—in the enclosed doorway of that business shut down for the night, places layers of cardboard down on the cold stone of the entranceway then on all fours crawls in, lays down, removes from his large traveling pack a blanket with a thermal outer layer to hold in heat, then covers himself into the inescapable cocoon which ones sees everywhere thru this big heartless city.

I approached God's temple & this is what I saw. These terrible crimes of misplaced persons.

This is the portrait of the future.

    ***

> Dear children, this current Empire is held together by a series of nuts & bolts at its joints, much like the connections of a great modern-age bridge, & it is here that Empire must be unworked.
>
> Red Jordan Arobateau, JOURNAL, 2007.

'This was given to me by God our Creator, any interpretation of what it means is up to the individual.'

Since America continues acting like the Great Beast* instead of a loyal, honest big sister/ brother of grandeur which she once was; it only remains for the people to do one thing--- shut it down! To put into the hand a new pen, to put onto the paper a new writing. What does this entail?

Work stoppage, boycotts simultaneously in every city & town on a national level, at first for a given period of 1 day. This to increase as necessary!

*Great beast of destruction devouring the lands, who sails out openly over-running the smaller nations in mayhem and avaricious stealing, while internally devouring with gnashing teeth its very own children.

What We Must Do Domestic & International:
Domestic:

1. National health coverage. Free medical coverage for all American Citizens everywhere in every state promptly when needed. (An International Healthcare must be established so travelers between national jurisdictions will be able to have a free coverage for any illness wither chronic or emergency.)

2. End to the barbaric practice of rentals—each citizen worker, or retired senior will have a suitable unit, which they own & is theirs! No more rents or fees will be paid! Just a mortgage, which will be 1/3 less then their former rent, and when this is paid off, they will own the unit/house free and clear, forever.

3. Employment. Each citizen will have a job. Everyone will work a humane schedule of 35 hours per week every week but for vacations, holidays etc. Everyone must be employed in some kind of work! Likewise, every citizen must be given a job and not denied employment.

***

Idea is not to meld all the nations of the world into one large centrally governed body, but to maintain he sovereignty of each nation in cooperation with each other.

The goal must be peace! Peace on earth! It has become the Prime Imperative! Citizens we must employ ways to install these demands now! The world must bring itself to peace! It must come into alignment with all of the prophets of God who ever spoke about reconciliation, forgiveness, and cooperation with one another! Humility under God and having civility towards all humans! Because other changes are happening as well, concurrently with our petty human dramas here on earth, change few of us are aware of. If we don't it may mean the end of civilization on our planet! We must be ready for the new age, which is swiftly upon us!

11.
'The will to power, to well being, to wealth triumph over the will to holiness, to genius. The highest spiritual achievements belong to the poor.'

Peter Maurin, circa 1930.

Transman had his layer of clothes prepared that night, for work the next day. First a used shirt--it need not be a fresh one since no where particularly nice to go, just the library, and the health clinic for blood pressure check and socializing w/pizza at Luke's group so, the shirt--hung on a rung of something, chair back, weightlifting bench, ertaz clothes rack, etc.-- immediately underneath that, first on the hook in fact, his same soiled tie--a donated one lifted from the Sach's Fifth Avenue dumpster at midnight by a transwoman friend Dominique--which currently being his favorite he was wearing night/day and would until it frayed, disintegrating to rags hanging around his neck, so, in their order, tie, shirt, then a fresh teeshirt--the only article of clothes guaranteed to be fresh from the wash by absolute necessity, and last, over this a pair of men's boxer shorts--with the dick in them, safety pinned securely inside the pouch so as his budge would be ready to slip on at convenience.

I have walked so many lines! Walked the line against racism, then again a little later in life, against anti-homophobia, walking in or out of the gay bar at night is walking the line. Being myself of the wrong color in the wrong neighbored—walking the line. Now here we are walking the line once more! Am I going to have to walk a whole new line now because of anti Semitism? When will it end? All this walking the line!

My pride my vanity and swagger helped get me thru the world. But frankly it is the spiritual stuff which sustains me deep inside upon waking up until going to sleep.

So let me say again, some part of the human mind seeks, needs, desires, searches for God. All voices & all languages roll up on a big highway of faith reaching towards Creator and Creator hears the children no matter what their language, custom or faith; these prayers in faith!

Seems there is, inborn, in all humanbeings, this hunger to know Creator—this itching for the Divine.

Furthermore, all that is accomplished in material, upon earth, is not done by works but by Spirit.

God creates hope. Its possible eventually some of our dreams will come to pass while others will fail, but there is hope! Hope, for however long or short a period of time this hope is temporarily created. That's what is important! That the people have hope. You lived *in* hope! You lived *on* hope!

12.
How long does it take for the people to awake? Until they are shuffling thru the streets, hungry cold & sick, bundled in 3 layers of rags, formerly clothes, eating at the church free dining room; no money in their pockets? Their faces lined with bitterness born of grief & seeing so much grief of others they once loved when their hearts could still entertain that emotion?

That is scenario is already here for many and other are fast getting to that position; this is the way-- inevitable which befalls all of us unless swiftly changes are made.

Have commented before on the stupidity of the minions of the ruling class, which governs the people; let us not delude ourselves! They have access to some of the finest minds in this world. They do know what they are doing. And to refer to them as 'stupid' is only a moral judgment about their bullheadedness, pig headiness, but in no means are they intellectually deficient. Only morally bankrupt.

Rich men are the same the world over; only some are better and some worse. The rich, of all different races, religions, and colors.

Incrementally they are aborting our lives piece by piece--- you are waiting for conditions to get better but its only going to get worse. Very nature of the economics of our society currently rests upon a faultline, because those well-off, seem to be very rich, yet just underneath the surface, are sinking too, and while clutching to save themselves & shore up their own ebbing resources they turn to grab more of what we have.

The rich ruling class would lie to you and say these accusations are not so. That your rent increase is due to higher taxes, when in fact it is only partially true—the rest turns to excess profits that go into their own pocket. Further, remember your teachings of a political nature! The rich landlords shouldn't be owning more then their fair share of housing, --one dwelling per person--- so as other people may own a house of their own also! Your boss will tell you their factory can't pay a living wage or it will be forced to shut down! But examine their books, and financial ledgers, it tells a different story! People study ways to win an argument and cleverly manipulate their speech, however that's no wining an argument, that's delaying justice.

And time is long overdue that these societal defects be set right! Ownership by the people of the places where they are employed! Each with an equal share!

See the faces of the poor. So many suffering.

God spoke to me upon awakening, when my thoughts weren't so much of this world:

'First I'm coming to My children the homeless—their needs *must* be answered.

It will be asked why have you treated My children so shabbily?'

Little children with their hands clasped praying; 'Please God just bring me a piece of bread to start out the morning tomorrow.'

I pray for you!

Just remember if you take up the struggle, you will be opposed. There will be places without food. Times of rushing currents with no bridge to cross, but I will see you thru. I will be your bridge.

There will be danger & you will cross, safe.

'I'm coming first for the poor. So if you want to see God first, become very poor.'

13.
The streets have been scooped clean! Not a pfennig! Plastic sack ready in my coat pocket to seize any cartons of abandon food on tops of garbage cans, quick and with lest amount of embarrassment. IE: "oh honey look at that poor old guy eating out of the trash. AHH HA! It's the famous author Red Jordan Arobateau!" ---Busted!

Well as friend L. said: 'They don't think that being a saint isn't a full time career…'

Anyway Children, poverty is an exercise in discipline. Everyone should undergo it for a length of time—at least 5 years---to *see* more deeply. Now it's a paradox also, that to dwell too long on the subject of poverty is unhealthy spiritually; it's the counter swing of the pendulum of obsession with having/getting/keeping wealth. Either extreme isn't exactly what Creator intended for us.

Every penny we stop to pick up along the road of life is a burden in heaven.

Red Jordan Arobateau
January 2007
6:04 Am Pacific Standard Time
San Francisco, CA
USA

Editors note: the following section was used in ACTS AGAINST THE POWERS OF AUTHORITY.

I must speak out in behalf of the animals of this earth. Because, to see the sea turtles penned, climbing upon each other, green webbed feet clamoring over and over each other's green shells, waiting to be slaughtered in the wretched Chinese markets of my beloved Chinatown, hurts my soul. There is a way we can raise food, utilize humane animal husbandry to ensure them a good life and a painless death, and feed the world plentifully and hygienically. Don't forget by livestock being used for food by us, we ensure them propagation of their animal species. But it must be done with humanitarian care. *Don't forget Dear Children, it's the spirit of the thing.*

14.
Dear comrades; comrades of the Resistance, freedom fighters, et all; words are not strong enough for what I have to say!

The sight of polar bears eating each other because they are starving at the former artic circle all due to human greed and selfishness of the civilized world especially America (who uses 50 percent of world fuel emissions tho we are only 5% of its population) and who insists on driving enormous Humvees and SUV vehicles that get a mere 7 gallons to a mile, costing $100 for a tank of gas; squandering huge expenditures of natures resources and Gods good will—something must be done! Anything!

ACT!

15.
Must speak finally, just a note, about good & evil. First to this fallen age of disbelief, inform you yes there is an actual evil. A negative & a negative state of being and we have the alternative of dwelling with in that realm or not and all beings have the choice of which to embrace the higher or the lower.

Now, to continue, there are those who say, "You are done! Write no more! Close your book!" But I must keep on.

Is only fair that we speak for all the people who have no voice—for the animals who have no voice in their cries for sanctuary, for peace & to have good lives with their own kind upon this good earth.

God sent many prophets to speak to the people, and they should be listened to. Otherwise Gods message will be missed.

The Creator has said to me: *'Write as fast as you can Red, as much & as powerfully.'*

How we sought God! How we salute Your perpetually burning lights! ---Now we enter the long corridors of penitence, grey stone leading finally to the grand alter of God so high up none can see around or over it, but where the tiniest being is accepted—with Love and with Grace.

Must say again that we are all equal in God. Some are higher up and closer to God according to the practice and devotion of their religious beliefs, but it does not make them better then the others. Because all people are equal in God. Because God made all people. This is the global human dilemma, the problematic human situation in that humans imagine since they are 'chosen people' or of a religion which has found out more about God, that they are closer to God in that respect. That they are, so following, better. That they are more deserving. They assume themselves to be superior over the others, -- when nothing so far fetched could be the truth. If anything they are chosen to serve the others who are blind! Who need them more! If anything they are called upon to climb down out of the high place with their knowledge and go among all the rest of humanity carrying food, knowledge, comfort and wisdom to those screaming in darkness for relief! They are in no way better then the others! God made us all! God loves each and every one! God loves the reflection of God's little selves gazing back at Her, the Devine, with their tiny faces—no matter how they practice their devotion of Her, weather be they primitive, or educated; simple or profound. Weather their worship be the strange and unfamiliar, the eclectic and arcane, to the common, well-trampled aisle of those worshipers who kneel down and shout out loud prayer. God is a just God, and is jealous of Her people, which is everyone whom she created! And She has created us all!

16.
The bleak poverty stricken west Oakland neighborhood dotted with loitering figures beside their corner liquor store; in the windows cardboard advertisement; where rag tag children go to purchase overprice treats, the bleak streets sprout like weeds, here and there the new condos, modern, sleek silver steel, glass, high standing, with clean lines. Luxurious lofts for sale, with redwood decks. Add a roll-on spiffy new portable barbeque pit. They overlook the old Baptist church, low lying, where tired 50 year black working men in blue shiny suits, women in their best with big hats, brown faces, black faces, tan faces all going to kingdom come via fashionable prayer in song. Old, and the new. The color us, the color another. Green weed-choked lots come up after the rain. Lots cluttered with rusty automobile parts, wheels off vehicles, spare tires, rusted axels. A few potted pots pets in someone's windowsill bring joy.

A box-shaped freight truck creeps across the horizon over a flat freeway on stilts over the city. A black crow sharply reverses its flight path in mid air, so quick and strong the move, swooping off the opposite direction after a 90-degree turn, following its mate.

Rich Starfucks pay more pennies per coffee pound to the small growers so they can have a life. The screaming, picketing and protest of activists has worked –a little bit. We must continue the fight! All meat process slaughterhouses must elevate standards regarding humane consideration in how livestock is raised & how it is slaughtered. Free range grazing. As many people as are able are becoming vegetarians.

I would write beautiful revolutionary poetry.

The commandments for human living was sent by God thru Her different prophets. God said: *These words which I command you on this day will be upon your heart, and you shall teach them diligently to your children.*

I see the old departing and the new. The new have no need of God, having so much material wealth. Will God die out entirely, until Her name is spoken only by the lips of the wind, from the echo of all these tiny poverty churches, long gone? When that day comes She will shake the earth! Shake it! Shake it until a terrified people rediscover Her and fall down on their knees begging for mercy!

***

There are some that say the revolution starts with each person, that it is not the one sweeping united front of many; an invading army changing a country, a century, some giant sweep totally from outside, but that revolution first starts as a human dawn inside each private heart.

So this leaves us with a conundrum. Isn't one dependant on the other? Neither can one change ones view of the outside but that they have had some interior epiphany first; yet, what catalyst is to cause this inner seeing? What dramatic tap on the shoulder, which awakes a people to reality? So that they can indeed claim, "I See The Light!" Regardless of this age old puzzle (what came first the chicken or the egg) change, is key. A mighty change is usually needed to aright a personal life, or the directive of a nation. Furthermore, sometimes to save the soul, to save the motherland, change must come swiftly! How difficult this is to act upon during times of citizen's dependant on comforts they treasure! Those brought up in an environment of plenty! For them to discover, *then act upon this knowledge,* that they must give it all up in order to ensure equality and justice for the totality of Gods creatures—and that they will not be held accountable for the hell bubbling over, this coming storm.

Now, in spiritual terms, another axiom. No one of their own is good no one on their own is right. Only thru God-the Creator are they good—the Creator. This is the center of a humanbeing. Here they have found themselves.

Here there will always be joy.

17.
What the human race is doing to the planet, to the creatures on it is so unthinkable, so unspeakable but ultimately it's about what the human race is doing to itself.

In nature's evolutionary process there are mutations—if some entity splits off being so severely mutated, so radically different that it can't survive in the environment it dies out. Human nature is inherently both good and evil neither being dominant naturally, but can be either by instruction or the education and guidance of its elders. If something goes to the evil side it will destroy itself, wipe itself out & tho that may benefit in some way some greater evil, the fate for the organism itself that was doing evil is that it is now dead and gone. So for human survival and for civilization to continue is to try to do good and to do the least amount of harm to itself and hence, to others.

Knowing this, it seems crazy that rich cities could sit easily on top of a gold mountain composed of so much evil, trickery, financial leverage against poorer citizens, and their animals. That it could lay its head on a clean pillow and dream sweet dreams in a condo conversion after kicking out a formerly squalid building-full of sick and feeble oldsters, struggling mothers with young babies, single people with their cats and dogs—leaving them nowhere to go! That medicine and aid is being niggardly squeezed off at its source and put instead into a fake war to grab oil overseas, so common people are going in pain, hunger and early death!

Furthermore it is ironic that so many of us are suicidal and depressed—when there is a world of humans around!

> Problem is isolation & loneliness, which is crazy because there are thousands of other people around, so it isn't a lack of people but of connection.
>
> --- Yvonne St. James Dutra Challenge Day leader 2007.

Remember you lessons of poverty. Remember them well my Children. Remember your pain. Remember the broken bones because state wouldn't pay for bone strengthening vitamins. Remember the extracted teeth because the indigenous dental program would not approve a root canal for 6 weeks lagging, waiting for permission to remove the decay, by then it was too late to save them. Remember your crying child in pain because of lack of $4.50 to take them to the 'free clinic. These charges! These brutalities! These laws of satanic idiocy! Remember! Remember the too-often ticketed car you couldn't move from its spot for lack of fuel or repairs. So it got impounded. It was removed and you too will be removed--- displaced by the rich who pour into this area like it was a resort luxury hotel beachfront paradise for a fucking life-long vacation, for their own private use, driving the rents and the property taxes of your abodes up, up, up.' Remember the gangs infecting your neighborhoods where you tried to stay alive stuck at a lower income. Remember! That the powers who rule us have abdicated our estate! That the rich have sold us out for their egos sake and for more gold then they can ever spend! Remember! And act accordingly!

As far as the Christian church-- I wonder why try to be a part of something God is getting ready to get rid of? Like so many other institutions of man built--- not women. It is so corrupt and worm-eaten it must fall! Or change. If it changes then it will be gotten rid of and replaced with a church more close to the heart of Christ. Well anyway, Grace is feeding me little sandwiches and coffee downstairs at the social hour. And amazing miraculous taps from the Spirit upstairs in the cathedral, both thru the messages delivered in sermon, and thru the breaking of the bread. I see how powerful it is, this bread breaking. Is it because the cathedral is so big and so many other believers surround me that God's message is amplified? Well I keep going to the 11 o'clock service climbing those 190 stairs to get there or whatever the count was…

Poverty. What a ragged bride she is; whose torn grey garment is made of cobwebs. —She seems mean. A tight mean line for a mouth. Is this the poverty I've embraced? Is this who our Savior has called me to wed?

In the high theatre of the church on pulpit the minister gesticulates. The masses attending are attentive. I am at my station in the back row.

I am sitting in the church, penniless, among those whose ancestors stripped my forbearers of their material wealth, stole the energy of their backs their hands, their feet, their legs, ---their wombs--- harnessed their labor unpaid to a slaves iron shackle. Now I don't have. I have not. 5 generations removed I only have a dollar, my spare change, to put in the offering. However this congregation, they give well. The well heeled master is still operating his antique machinery whose wheels grind on and on set up to enrich them daily, and somehow siphon my last dollars away from me. Either thru rent, buying of food, or necessary purchases, medical aid, transportation—all the infrastructure of civilized life!

I am raised up so that all might see! That's what Christ spoke. And we are suppose to follow in her/his footsteps and be like Christ. We are citizens of heaven! Maybe other citizens will see my bridal gown of holy cobweb poverty and get a clue!

The preacher is far away, but lifted up over 40 rows of pews which stretch from right to left, a ship full of parishioners, now he preaches: "Jerusalem, Jerusalem, who murders her prophets, I would have gather you up like a hen gathers her brood, but you would not!"

God has whupped my po' ass good. God has whupped my po' ass down to 9/10ths of the last degree. God this path is whupped, it's a killer and its me doing all of it! ME! Doing the actual flagellation of self like the monks in hair shirts in medieval epoch in stone monasteries…

The devil triumphs in the uncertainty of human beings—but God triumphs in our uncertainty when Her will is manifested out of it. Faith. Hope. Charity. —The translation of Charity being to Love. These three.

I uplift all those I love to You.

Forgiveness, forgiveness, forgiveness! Says the Lord(ess).

Mighty chorus of Amen's, Amein's, Blessed Bes.

    ***

Charming studio for rent—over priced $1,000 a month; yet homeless persons used syringe drug needles, slender clear plastic with orange caps, left on the door stoop.

The police & medical examiner cars waited outside, they were up there in the hotel ascertaining cause of death of a transsexual women. Prostitution is involved. Most of these cases are never solved. Down the street a transient man has collapsed moments ago, seeing the cops not far away, his companion, another tramp bent over his fellow tramp to see what he could do, nothing--- hastily gathered unconscious mans bedroll into his own, prepared to take his stash & run—so it would not be confiscated & thrown into dumpster by cops. Gone, when he awoke in the hospital—if he did ever awake.

Drug hypes with their crack pipes firing up in the streets, suck from a cylinder of battered metal, inhaling clouds of death. Negation of life.

Birds, children, puppies—the squeaking of life.

**

There are very few of us who undertake this journey… This transsexual path.

More and more can't see the wisdom of transsexual people ghettoizing themselves, digesting the poison of their repeated wounds over & over, together. The empty promises we make to each other. Things never done. Run in off the street into a support group. Spit up the evils of our days, all our pain centered around our unpassability, or those living on the opposite end of the spectrum, highly passable, who live in secret stealth hiding clues to our previous identity, spending a precious lifetime in concern about being 'clocked'; in loneliness out somewhere being that man or woman of our dreams if we can't be 'read' & nobody knows our 'secret'. Rehashing and regurgitating all this garbage centered around our sex & gender which is after all only a genome, a microndrial pattern set before our birth & what we must suffer down an eternity for.

Learn to love self no matter what! Then acting on this information, love each other! This is called the holistic way. If we don't do it this way, we suffer.

    **

Holy One, they walk to you backwards because they can't bare to look at it, the truth is so terrible!

    **

I know why you hate the white male preacher,
Because he is the status quo.
The status quo was against me too.
That's wisdom.

    **

The mental spikes they nailed thru his hands sting my hands too.
I love the Lamb.
I take his head between my hands and embrace him.

The Lamb who was slain.

    **

Cast out your rage.
It has no place with thee.
Come let me
Set you at liberty.

    **

I extended my hurt hand,
the one where the arthritis is worse.
And Jesus took my hand and examined it gently
with no pain began to unwrap my skin and veins and nerves as one does a bandage,
and healed me.

Editors note; further segments from the novel.

> What are the measures of resistance? They are the level to which the individual is capable. First we must divide the means of resistance into 2 categories:
>
> A. Peaceful means.
> B. Violent means.
>
> Here is a small, escalating list of measure of these different levels, choose yours:
>
> --Passive resistance. In which the protesters, picketers etc., blocking the sites of cruelty, go limp and must be dragged off to jail.
> --Aggressive action. In which freedom fighters invade various offices of cruelty & drench them with thousands of gallons of water.
> --Violent terrorism. Involving execution (murder) of top level personal from which or thru whose hands these cruelties are ordered or dispensed.
>
> ---The Prophet quoted in The Red Jordan Arobateau Reading Society

***

In the beginning the old prophet had said:

> Acts of revolution to be made against the ruling classes & all its government underlings must not falter! Even those involving murder, executions, and great public destruction including dams which have stolen water from the natives and destroyed the ecological infrastructure of Mother Nature, gross institutions of torture against animals and people—such as 'sex-role/gender dysphoria, reprogramming clinics' for underage teens & children, transsexual youth of the future.

18.
2 pigeons romancing on a deserted restaurant fast food booth.... I wear my halo like a hat that must also keep me from the rain, sun, and other bad weathers of the heart.

Looking around at every noise furtive, animal-like. Transman Red had worked 40 years on the wage-slave market. Now he was free.

Limping down the street between free computer @ public library, and Xeroxing at Korporate Kapitalist Kinko's Kopy Center.

The life of a food gatherer in prehistoric days was a daylong enterprise; picking berries off certain bushes—knowing which ones were poisonous to avoid. Certain roots could be dug and eaten, scavenging of dead carcasses, chewing a leaf here, moss there, eating a swarm of insects in one place, savoring their larvae in another. So the life of a food gatherer is exhausting. 60,000 years later, today also; the stress of the free food line because of some of the rotten people in it, also some who work for it. A food bank on Monday on a weary trek over a hill, to get supplies of cheese, peanut butter, caned fruit, canned milk, and a can of beef, then the food vouchers redeemable at Mc Crap a junk food palace, scurrying about the city picking up spare coins (two 25-cent coins, numerous pennies, a dime and a nickel); any Aluminum cans which cross my path. (On return jaunts only, so they don't stink up my backpack at the places I visit.). Fridays, food bank across town. Up and out, scrounging for discarded transfers in the streets to save bus fare. This church food bank yields 8 red/yellow tomatoes, a green head of lettuce, a box of dried mash potatoes, a log of frozen turkey, a gallon each of milk, and orange juice, one large thick orange/brown sweet potato, a sack of pinto beans, a sack of peanuts. The synagogue and church oneg/hospitality for slices of cheese, grapes, little sandwiches, lots of coffee, fruit juice and plenty of sugary cookies, brownies and slices of cake. I have spent only $1.89 this week—for chorizo to cook the beans mixed with whatever meat I have.

"You aren't a man!" The ignorant ones, accusatory, jeering. They said I wasn't a man! But their hate doesn't hurt me as much now. —I been a queer so long—I inhabit the middle ground. They inhabit the absolute ground.

I got to represent who I am. I can't represent tradition. And reject its stupidity in the way of its placement of individuals, hierarchically, much to their suffering.

I've experienced what it was like; border line mentally ill walking in the cold rain in a thin coat, only books and paints with me, walking. Solitary friends are the green grass, the silent buildings, rain falling on my drenched trench coat, getting wet and feeling it is a relief to be cold and wet, better then those killing emotions going on inside.

'I can't give up hope' you croak feeble you said this all during the cold years, the loosing years. When you are still saying this 30 years later, body disabled; without funds, when hope gives out, having seen nothing yet made material? Faith. Then will you say Faith? After this?

What is faith?

Faith is the substance of things hoped for the evidence of things unseen.

Faith, it is the spires of mosques and churches and temples beckoning us from a distance, waiting, perpetually waiting to minister to those hungry for spiritual food.

Faith is the reason I am still here after half a century.

    ***

Go down a street in a neighborhood houses lined either side, facing out. There's a story behind every door. That one, the husband is a wife beater. This next door a schizophrenic woman and her child. That was my door. This door, a poor family struggling to send their kids to college. Behind another door is a struggling painter who must subsist on minimum wage. His paintings number in the 100rds now. In reds, blues, yellows, greens, violet. Mostly stiff amateur renditions of people. He has little talent. Will he ever receive any award or attention for his efforts, if not his work?

Here is one of my sisters who tumbled out of a worse door then mine. One with practically no support from anybody. One of the dropout from normalcy. Former dike brawler; white/platinum blond hair; Hells Angles pussy-trade dressed in standard castoff freebox blue jeans, gymshoes and teeshirt, holding 5 stained plastic sacks into which she is constantly digging, delving into them with tan freckled long scrawny arms that bare blue tattoos of when she was a street rich fuckable female, a prize, a commodity, once proud, now forgotten, faded in time. Cheerful bright drug hype survivor, buoyant, adaptable, ever changing with the instance of those constantly hustling.

I've been among pimps & pirates & thugs--- & I don't want to know their names, never did want to know. I don't want to turn states evidence against any particular individual but to learn from who is there. Tell us now & the shape of things to come!

Continuing our parable of thugs & criminals-there are persons sitting on top of this United $tates, and the world in fact which are far greater then its stolen-vote elected puppet president. I don't know their names, I don't want to know. But I bet we'd all be surprised… American poor, elders, our money for pharmaceutical goods is being drained away, it's a pretty price to get the pills I need to keep me sane, blood pressure down, breathing thru my allergies, and a few other aliments. It gouges away at my flesh. The rent increase gouges another hunk out of me… All our money is being sent overseas to buy bullets and bombs to kill the Iraqi people, (Arab's) in this continuation of the Medieval Crusades, 1,000 years ago, new millennium style.

I walked among whores, hypes and the mad. Also searchers, seekers on higher planes. Went to Mario's men's drumming circle @ City College, the next day, Sunday, partook of Grace, after, to the Faithful Fools in which we were seated in a circle and invited to write on our events that day. Since I did not get to read mine aloud, here it is:

> 'Thinking what is God's purpose for me, what is the direction followed obediently in the path I had not intended to go. Fed pigeons. Bread from the free food lunches I got. And collected 8 aluminum cans. Took notes. Prayed & wondered. Also see the rich are encroaching on the TL space. All this might be gone 10 years from now. We will be like apartheid of Johnsonburg South Africa all over again, in which brutal police questioned impoverished black Africans demanding to see the loathed pass in order to travel thru their own land! This will be us! Needing day passes to enter this domed, walled, gated city, passing thru scrutiny of gatekeepers at

dawn to labor, then back out at dusk to the barren lands, to live in our cars and trailers.'

The others recounted approaching TL homeless, talking to them, I said, I try never to talk to them—I share the same food lines with them daily and sit in the same support groups, I already know what they have to say! I don't want to be encumbered by their schemes, insanities, drug deals. I'm afraid of the criminal element laced thru this population, winding, twisting like an evil snake. I'm in competition with them for food, for space! I just go thru the TL on my way to free library and the shortest path to public transport.

Well anyway, I always wanted to do big things, because I had big pain.

I have prayed, searching.... Maybe somehow I will dig thru the hustlers, cheaters, evildoers to find the miscellaneous Van Gough— who can't really paint-- who is suffering, who has no market value but his soul. The fallen woman, who has discovered innocence. And be able to attend to them in some way. And the Holy Sprit has come to me saying part of my mission is to do a restorative work.

19.
As time slips by, there's just a decades difference in when we all came out, (as some kind of queer or another) back in the 50's as opposed to younger ones who emerged in the 60's. Or later, in the 70's as opposed to the 80's—When we 'found ourselves' then acted on it, made a tremendous difference as to the availability of supportive queer community at the time. As to the treatment of us by the world in general. Were you one of those silent men-women passing? Back in the day we employed styles and methods of passing which were not holistic, but brutal silent, individualistic, living on he fringe in a state of raw survival and little else.

It's time dear ladies... it's time....

Time when all my mistakes, & losses have faded into the past & can begin to build on new uplifting architectures.

***

TG/TS Clinic. Adjunct of the City Public Health Department. Free. Another blood panel. Needle in vein, friendly nurse. Lollypop after. Transman grabs three, red, blue & yellow. They are the worlds first major clinical information gathered report on the health of transsexuals who undergo hormone treatment. Transman's statistics date back ten years.

Transgender are crazy because of a higher level of stress then normal people.

I am convinced that transsexuals and gay & lesbian people belong in the greater community. Amid our straight sisters/brothers, which is how we were born. We don't belong in ghettos. But are driven there by bullies, ragged outcasts from polite society themselves, raised fists, taunts, curses. And on the higher end, by preachers, rabbis, mullahs, and other spiritual dictators—who denounce us because of our chosen sex preferences and gender.

Most TS concentrate on their outward presentation only, which is well expected, as failure to pass, or to pass badly, can have deadly consequences in hostile society—beatings, murder, or daily murderous insults and hurled threats. So one finds transsexuals doing all the outwards things. Body building or practicing swish, feminacy in full length mirrors in their small hotel rooms with nylon stocking hanging over the edge of fly-by-night suitcases, having tried on every pair.

Do they work on developing their interior? By being inside so dainty swish, so swish with vigor, so feminine with a hope-to-die-passion is masculine outlook. A male behavior. Likewise the muscle-bound man posturing in his teeshirt—sporting a new phalloplasty, a meaty 7 incher with a manly dickhead, wither real or silicon, but inside still girlish ways. And if your course of life doesn't take you thru those necessary changes in during the due process of daily routines, your mind never will encompass that new female or masculine scope, and sadly not much true transition occurs.

But, so what. After all is said and raved about, it is God to whom we bow and no other. Not mullahs, rabbis, or preachers, & not our next door neighbors opinions. Only God Who has created all genders, in Her grand diversity.

Its funny how a queer friendly venue, tavern, restaurant, hotel can turn hostile—thru a change of ownership, or a change of the neighborhood... Along Polk & Post, site of the famous transgender venue Diva's with its crazy trans hooker girls, which the neighbored is trying to get rid of... They gentrify, put out potted palms on the sidewalk, cheep rent rooms are renovated into little boutique pretty expensive bed & breakfast inns. As said previously, the rich are overrunning this city... its just a matter of time before we are all gone, gone to traveling the world in busses like Gypsies, staying here and there at cheep motels...

For a moment the ethereal plane opens up out of the common grey cigarette squashed, stained streets like the opening scene for a play. Sound of a deranged Chinese woman hollering about her green goods for sale cheep in bombastic Mandarin...Foggy Chinatown alleys, the slap of pakow cards onto the table behind locked iron grill doors.

Here is some facts to put our human condition into perspective:

Earth formed as a planet 4 ½ billion years ago.
Single-cell organisms, 1 billion years ago.
More complex plants & animals evolved after that.
Invertebrates, at 650 million years ago.
Fish 500 million.
200 million, the first mammals.

Or, in simpler form:
Earth formed on January 1st.
Bacteria—the first living things formed March 22.
Invertebrates first appeared November 9.
Fish evolved from invertebrates November 22.
Mammals evolved December 16.
Monkeys and apes evolved December 28.
Humans only appeared a few minutes before the end of the year, on December 31.

World Book Encyclopedia 2007.

***

I was taken on a brief descent into hell
So I could see the future & the past.
Saw a hall of mirrors; ever-reflecting back & forth.
Where all souls vanity admiring self
Now cast image of their truth, which was ugly flaws.
From east to west an west to east, for eternity, back and forth,
in great horror at their grotesque faces, hideous malformations.
But this was only the vestibule of hell.

I cannot tell you all what I saw;
it would be as great a book almost as heaven's is.
But here is the most important essence of what I saw, all of it.

Pride,
Covetousness
Lust,
Anger,
Gluttony,
Envy,
Sloth.
All these cause spiritual death.

***

Many have come to save.
Down the slippery mountain into hell.
I appeared in the form of a mighty stag
and went down to the flock,
They followed me; I led them up to the high places
thru the rocky craigs
Thru the narrow passages with width
only for one of them at a time.
Thru all the strange turns and places they would not have gone.
And led them to the mountain top
where they were safe from the lion.
Safe from the hunters of skins.
And on I led my flock
into the valley on the other side where peace reigns.

***

Creator: I am the keeper of Records. I remember everything. The past, set it aside. I'm getting ready to do a new thing.

The People: If all peoples of faith, Wicca, Christian, Muslim, prey out of their masses, their synagogs their churches with the message of peace and take this home into their world, take that same spirit you have learned, which you have sung about, to the spiritual heights you have chanted to attain, go home quickly and wipe off your desk of all the impending evictions, the debts, the schemes for revenge, lawsuits, plots against enemies.

Creator: Do not dwell on the past. Or consider the things of old. I am getting ready to do a new thing; it is about to spring forth. Do you not perceive it?

Chants of a liturgy in Latin die out supplanted by a girl child crying. The scene opens, it is a large grey structure of worship, whose mighty walls crumble down in places to reveal the great blue/white sky & universe:

Holy Spirit: Turn your thoughts to that which is holy.
Strike bell in the bell tower first time. It is all set out. It is all mapped out in a plan.

The People: We want things to be set right! How are things set right?

Holy Spirit: Repentance. Recompense—when ever possible.

Creator: Don't remember the things of old or the things of the past. I am about to do a new thing.

First this must be wiped away.
Strike bell 2nd time.

Holy Spirit: The judgment is Mine. Says the Lord.
Strike bell 3rd time.

The People: God sees your worn trousers with holes at the knee; thread bare, too large one season, too small the next, from eating nourishing yet fattening preserved food donated by the food bank, a pair of donated shoes broken down from walking; stained & spotted tie a gift from friends, your whole life from the Good Will 2nd Hand Store.

Jesus (or other Prophet): I come that the people might be lifted up with Spirit. Freely given.
Strike bell 4th time.

Creator: I am God to Whom all pray.
Strike bell 5th time.

They came to me in the desert with 1,000 miles behind them and no returning. & a thousand miles lay ahead, famine, sun baked, drought. They turned to Me then.
Strike bell 6th time.

Turn to Me now.
Strike bell 7th time.

The People: All that is prays to You.

Masses of people bow deeply, bending down deeply, prostrating themselves upon the floor, drinking deeply of the Sprit of the Most High.
Strike bell 8th, 9th, 10th, 11th, 12th, times.

20.
When I was young and there was so much promise for the future those were my happiest days. I was full of hope, had energy, strength in my body. We walked the avenues lined with secondhand stores, coffeeshops and bookstores, talking of our victories to come. We assumed the goal of all our hopes was just in sight. Laughed in cafes, drank coffee and together discussed our wisdoms.

For thousands of generations back into history people of earth worked lands, fed themselves & fed their families. Lived, died, leaving no records, but their communal legacy--- skeletal heaps of bones and broken pots & tools. Some among us do leave a remarkable record.

Is mine a work of ugliness?

I'm not sure, but do know that God has need of it—my art. For some reason not yet clear.

All creatures do good and do bad. Better that I do nothing at all then do bad, but better that I do good.

All the Crucifixes are covered in grey cloth. It's Palm Sunday.

Have mercy on me Creator, because I am in trouble.
My eye is consumed with sorrow, and also my throat and my belly.
For my life is wasted with grief, and my years with sighing.
My strength fails me because of affliction, and my bones are consumed.
I have become a reproach to all my enemies and even to my neighbors,
A dismay to those of my acquaintances;
When they see me in the street they avoid me.
I am forgotten, out of mind, as if I were dead;
I am useless as a broken pot.

Psalms 31 9-16

I am old, I am old, I will wear the bottoms of my trousers rolled....
--T.S. Eliot.

Here it is, all written down, as fine a book as you will see, documenting those strange and wonderful times...

Well, one thing I must say... dear diary... dear JOURNAL... In the bible there is a scripture that tells how Jesus needs a lift into town, being dusty and tired. So some Apostle or camp follower is sent to find a donkey... Jesus says, "Get me a donkey and if anybody asks why you're taking it, just tell them, 'The Lord has need of it.'"

So this JOURNAL, like all my books has been my donkey. My ride out of one town on my way to the next...my art, my work. And I justify every word of it because, *the Lord has need of it,* and She has told me so!

    ***

How they mourn her—that city which will never rise again.
How they mourn her, that nation which has fallen.
How they mourn times passed,
 that will never come again,
 of such great prosperity & knowledge
now undone.

All is lost.

---From JOURNAL by the Prophet.

To every thing there is a season,
 And a time to every purpose under heaven:
A time to be born, and a time to die;
a time to plant, and a time to
 pluck up what is planted;
A time to kill, and a time to heal;
a time to break down, and a time to
 build up;
A time to weep, and a time to laugh;
 a time to mourn, and a time to dance;
A time to cast away stones, and a
time to gather stones together; a time
to embrace, and a time to refrain
from embracing.
A time to get, and a time to lose; a
time to keep, and a time to cast away;
A time to rend, and a time to sew;
 a time to keep silence, and a time to
speak;
A time to love, and a time to hate;
a time of war, and a time of peace.

--Ecclesiastes 3:1-8. Holy Bible

21.
Listen to me and be still for I am God! I'm talking to you for the last time. —I will destroy My world and the people on if they don't change their behavior. Aright their lives and live in consideration and just behavior regarding all other beings.

I have brought you out of a long way & Am still among you—but not for long. I will disappear and take My heaven and My earth with Me. Then what will you have? You will have all you have constructed, all the things you built and worshiped, the full extent of this—but nothing more.

It has been said God is the sculpture of mountains, the potter of earth, the fisher of oceans, the jeweler of the sky. That all the universe is God's pallet to design upon. So these words are terrible indeed.

22.
Dear children, listen carefully. This is the last time I will speak to you. Revolution now! There must be change. Change is dictated by God (in all Her different Names) because Her world has grown so unholy. Change is mandated by the very stars in astrological formation, this day and age is the time prophesied. Change is long overdue by the persistent sufferings of so many many humans & animals. Change must come to pass to fulfill the longings, dreams, and prayers for justice from so many children's throats in this world today & down thru time.

There is only one reason to stop the quiet but inexorable raising up of a machinery, which is rolling, speeding speedily towards the abyss of change carrying everything with it & its uncertain outcome.

That is if sufficient powerful persons/nations on earth in unison or individually but at the same time, form themselves together as one to begin this Herculean process of change themselves! For sufficient numbers of the rich to give back what they have robbed. For sufficient number of the poor to come clean with the wrongs they have done against others. For the people as individuals to come clean of their vices & their predatory ways which impinge upon other weaker citizens & to voluntary join into the grand parade of change, making due recompense in all thefts and injustices even of the lowest and most petty nature & march victoriously over this earth creating a new heaven—one of terra ferma--- so that we may be closer in alignment with the commandments from the Most High. Not necessary the convoluted laws of men, but of the basic structure of a humane humanity. But since this will never happen (?) Revolution Now!

I leave you with this wisdom. Be reflective.

Consider inner self always—to the measure of all outward ventured deeds.

Embrace some religious faith, (one of a higher nature) Buddha Of A Thousand Smiles, the Compassionate Mohammad, Christ the Savior, Great Mother, She Who Is Ongoing, All Nourishing, All Powerful, All Embracing, All Loving.

Once taking up your sword of truth don't look back in doubt nor waver!

Make your peace dear Children, make your peace, & fight like hell!

Be ready.

Supersede any existing laws if they are unjust. You know in your hearts by now after all I have taught you what laws are right and what are wrong! (Thou shall not kill, do not steal, practice mercy, do not turn widows out of their houses, do not rob the poor.)

Don't forget children the greater humanity dictates that we act!

Keep on with your struggle in your revolutionary ways & cast your compassions up to the immense heart of the Most High beseeching for justice & mercy to flow down upon this earth—if not for yourselves then for all the confined souls, the sad & the sick, including animals; the sea turtles, the elephants the Orangutan, the whale, our mothers and fathers violated, the children small & the child-self with us, for this good earth as we orbit, 3rd planet from the sun in the solar system located on the edge of the galaxy Milky Way. *This was the end of diary JOURNAL by Red Jordan Arobateau.*

**Documents prepared by
Red Jordan Arobateau
For the Comrades of the Revolution,
Red Jordan Arobateau Reading Societies, Comrades everywhere.
April 8, 2007
(Unity Of Utopia
Lovely Hill View Beside The Bay)
18:00 hours.**

INFINITE LOVE
JOURNEY 2

YOU SEE

Momma said, momma said,
'you betta get tough'.

Momma said, momma said,
'things gonna get rough'.

Momma said, momma said,
'there be days like this'.

Old Soul tune, 1950's,
sung by blax street musician 2007.

23.
A milk carton, which was someone homeless seat is vacated. It is only temporary like they are…

A street hag is dancing in glee. Wizened, black, mismatch skirt, pants, socks, a crooked pair of boots, a sweater, jacket. She has discovered a broken crack pipe with resin in it. Fired up, snorted. Now she's tweeken'. "They got everything heah in San 'Sisco. They got it all heah Ah'm tellen' yo', they got it all heah. Ah seen it all now. Crack pipe full of resin, layen' on the street." These are our once-mothers. These are the grandmothers of wisdom rendered ineffectual---stillborn children who did not grow.

If not by one way, then by another. --Remember that.
Somehow we gonna make it.

Tenderloin. Downtown San Francisco. These tired grey 5, 6 story tenements have seen different cycles of humanity, waves of immigration of different kinds of people. Today the un-housed forces itself upon the retina of the eye in a sour circus spectacle.

A woman does her face make-up gazing at her image in the window of a parked car. A man uses its side view mirror to shave. People, who lack the essentials. All I see is empty cans, used stuff. Nothing is full. Emptiness. Nothingness.

You thought you had glimpsed the shadow of the thing—but were not sure. *'Is that it? It looks like it? Could it be?'* When you see it you will know it.

Out of nowhere, maybe hell appears a very large human rat in the form of a hostile black man chillingly angry, wild. Goes up to Transman Red, messes with him—"do you know which way it is to the Federal building? The Federal building! Where is it? You lookin' like you don't know…"He doesn't finish the sentence.

"It's down there, across Market Street! You'll see it when you get there."

"I know where it is."

He wanders off, aimless, hostile and messes with someone else, a young white woman, street wise, with her boyfriend. She howls; "FUCK YOU NIGGER, I DON'T PLAY THAT SHIT! WE ENSLAVED YOU BUDDY! WE ENSLAVED YOU NIGGER! DON'T FORGET THAT!"

That's what she said from her mouth.

Ugly hate is built this way. Action, reaction. Cause/effect. And, subsequently I carry my hate about him onwards into the group where I'm going, a poetry reading. Hate which finally is triggered by one loud black man too many—this one harmless, attired in a turban & a colorful robe, a fellow poet, but mouthy, seething with anger which is not directed at any individual but is a hostile reply to some small woman's statement. I get him back with the right word at the right time. After his outburst of hate non-stop, I wait, then later when he begins speaking I begin talking over him and kept talking and when he complains someone is talking while he's trying to talk, I inform him 'I get to talk because you talk too much.' A cold steel shank knife plunged into the belly of his ego.

Those who tried to make peace on earth will live in peace in heaven.

Aw well. Upstairs in the same group a homeless bum of a man says it all:

> "The gentle sensitive soul of the poet is not recognized in the business world."
>
> ---George, a street man.

All the love in the universe is here beamed down from the Creator Almighty. But humans are little repositories of negativity; compiled soot and debris of all their hatred and pains and fears retained. ---Is this the thing which we call evil? Or just closer to it's root?

Eat the bread of Dachau made of grass.

If the theory is true that life evolved out of a bath of chemicals and bacteria 5 million years ago, ironic, now bacteria is using us as a host to keep itself alive... over the eons a symbiotic dance. Bacteria is formed, becomes the host for all life, single cell organisms spring out of it and evolve rapidly into plants, animals, humans, birds, reptiles, and a minute bit of bacteria remains in each strain of life, valiantly holding on... sickening us... weakening us...

Toadstools, brown, speckled, their heads bowed unfolding beside the sewer, Baudalaire's Flowers of Evil. Another college campus shooting rampage, using automatic fire weapons. 23 students murdered in cold blood.

***

SF is faintly taking on the flavor of NYC. Or is it just my mind? Bigger, bustling, variety of foods and stores and peoples and languages, anonymous, more densely populated. Skyscrapers going up, up, up. City growing taller---- and more expensive. Hustling, bustling. Tour busses.

Chores & duties to do. Suppose I was like a clock & just stopped?

None of us were actually born here---born and raised from childhood, but felt or heard the call by some kind of means and got here—as our life depended on it.

I might have turned into a dope addict, denied, and without hope if I'd stayed back in Chi-town site of my former fall and decline into drug netherworld.

As they say I'm waiting for my ship to come in…. I'm still walking around town on a pair of borrowed shoes…

These streets have been picked clean because they've been marched by 10,000 homeless & poor already.

Why am I so poor?

Chances are if you're an old enough gay you've run up against the Amerikkka jail system--for being homosexual, being in a tavern or a club, which served gays. ('House of ill-repute.') 1950's, '60's.

So my generation was criminalized in their youth. Wasn't like today when youth take their queer freedom for granted. And step right over the failing bodies of us older soldiers who made this future possible without a thank you!

It's the criminalized outlook on life, plus my mild mental illness, which impeded me, plus the hatred of society for the outsider, combined. Mental illness. Psychiatric pills just suppress it. The power source down below must be turned off. Science hasn't figured out a way to do this yet. Am glad for my medications. Anyway, this antidote was just discovered ten years ago, so it couldn't help me when I was a teen and in my young adulthood. Time when careers in the 'business world' are born!

I most likely was born with a big ego—despite my teenage shyness-- as I grew up this ego only intensified when confronted first by racism, sexism and gender stuff and later the gay stuff, and my growing apparent mental problems, then the artist stuff. I was fighting on every front. This either destroys you, or makes your ego grow into a hard shell. One of the biggest battles one fights then; safe within their protective shell is isolation loneliness and depression.

> I remember so long ago
> when we were a family
> & I was safe and warm
> and my mother still loved me,
> how good it was….
> Then later, when I wondered,
> why we couldn't go on picnics
> they were so much fun.
> *Why?*

Here's an explanation why religion elicits a higher emotion—it gives flame to the human spirit where everything else is mere survival, toil, generation unto generation. What a big earth, a big planet, human dynasties untold hoeing of the vegetable rows, planting. Living, then going to their grave. The people, with no voice, eking sustenance out of the soil.

The lonely Transman continued to work on in comparative silence. Unheralded, unsung.

A baby remembers everything about the womb, its life there--- and maybe the heaven its just come out of before. A baby doesn't have the brain capacity to think… As the enfant grows into a small child it gradually looses this memory, just as its mental capacity is beginning to form. So the adult vainly struggles to recapture paradise—which visits them seldom, in dreams.

Out of this ambionic bath, as all children, we come. We, who inhabit that twilight between female & male. As Radclyffe Hall puts it; 'The no-man's land between the sexes."

> 'She was learning how to survive as a man in a woman's body in the outside world. Or, rather, she began to understand that such an existence would not be possible—that she was an impossible being.'
>
> The First Man Made Man by Pagan Kennedy 2007.

Maybe I'll be like the Trapist monks. Living a life dedicated to God, work, and silence.

I will start a work, it will involve the healing of the broken, and housing the homeless, and the raising up the stature of females.

Well this is an introduction to my world; this is the geography I live in. A transsexual male, in the year of our Lordess 2007, upon the threshold of space. Outer space, and space travel thru the voids to distant worlds!

PS, am setting up to begin writing Sedna my 4th science fiction book in the Unity of Utopia series.

As you get older certain things become apparent, for years I assumed I was writing something beautiful—the strength of my words, interesting characters and fascinating dialogue, a story to make the mind and heart soar. To add my work to the great body of works on the side of the resistance against the fascism of greed, of power for powers sake, which lead to ultimate sadness, and the absence of joy everywhere. But as the years passed on and my topics were no longer current, those particular battles fought, won or lost, then forgotten, looking back on them 20, 30 years later, saw I had written a historical document, valuable in its own right. But that's nothing I would have thought of before. Books with humor, sex yes, but also, their plots being situated in historical content, which younger generations find interesting—brushing aside my well-crafted scenarios. Now, in my sci-fi books, on the verge of outerspace, my toe on the threshold of the galaxies maybe I'm creating a prophetic dream!

This document JOURNEY is like PASSAGE was before it, and AUTUMN CHANGES before that. My autobiographical/diary years. After a 40-year span of primarily fiction. 'Dis here be my clef d'oeurves.

    ***

I am a font of tranny knowledge.

Miss lady & Mr. Man wait in the hallway of the chamber of horrors; the corridor of transformation. The sex-change clinic.

There is a group worse off then us. Those shunned. Those disfigured on the outside. Cripples, and the maimed. Seeing them people are horrified, politely turn aside. Amputated arms, withered legs. All torso nothing else. Human beings cut off at the waist. Faces with holes cut out where there once was a mouth. People severely disfigured by car accidents, by fire, by war. This group also is shunned, avoided. Asked to leave public places because they frighten off other customers. So too we freak queers who nobody understands. If there was real love in the world, all would be accepted—including my kind—without a problem.

Here comes one now, some lithe 'girl' Red has a crush on. A lovely, near his own age, quite intelligent, quite damaged. Every manner of cruelty of word and physicality done to her in those years before she became passable. All the estrogen she'd taken---bringing out her female intuition like mining for gold or drilling for oil, down deep she had struck woman! However thisdeep plumbing does not connect itself often. Mostly she is catty, mean to others, relentlessly cruel to herself.

Trannys. When I'm dealing with trannys I feel I'm dealing with skeleton people with no meat on their bones, just enough sinew and muscle to keep walking down life's paths. We stand face to face, their ribs are showing, the slightest hint of a mean word, out of them erupts raw hatred. --Its waiting just below the surface and the surface isn't very thick. So much negativity it becomes familiar. A comfortable zone in which to store ones head. Retreat to it. As a community we are so ready to fight ever–vigilant and all the good deeds done fail; we turn with venom hissing to plunge an icy dagger into someone's back.

The females (once male) have been so outcasted if they were men they would be violent, instead they are women trying to emulate women and they hold the anger back, tuck the violence under, because it harms their own image of themselves as real women. So instead of violence they are catty. Sharp, and catty. They bite. Cutting to the bone. One good part, since they aren't as violent nor crude--more like women--it's easier to hang with them.

  ***

Female behavior, male behavior, is biologically based & societal enforced.

Power dynamics change upon transition. The former female-on-female of two lesbian friends changes to a female with a dominant male. This female transitioned to male upon whom the world bestows greater benefits. Even among two female-to-males, power dynamics can shift; for instance one FTM who transitioned 5 years before the other for period of time has been 'the man' while his friend was 'the woman'. One has been female with female energies & butch energies; the two perceived in public as male and maybe dike, suddenly upon transitioning the new man might gain more power, upsetting to the old arrangement between the two. So transition does change things first by energies of the individuals, which often readjust; second in perceptions by society which exert a slowly steady, maybe unwilling, tug, thru their viewpoints, treatment and expectations of you. Things have changed. --- In ways deeper then simply on the surface. For instance the donning of drag king apparel, or in the case of a woman transsexual donning of a feminized wardrobe—when they take it off, go back to role play of their born gender, dynamics still remain the accustom ones. But upon chemical and surgical transition there is an inner alteration accompanying the outer surface changes. However all inner change itself is still only a superficial state to what lays deeper in the heart and personality and mind of the person, which often does not change. For better, or for worse. What is really important in life, the bonding, the loyalty, the friendship, the caring for, the love between people, this should not be altered by the mere surface re-arrangements of hormones, surgery & dress, no matter what. – If these friendships were real and true to begin with. So this should not change connections one has made with friends, lovers, and family--- persons to whom one is close. However we know, sadly this is not the case, that often friendships are broken, marriages destroyed, and circles of friends disturbed—ejecting the new man or new woman. This in part, as previously stated because it is a superficial world in which we are living, and the self is informed by shallow reactions daily. The style and way of this unnatural, artificial society at large does not make for bonding people together, nor holding relationships—because it holds nothing dear. Nothing of the heart is important—only the pocketbook and the ego. If we are constantly living while dealing with the results of a world of spiritual artifice without seeing thru its delusion, without overcoming it's strong hold to some measure. So to a greater part it is the outer world, which helps break apart our fledgling unions. Unions not strong enough to make readjustments. For relationships sake we must make spiritual and emotional growth upon a person's transition. Both on the part of those who change, and those who view this change. It is not easy to be a soulful, heartfelt and true person in this artificial world built on commerce, greed and ego, and many bonds go crashing, not only those of the transsexual.

24.

> *Money—keep it as far from yourself as you can. Do not take it into your heart…*

Words to the Prophet--2007

There's is a lot of money in this town and I see it walking in front of me on the hoof in the form of 2 elegantly dressed gentlemen; distinguished, one grey hair, the other young, both slender, and towering over my small 5' 2", at nearly 7 feet tall in bleu jackets, brown shoes, kaki slacks, padded wallets. Down Grant Street classical music spills out of a store with art artifacts on sale for a fortune. Replica bronze warriors squatting, ready to spring, each weight 900 pounds apiece, to guard your living room.

Chinese store--hover there too long absorbed in perusal of the mass of cheap trinkets 99 cents up to $5.99 a little Asian lady will come darting over pleasantly to inform you its price (cheap) urging; "You buy one now!"

Bronze lions cuddle beside the bench where a pedestrian stops to sit-- their fangs barred at her elbow, their jaws open in a silent roar from the jungle. They shall be my symbol of capitalism, of money, of acquisition and greed. And will sit here ravenously waiting to see who they can destroy, before for the following dresh. —Which is like a Buddhist meditation.

Am so concerned by saving 5 and 10 cents it becomes a goal to which I'm almost attached. Buddhism informs us we must loose all our attachments to things. The way of Jesus Christ and probably heaven too, is not these low attachments.

Transman had looked into the metal/plastic coin return slots of 20 newspaper vending racks that day, pausing for 2.5 seconds to scrutinize each, an interval in which his face puckered up, eyes squinted, mouth pursed, before he'd turn on his heel and walk away. Having gazed into them thoroughly. Yet, after that day had passed he still didn't know what the newspaper headlines read -- even at 2" high black bold font--because his scrutiny was directed solely at the money return slots. He was looking for spare coins.

***

Case History: The oldster lives in a tiny room, which faces upon the street, having for a 'balcony' a public fire escape. He/she dwells there in semi-poverty 37 years. They inhabited this room while simultaneously passing thru a progression of jobs. A laundry worker, a facility matron, and a coin-counter for some establishment. By which they acquired a tiny social security pension upon retirement, with which they can now continue to pay rent on the room and buy sufficient groceries, --- when supplemented by free food lines. Often for pleasure they go out on this 'balcony' to stand watching the populace below. Their small pleasure for decades was to observe the same congested street, hollering of the teeming populous there. Thankfully that noise and mayhem is immunized from them somewhat by being several flights up, on floor 3. In the last decade they marvel at the great strides this city has made! How beautiful it has become! Much of the congestion has been moved, and how much more pleasant it is for the person—now an oldster to enjoy! What a scenic community rich in diversity of pleasant (tho now unaffordable) restaurants. But the cunning city has tricks up her sleeve! One day the oldster, shuffling painfully into their doorway sees that their building has been sold! The new investor immediately evicts the old tenants, remodels each unit, and resells them individually as condominiums—owner owned units, for a gargantuan fee the Oldster, jokeably, cannot afford!

Devils laugh: HA! HA! HA!

From its ritzy end near the water, go down further on Fillmore Street & you'll see where it use to be ghetto. From 1950's on when redevelopment began to destroy it. So little capital, so few resources; it's sour, fonky, yet it's home, a place to return too. Slap an affectionate nickname on it; 'the Mo'. Fillmo' Transman Red arrived here, in 1969, living just below, in the Western Addition, seeing the great demolition all around him—the vacant lots; his own building condemned, set for removal.

***

The naive of the cathedral, stretching 3 levels vertical, is round, like a birdcage, with lovely stainglass windows which glow from sunlight shining behind them until day wanes; reds, greens, yellows, shades of blue. The Spirit passes thru here... can you catch It? God sees all who come in this place dedicated to God. This place, of cold stone, and of the Word. *How could they have forsaken You? The Holy Smoke... no one can see You?* God knows who passes thru here and their reasons. God knows who employ themselves in Her service for gain. God sees the hearts that are true.

I have a salve for you. An ointment to apply.

'Put it on my knees, my ankles... my feet, my crippled-up fingers, my sore left arm... no. Put the salve on my spirit... My heart.'

A rude happening at shul. After all this congregations' generosity in allowing him to eat up all their food at oneg, at a particular event before service, he is finally confronted by a Food Nazi. "The food is only for families with children! It's a potluck and you never bring anything!" She snaps in ire. Two congregates tell the fascist that it makes sense that strangers eat all the food because there's too much food anyway. '*I am hurt and angry.*' "BUT DON'T FEED THE POOR!" Red screams. There's no advantage to turn down a newcomer, to exclude someone--- especially a writer who will make sure to shame shuls everywhere via the printed word down into time immemorial in their Journal!

This world. They worship the almighty dollar. What a joke. The most precious thing is human life. Human hearts. Human beings. They are thrown away.

My face hardens. My face reflects its anger back to you!

>A withered leaf
>fallen off the tree in autumn
>scuttling in the street is more beautiful
>then a green dollar bill.

"Sir can you spare a coin? I have nowhere to stay." A skinny white arm sticks itself out of a frayed jacket sleeve, proffering a trembling upturned palm. A wan voice, a dying soul. A humanbeing tho young, is dying… A plea whispers wraith-like from a weak-appearing woman in her 30's seated on the cold concrete in thin, threadbare clothes.

Where true charity abides, God Herself is there.

Oh God its too much, its too much this society is asking and everything suppose to be free, what You have given us, but they have put a price tag on this whole earth.

I will start a work; it will involve the healing of the broken, and housing of the homeless, and other acts, which involve the rising up in stature of a (female's in particular) mind, body, & soul.

I must follow instruction from God to do this thing. Spirit tells me:

That none be hurt by your laws & statues & none be harmed--those under your jurisdiction.

Grey stone towering edifice. Medieval. Rising up tremendously in a cross-shaped foundation, grey stone wings holding pews, paintings. Alcoves of prayer, votive candles. The service @ Grace is beginning, it s like opening of a giant prayer book carved from rock out of a mountain.

An usher dressed up in a red outfit like the whore of Babylon offers me a wicker collection basket.

Well, there is surely a heaven! At Chinatown branch of the Public Library picked up a pink covered book by psychic Sylvia Brown and immediately it made so much sense. Thought; 'I want to thank you for your good work'. I flowed right into the understanding of it. Sylvia was saying how some souls weren't ready to die yet, like those people who die insane or who were caught up in torture, mayhem, survivors of the holocaust, of shipwrecks like the Titanic. When they go to heaven they go to a special place where they receive tremendous love and compassion from God and from the spirits there and up there are set to some healing task. Gardening was one of the tasks-- and I had already experienced about 6 months ago now, on awaking, the vision of friend Suzie De Young, she had died much too young, of breast cancer. She wasn't ready to go yet, and her life work had not gotten far. A room full of photo negatives not printed, those printed stuck in bulging envelopes & boxes, their edges curling up, with no money to format. She had said for several years she was sending me a collection of prints but never did. There Suzie was--- in heaven-- taller then she'd been, and slender, not plump. Still young, elegant, her same voice-- and she had been gardening when she saw me!

> *Psallite deo, psallite!*
> *Alleluia, alleluia!*
> Praise God for S/He is good!
> Hallujulia!
>
> Laudate Dominum omnes gentes. Alleluia.
> Praise the Lordess all you peoples!
>
> ***.

Again Transman enters the halls of Grace. Stumbles in, hair tousled, tired from the uphill trek. The priest speaks from the pulpit to a congregation of one thousand: 'Independence is an allusion. Our existence is that we live in relationship to each other.'

Transman Red sighs. How well he knows this. How poorly his life has gone, not having family or sufficient friends.

Some chose to self-segregate themselves away from other genders or races or classes of people—for their own self-preservation. A lot of lesbians do this, dwelling as much as possible within a lesbian women's enclave, so as not loose power to men. Blacks do it, remain ghettoized. Patronize a small circumference of local Afrocentric stores, churches, beauty shops, and hangouts as exclusively as their availability permits, to try to combat the omnipresent image of the Caucasian man who plasters images of his pale face over every billboard, newspaper, magazine, movie, and television ad. Many of us transsexuals do this—especially those who can't pass; -- it's almost a rule by which we must live. Some of us want to remain in-between the sexes, or transgendered and feel more comfortable in a gay/trans ghetto where nobody gives them a passing glance.

Although passable he has so long found refuge in the gay Mecca's of Amerikkka in his years as a dike, that they have become home. Plus, Alice, the straight, non-artistic world is boring! This Sunday the Transman sits on a pew surrounded by a sea of heterosexuals. No telling how much 'family' is seated right alongside—but shows no clues.

The spirit spoke to me at Grace, with a vision:
> I am covered in blood head to toe--- I'm being born. It was a difficult birth—most are not born. See among all these heads at congregation, so few born. My work it is a work only I can do. That few can do.
>
> *I have given you clear sight. Better then the others have. You see!*

25.
Jesus is the only person I know.

For some, Buddha is the only friend they have. For some, Mohammad is the only friend they have. For some Jesus is the only friend they have. —On this disconnected earth.

One of the first times he remembered making the acquaintanceship of loneliness; born & raised on the racially segregated black-tan south side of Chicago Illinois, he-she was sent to a special school—the Laboratory School, an adjunct of the University of Chicago, which comprised kindergarten, grammar, thru 4 years high school. There a semester was shorter by 4 weeks then the public school system in the neighborhood around Red where she/he was raised which the kids, Red's friends, attended. For these 2 weeks beginning the new semester, and 2 weeks after school let out for summer recess, s/he had to play by him-herself. No longer were companions funneled into his-her life by an organization nor environs, so Red was left to his solitary books, toy trains, the chemistry set and the great outdoors.

The yard, sunlit, the front yard and the alleyway where they would play baseball soon, that alleyway —thru which it seemed some great escape into the adult world, might be possible.

The green wooden picnic tables stand empty.
They are ready but there is no picnic.
No food prepared because there is no family.
There is only the father & the child.
A very good father. A very kind father,
 but only one father.
Not a big enough family to fill even
 a single big picnic table with joy.
Where is the family in the full extent of its being?
The mother has been broken.
Discarded by society.
The family has been torn apart by race hate & gender hate, generation unto generation,
so now the family is no more.
The child is so lonely!
The green wooden picnic table sits empty.

I knocked on many doors—the art world, the queer nite-life, the political--- and none of them opened, or opened only partially.

Grace Cathedral. Because it's such a big church it's like a spiritual drink

If anything a person does in this society if they can't make friends, if they can't be sociable, it is to go to a church, synagogue or some other religious institution weekly, to plug into the Divine. The divine-in-community. For the upliftingness. To plug into the higher aspects of human existence.

Its ironic but if you're really poor one of the few places you can go is a religious institution—a church, I know for sure, maybe also the other religious disciplines—ashrams, synagogues, pagan rituals. So being poor I've gotten a big dose of spirituality.

Whoops Alice! In both synagogue and church there are those 2 lovely preacher-rabbi men—hands off them! He's Gods trade!

And by the way, this anti-Semitic fervor among some idiotic born-again Christians is so stupid. All of you are Jews! All of you! All of you will say you are Christians, but you are Jews. Who do you think Jesus was? Who do you think his apostles were? Who do you think was his mother? Jews!

I enjoy this shule, watching the ceremony, singing the songs, one can feel how this was the original tribe in which Jesus came out of, and be momentarily transported back to his time and place on the sands of the Sinai desert.

Film night down in the Crypt; basement underneath Grace Cathedral. Green Pastures. A 1930's black motion picture classic. Discussion after:
> "Life was so tragic, so horrible under slavery. All they could think of was going to heaven. That was heaven to them—the end of this slavery."
> –86-year-old African American woman, San Francisco, 2007

All the human tribes sold out by a few corrupt individuals for power, for greed.

God knows the many deals made in boardrooms, behind locked mahogany doors, whispered behind back of hand of those in-the-know, from corrupt dynasty's since before pharaoh.

Some hide from God, because they have something to hide.

The strongest man in the world, armed with all the most modern equipments of war, is not as strong as the weakest one who has sheltered and loved some other beings thru their life. Crippled, halting, they stand more mighty.

  ***

The first lesson. Everything is Spirit—even the physical. It begins & ends in Spirit, only. The physical 'state' what we call the material plane, of flesh and solids, is a transitional stage.

26.
I always liked the word university. It reminded me of the universe. Great. Vast. *& I would serve God.*

Universe. This is why he was writing Science Fiction and pondering the incalculably enormous distances of spatial time.

When he got too egotistical, the voice of the Lord spoke to him: *A lot of people have sat in these seats (pews) before you, Red.*

After its wine communion Grace Cathedral smells like a brewery & many a bawdy barroom where I have been before. Why they don't serve up grape juice for us (recovered) alcoholics? After it is pointed out that alcoholics must never touch even a single drop of alcohol. Tradition. This is why people refuse to move foreword on the road of progress. Those possessed by old-time minds, whither they be young or old. Those resistant to change.

***

Sweeping up fur & feathers off my floor. Its spring, everybody is molting.

As said my cat is a Maine Coon—the largest breed of small cats. Some attaining a weight of 30 pounds. He is the largest cat I've ever had. When Mr. Fluffy was young and had a full set of teeth, must have been a formidable sight as he went charging out of the shrubbery at the other males invading his feline territory.

***

For some of us in the gay-trans community, the acknowledgment in a 'hello' is the only interaction they ever get from brothers/sisters. No one knows them. There is no love.

>So much crying.
>*So much crying.*
>*So much crying.*

It's so hard, damaging myself crawling over this broken terrine of souls.

Spring 2007, the Transgender Law Clinic gives a public affair. A lovely transsex girl flits across the reception area in a nice downtown hotel in men's bluejeans, a teeshirt over budding breasts, her hair, growing out 2" 'She' is coming back. After being in male garb for several years. Her sisters have informed her; 'oh you'd make such a cute boy', but she'll have none of this, she is a woman. Destiny bound for feminization to the last degree possible built upon a male genetic structure. Her in-between stage reminds me of trans women of the long ago past -1950's, this was about as far as they could present themselves in public, without being arrested for 'female impersonation'.

It was nothing but us gay kids dancing, shrieking, flirting getting drunk battling the urge to kill ourselves, those apex of days—the few hours at night in the gay club after a daylight of solitary exclusion by the straight mass; poverty, loneliness for the unemployed, and scapegoated; a stream of constant two-faced lies pouring out of the mouths of those stealth. It was around 12 midnight, fun, laughter, song, gay kids gathered. Suddenly the lights went on…that vice cop hollered how it was a raid, and how we had been fooled. And some of those fooling us were our own queer people. Queers living a life of subterfuge. Of stealth. Of lies. Acting as agent enemies to our suffering, criminalized community.

That handsome vice cop sitting near me, dressed in dark trousers and jacket; arched both of his plucked eyebrows, his upper body heavy from weightlifting; takes off jacket there's the silver star of the police department. Badge of authority. A strange smile flitted around his lips. All of us gays to be transported to jail. We have come so far, up to now. From the old 1950's burden of the raids. Now tonight at a reception, on a podium, the superintendent-appointed Police Commissioner, a transsexual woman, is sworn in. She stands with dignity. Slowly we climb into the positive light, over a progression of time. Some landmarks: In the 1980's see sister trans woman clerk in a 2nd hand store. One of the first transsexuals obviously, openly employed in public. Another decade, 1990's more transsexuals seen working in shops here & there. Change slowly pushes some of us upward, leaving behind their fallen sisters prostituting in hotel doorways watching on, enviously, as their contemporaries catch the bus going to 9 to 5 jobs.

God never disbars us, never.

The transsexual is always going to feel a virulent rage that they cannot be the sex they were destined for before birth, and the superficial sex change, a later date transition provides relief from this situation, although it isn't a complete answer.

Any transsexual to truly transition must undergo spiritual transformation as well. All those who don't undergo this are only rearranging body parts without true meaning, and their 'happiness' is only temporal. For a transsexual to transition truly they cannot hate either sex. Men who hate women and do not undergo spiritual transformation just become men with neo vaginas and feminized secondary sex characteristics. They remain men.

    ***

> *"Life was so tragic, so horrible under slavery. All they could think of was going to heaven.'*

In casual passing by what black people receive in the street from other nationalities---is aversion. Aversion, which is fear-based. Not simply hating of blackness, or loathing of African persons, but fear born from some previous experience, for, after, they see every other black person as a threat. & people not taken on a individual basis, but preconceived notion about the whole group to whom they belong.

Now here's another group—which time might have forgot—women artists of the past.

> It matters far more then I can probe in an hours discourse that, women generally, and not merely the lonely aristocrat shut up in her country house among her folios and her flatterers, took to writing. Without those forerunners, Jane Austen and the Brontes and George Eliot could no more have written then Shakespeare could have written without Marlowe, or Marlowe without Chaucer, or Chaucer

without those forgotten poets who paved the ways and tamed the natural savagery of the tongue. For masterpieces are not single and solitary births; they are the outcome of many years of thinking in common, of thinking by the body of the people, so that the experience of the masses is behind the single voice. Jane Austen should have laid a wreathe upon the grave of Fanny Burney, and George Eliot done homage to the robust shade of Eliza Carter—the valiant old woman who tied a bell to her bedstead in order that she might wake early and learn Greek. All women together ought to let flowers fall upon the tomb of Aphra Behn, which is, most scandalously but rather appropriately, in Westminster Abbey, for it was she who earned them the right to speak their minds. —Shady and amorous as she was.

A Room Of One's Own, Virginia Woolf, 1929.

Virginia Woolf documents in her immemorial essay A Room Of Ones Own, going to a library and on the shelves of 16th century women writers there are 3 volumes of work—compared to shelves and shelves of men's. But the 18th century there are many shelves. So was my experience as a queer. In 1960, there was only half a shelf of queer writing, ten years later in the advent of women's publishing, there were shelves and shelves, and soon a whole bookstore of it. Transgender followed the same pattern. My MTF study The Big Change, written in the early 1960's, which became publicly more widely available in 2001 is one of these early, fictionalized transsexual novels. A friend declared yesterday that ten years ago— in 1995, there were very few TS/TG books, it was a rarity, and now everybody is coming out with 'their story.'

So, there's whole groups of 'outsiders' depending where you are and who you are.

There's whole underclasses, and shut-away statistics which compose the demographics of our life, the rich mosaic, the tapestry into which are woven so many individual threads, most of them content, but a few, suffering. Being plucked out.

Some people just live a life of pain & like all everybody's got is hope but some people find that, after a long time in pain—with just their hope--- at some point when it becomes apparent they never will shed their pain, then they begin to cast around for a way out. Meantime they frantically seek methods to change their lives, to find happiness; look about at various steps for relief, turn to self-improvement but if they cannot change what they are & if in whatever they try they still don't connect with happiness, no matter what they do, they can only hang on for some great shift in the future. I hope time marches on.

***

I look at these white upper class girls get on bus; long straight hair, long transfers too—blue/white strips of paper, good for the remainder of the day, while my own is short, due to expire. *'Don't be jealous'* says the Lord. *'I have given you something they don't have.'*

Everywhere I go hear voices talking about 'selling their house' or 'fixing up their house'.

What I don't understand is if the rich think communism & socialism is so hideous, so evil, in that it spells the end of freedom and individual rights, then why are the rich making communism and socialism –and anarchy—inevitable, by acting so atrocious in greed and by leverage using money? For as it now stands, and for *all it may become in the future,* communism and socialism when compared to kapitalism is the better of the two evils.

The further into hell I went—the lost souls--- their clutching grasps. The rich grew more and more monstrous till some no longer had bodies, just grotesque faces gnarled hands grabbing; beckoning, calling, "save me!" And here & there a once human form sank into a small pile of solid gold, riches, jewels, diamonds, rubies.

Ornate buildings leftovers of yester years 1920's opulence, and even older, fancy decor of the 1800rds. Inside just as much poverty as the rest, a quick sight betrays it; an older man, tousled head on a worn pillow lays on a cot facing the window cracked open for air.

What is this older China-man's story? Don't you sometimes wonder about the lives of others? The priest says it @ Sunday Service 11am April, 2007:

"To imagine yourself inside the mind, and thoughts of another human being is the start of compassion, & the beginning of morality. It is the beginning of religion."

Teachings @ Grace from Dean, Allen Jones.

Walk by ancient buildings of the old Chinatown to get some cheep meat for my dinner. Brick masonry decaying. "All the shops begin to look the same." A tourist says, but I've located mine after months of maneuvering thru this area between the library here, and searching for a butcher shop, hungry, days before me with the prospect of hunger, with only $3 to spend.

On & on tourists exclaim, "That's over a different hill." And etc. Forever searching the Holy Grail of some special Won Ton they have savored before.

Its so congested here that the intersection at Stockton & Washington streets both streetlights flash green, go, and pedestrians can cross either street, the one across or the one diagonal, crossing 2 lights at once, forming either a box pattern or an X. This speeds up the volume of motion. Then the light turns to all the cars again at once, then all the cars and pedestrians of each street individually.

***

AW MA GAWD! Just heard the news! The Episcopal diocese is falling into poverty! Also it's jewel, Grace Cathedral, its very structure is crumbling! So this is not the rich church of former years—just 10 years ago! The reasons are many. Time has eclipsed the lives of many old rich donors. The diocese is divided by an ultra modern theory set into practice, of inclusion—women priests, gay weddings. And decades earlier, inviting blacks in to sit in the pews with whites; and opposition to the Viet Nam war. Its outreach to the poor is bringing in new, challenged groups, and driving some affluent members away. And last, church-going is declining in Saint Francis's city. Due to the fact this place grows increasingly wealthy and preoccupied with vanity, with little time for Spirit. Furthermore despite all my loathing of the rich—I see even this great Mother Ship the cathedral is in trouble! Each stained glass window, which extends several floors in length, costs 1 million dollars to refurbish, because it must be disassembled by hand. Worse, the poured concrete structure is slowly crumbling! Sadly it was built using modern techniques. Old St. Mary's down the street near Chinatown built in the 1800rds with old fashion methods will probably outlast Grace! The same for the 'Washing Machine' church—St. Mary's' cathedral up on O'Farrell & Laguna, it too, sadly was built with the new methods!

The sound system is kaput! The cook has found another job! Oh sad news Grace!

I saw a terrible chain, 2-inch thick links, gray, turning green from age—unopened for eons:

God: I'm going to put it on them!

Holy Spirit: The Nation.

God: I'm going to put this chain on them because I love them. I've heard their prayers for justice! For the end to war, for peace to reign in their world. So I'm going to bring them down the level of the underprivileged all over their earth. So I can love them and so they will learn to truly love Me!

The Prophet (Red): That means so much pain. Death…

God: I am the Author of all things---even darkness.

The Prophet: One might think it strange, at first glance, for You, Creator to take into your Ears and Divine Heart a peoples prayers for condo conversions to be approved, for prime interest rates to remain fixed –then strike them into poverty by Your Hand! Even as they kneel in supplication God! Yet, their souls are at stake! They must suffer so much so that they can walk right into Paradise without even a thought if they'd be excluded or not. (Surely the rich cannot enter heaven no more then a camel can pass thru a needles eye.)

    ***

They all come to God for different purposes-- & reasons. Some to sing. Some to serve. Some to add to the substance of community. Others to preach. Some to extol their acquaintances to come and join the Great Spirit's House. I came to Creator's house with two talents—to write, & paint. What my purpose with God is, I'm not yet sure. Maybe to heal thru my words, and inform thru the visions painted down in oils on canvass.

No one iota of the sounds of praise will be withheld from our Creator.

***

A band of angels rolled up too near earth, & got wet from so many human tears. To dry their wings they flew up to the sun. The earth rings with praise!

***

Wet laundry hangs in the kitchen window, and on a rod over the doorway between kitchen & main studio room. As they get dryer the sox and shorts are transferred to the doorway between studio room and the walk-in closet which serves as his first office. (The second office being the other half of the kitchen, which is now cleared away in anticipation of finding/procuring, lumber to build a loft for storage in that small area. The dimensions of the loft: 5'6" high, 5 deep by 4 across.) Hasn't been able to afford Laundromat for 2 years since he retired.

Out on the street en route to animal shelter to volunteer, stepping into cages to hold lonely dogs in his arms and do their dog laundry, he encounters another forlorn creature. A street hag with a foreign accent (German?) cackles, holds a green dollar bill between two sun-brown gnarled hands with wizened fingers; she is ruddy faced from enduring the weather outside 24 hours 7 days a week, 365 days a year; wrapped in 3 layers of clothes; "It would be nice if this was a $100 heh? But a dollars good enough for me!"

Already wind is blowing...

More notes on queerness: The FTM-SF meeting was a workshop led by a noted Bay Area personage.

Some people can only have sex with a woman who was born a man, and with a man who was born a woman.

> Some people are just attracted to trans people it's a whole queer dimension. There's no way to name this sexual experience, & its something not talked about.
>
> Patrick Califia, 2007.
>
> ***

There is confusion in our transex world. There's a lot of sadness in being a thing unnamed. It is cold winds blowing inside the heart. It is being an orphan on the storm. It is being imprisoned in a cage with few arms to embrace your loneliness.

Well, this obstacle too will be uncovered. There's evidence—haven't we already come so far?

Why I remember those distant days of adolescent sex. Of spit and lick. Crisco. Back in the days before we knew what lube was! Out on the avenue loitering in front of the gay bar. Our skinny butts sliding off the hoods of parked cars, whooping & hollering! Mere kids at play, in our teens, bright as the sun, burning!

One last word of our evening after the FTM meeting, about one of our members, a crazy young kid. We are seated at a long table at restaurant. After the meal there are food scraps on several people's plates—Transman Red being frugal out of necessity wraps up his leftovers, carts them off in his pocket. This young kid is to be seen changing chairs from place to place, slowly eating up all the food in finished plates, which remains on the table! Poorer then Red! Why? Because all his extra money goes to nice clothes. Men's. After discarding each skirt, blouse & dress. He must build a new wardrobe.

Everybody goes back to their room to digest the day after its over – its the moment of truth the 1950's vice cop after that raid on his fellow queers must have felt. We take stock of ourselves, look at ourselves in the mirror shaving and, at the end of it all must ponder, 'what have I done with my life?'

It is logical that those marginalized, ghettoized would begin to make a lifestyle inside their segregated state, evolving their own language, customs, and relationships with each other—high camp in the case of gays—a lifestyle which does not end once the barriers against that people outside in the greater society start to fall. For some like myself so long dwelling behind its bitter-safe confines, now so sick and tired of faggotry, of cold dikes who exclude me, now that by my appearance I'm not automatically shunted away into an eclipsed margin by the greater heterosexual society—them taking me for a straight man--- maybe I've seen the ray of sunlight falling thru the cracks in the prison door and want to follow the path to freedom—freedom from The Life I've always known since 15 or 16, which had been increasingly ghettoized as the years marched by with social life exclusively confined to lesbian, gay and now transsexual people. I'm sick of it! Sick of the queer party!

Me-- Just another pretty face in a room full of whores!

***

My goal? To begin a more positive JOURNEY. So far this volume has been about all the pitfalls & stumbling—let us move on to the upliftingness of it all!

Do these things now Dear Children! Before the raw fire burns out!

I feel a great show coming on!
Fine black jazz music like a dance…
Hearing Dalila Jasmin in costume
waiting in the wings for our command
performance
at Club Eros;
shimmering her bells & bangles in the
background,

giving a glimpse of Higher Worlds!

27.
I guess we are forever seeking the lost part. I am looking for my mother—so the man won't do. Jesus will be my mother we will sleep together, maybe carnally.

Love that's what I want. For you to love each other. No loneliness anymore. No heartbreak.

> Praise the Lord from the earth,
> You sea-monsters and all deeps.
> Fire, and hail; snow, and fog;
> Stormy wind doing Her will:
> Mountains, and all hills;
> Fruit trees, and all cedars:
> Wild beasts, and all cattle;
> Creeping things, and winged birds:
>
> Psalm 148:7-9

***

Regarding this JOURNEY; what a price is paid for these words!

I speak to validate myself. But most often am not allowed to speak by those in control of various assemblies. So I will speak! On these pages!

I am not allowed to speak in Grace Cathedral!

The priest strides up and down the aisles, black clerical robes fluttering along his majestic patriarchal frame, microphone in hand valiantly searching for anyone to speak but me!

An Asian lady comes up to me after the meeting, making a 'hush!' sound. With a sweeping hand she indicates the congregation that swirls out of the doorway and whispers; "Here, at Grace, never say anything about rich or gay—they will attack you!" She must mean this, saying it 3 times.

Only 8% of San Francisco inhabitants attend church or synagogue. If ashrams, mosques, and pagan gatherings had not been withheld from the study maybe that would raise it by 3%-- a little over 10% of the population. The typical churches I've attended are so traditional it is no wonder the most in need will not have it. If all the disaffiliate artists, radicals who would reshape this nation into a democracy more equitable for all—including global justice—especially justice for female born persons, and if many of the city's 30,000 homeless could be reached by these religious institutions other then thru a free meal, their populations would swell. No wonder! I am a Christian and they can't even reach me! And my associates have no worship, no religious discipline. Instead they are spiritually mad, rushing about with heads full of brilliant ideas, but as friend Hugo observes from his little cabin in the tranquil desert, they are like a crazed child who runs stumbling from one corner to another. Each must eventually abandon the strife of their hopeless battle against this world to rethink, to contemplate, and to do so must retreat to their private cabins on some hard to reach Mountain Top. Whither this be in fact, or symbolically. Often I must go there with my private liquid fire!

So this is why I got mad at Grace Cathedral:
There is a panel on racism (black), which I attend. Naturally the stuff, which is said by the 3 African American panelists, drives me wild as a mixed blood who has lived this shit over and over since childhood ears began to fathom race's deep dark meaning. Once the panel is done with and the room opens to discussion my hand shoots up to make a statement. I feel bursting inside and must speak of it because they have raised some issues: -- Light skin, not accepted. -- Gay, not accepted. -- South Side Chicago nostalgia. –I am a published author. -- The race discarding their finest and best, throwing away their mixed raced children, their gay children, their radical voices. I would speak about glbt authors! Us, who are their mixed race cousins. The highly motivated black entrepreneurs sold out by Fillmore gentrification. Can you get me hooked up with publisher? Yet I did not get called upon! The handsome yet conservative—*Tenured*—priest ignores me. So later I simply vent my feelings in another church congregation meeting. Howling vociferously at the top of my lungs!

God shows me how angry I am. *All you people are angry* says Jesus. *Because they don't belong anywhere!*

Every human wants to belong somewhere.

In a panel discussion @ Faithful Fools, Scarlet Harlot talks about being criminalized for her lifestyle, which consequently causes her to make it become an identity; the whore as an identity as opposed to what she had once viewed herself just living her life and doing prostitution for a career. Each of us, once a baby, then an adult, becomes typecast by others, become some ironclad identity. Becomes that thing! No longer human, no more a sister, or a brother in a human family.

***

Pigeons peck the last afternoon scraps before night falls.

Red Jordan Arobateau won many awards. He won the Macarthur Foundation award in 2034.

Honorarium For A Life...

These are the scraps our Good Creator will feed Her/His servant!

Oh well. Am growing closer to the mystery of God. Affliction is not to torture us but to draw us closer to God. This according to a revelation given to Julian of Norwich, who lived from 1342-1416. She wrote The 16 Revelations of Divine Love. Julian was a nun who became sick almost to death at age 30, at which time she had visions. She described seeing God holding in Her hand a tiny brown nut, which seemed so fragile & insignificant that she wondered why it didn't crumble before her eyes. She was given the understanding that this brown nut was the entire created universe, which is as nothing compared to its Creator & she was told: 'God made it, God loves it. God keeps it.' From Julian of Norwich; 1342-1416.

***

He traveled in the better neighborhoods. Stuffed his pockets full of crumbs and fed Gods grey, winged birds with warm bellies & pink feet as he shuffled steadily about the city upon his routes of survival and of inquiry and of sociability. Soon arriving to the pet shelter, here he sat holding little dogs in his arms for 2 hours.

Feeding pigeons in Union Square Park one afternoon with a fellow trans, a beautiful, barely readable woman who, upon observing the birds said 'they are like tiny machines running around'. Yet the Lord has told me, *'they are more then machines.'*

It's always the big strong healthy ones—with no compassion who without a single thought chase off the weaker ones—because they don't understand. Never been sick a day in their lives. To know suffering is at least to have an idea of the beginning of empathy. They who suffer at least have been shown an intimate knowledge of others plight, because they remember their own pain, and what they once were themselves. Worst part of our transsexual lives, us, our generation passed is made of so much pain it's turned us to vinegar. Evil. We turn upon each other & fight internally. We bite the helping hand who feeds us. As I said, I'm sick of queers!

Many young TS ladies don't just need plastic surgery, they need in-depth training on what it really means to be a woman. If that's what they intend to be….

This point is very confusing because not everybody who says they are transsexual really is--- with every detail in place. Society may not understand what strange new breed the third sex is. Some who are transgender don't truly want to become women, nor in the case of some FTM's, to become men, but to be a construct of their own imagination.

Regardless, we as a people, both TG and TS, ultimately what we need is growth. Personal, spiritual, and cultural growth.

28.
>When April with her sweet showers has
>pierced the drought of March to the root,
>& bathed each vein in sweet moisture
>as has power to bring forth the flower
>when, also, Zephyrus with his sweet breath
>has breathed spirit into tender new shoots
>into every wood & meadow, & the years sun

> has run half his course into sign of the Ram
> and small birds sing melodies go to
> sleep with their eyes open all night
> (& so Nature pricks them in their hearts);
> then people long to go on pilgrimages,
> and palmers long to seek strange shores
> and far-off shrines known in various lands
> and, especially, from lands of every shore
> in England they come to Canterbury
> to seek the Holy, blissful, martyr
> who helped them when they were sick.
>
> Geoffrey Chaucer, Canterbury Tales; 1500rds.

So my JOURNEY is a spiritual pilgrimage. My retreat into private space. My outward journey to the reclusive Mountain Top.

The importance of being positive must not be underemphasized!

Keeping an uplifted mind and a good attitude.

   ***

Friday finds him on route to yet another church food lines offering hand. —This smaller Episcopal Church has mucho vegetables & other stuff.

> Lettuce, tomatoes, cabbage, sweet potatoes, carrots, squash, artichoke.
> Apples.
> Can of spicy beans.
> Bread.
> 4 pack of chocolate drink.
> Beef jerky.
> Rice.
> Cottage cheese.

On this bus the Chinese driver gives Transman a short transfer— barely enough time to get back home without having to duefully put out even more coins into the steadily gobbling capitalist time-clock machinery set up to rob people. Of course he is worried about the too short transfer, where in sets up the drama.

Incidentally, 3 transwomen get on the next bus, they travel in bands for protection. Two white, one pretty brown skin. Two over 6 feet tall one 5'10', all husky builds. He has the following thought: *'On observing my sister MTFs, can't but help be impressed by heavy musculature & physical size of many of them—born with male genome thus subsequent physique and skeletal size; they can hold their own in a fight. They look like half an Amazon football team climbing up the stairs of this bus in all their bells and bracelets, dresses, lipstick, long hair and dainty women's shoes.'* A physique which many regret. All three of these large girls must maintain a highly charged positive attitude to push them thru the world—as obvious misfits, since none of them are passable. On the sex change combo of Estradile and Spireolactin--a feminizing hormone and testosterone suppressant-- they loose muscle mass, many lose pounds of weight—until it's replaced by womanly fat. And these new women say how they feel more vulnerable, believing they don't have the brute strength they once did—to combat any attacker. But this is part of feminizing. You can't have both.

Now the petty drama of a poor soul with little else of importance on his mind but survival… As he exits, T looked down nervously at the heavy-set African American bus driver ensconced on her throne of small power—the bus driver's seat. She commands a thick wad of bus transfers—this month's color, sky blue—which, are time dated & there in is the crux of this difficulty. Still worried, believing the previous driver has shortchanged him on his transfer, he sees this new bus drivers transfers are ½ hour longer! Whereas the hours of his transfer are shorter—he is afraid it might be insufficient time to return home! –And stupidly says so aloud. And her reply; "I wouldn't give you one any way!" –Alligator snapped --- belligerent, indigently with a simmering outrage underneath of inheritance of slavery, years of poverty & subsequence protective hardass shell, (like a turtles shell) of ignorance. T is slightly taken aback. It wasn't necessary for her to jump into this hostile agro stance. This situation can fast turn into a verbal assault between them. This driver could have said anything, but chose the raw, sour negative retort. Chances are she lives out her life this way also—in disappointment, un self-satisfied. A mountainous brown volcano, constantly spewing out sour gossip with vehemence, & elaboration, berating all around her right & left. Transman is no better; his acid tongue states; "Well have a nice day Miss Sweetness and Light." At least better then he would have in the past have been, yelling at the top of his lungs. Sees now he will have to leave earlier to get the earlier, direct bus and avoid both these wretched drivers!

Attitude!

So according to the Gospel, I'm suppose to love this bitch! And she is suppose to love me!

During the evolution of times since I was a child, our country America has seen a whole new wave of immigrants, from South America, and Asia, just as earlier in the 1800rds they came from Northern Europe; English, Irish, and later Southern—notably Italian. So many minority groups seem to have set themselves up with beneficent societies, they learn to help advance each other for the betterment of their race, they've set up infra structures, yet still others are not prepared at all. Especially blacks, who have been a minority immigrant for the longest sojourn here. We, whose natural progress of historical racial development was interrupted by slavery.

Transman Red thought; *'no one is helping me, along my path of a fine arts painter & writer.'*

    ***

Universe is like university. It is from this university that he graduated. Not the university of dick-torium.

So, my message is to make the children see deeper into the meaning of life because they will fare better in the end & their way in-between will be strengthened.

I report what follows because people must be made aware of evil forces in this world; they must be prepared: There's evil in this world, some negative force greater then each individual person. Evil, down deep inside our finer hearts and minds. And God has created this evil perhaps so that all people will have a choice to be either good like God, or evil, like this negative force. If God has created this evil then evil is not only greater then any single individual, it is also greater then the collective evil of all humankind—all evil done by all people put together; added up since the beginning of time.

Satan hates to be exposed. If you even use his name some people think you are a Satan worshiper—or why else would you even bring up his name? Nothing could be further from the truth. You are an ardent follower of The Light. A being of peace, of love, of the Savior, of grace, of our God, Who also is a Being of intelligence, Who would not have us remain ignorant.

Actually no matter how much pain a person has endured, nor for how long, to embrace negativity, in some horrible paradox, is to be clinging to the dark side of things, and not the uplifting Light. Thus in effect, remaining in the imprisonment of the negative force, hence de facto, worship of it! This does not seem fair! To carry this double burden forever along their life's path, burdens seemingly not their fault. The first being the original offenses which came against them when they were weak and vulnerable, such as living thru a war, being raised in a home of physical assault or mental abuse; the second, that subsequent eternal fearfulness & sorrow they bare, still marked indelibly by their life-altering experiences. But each individual must be accountable, and shed the burden of the second, somehow. If a person has been so hurt and tortured of course they may find this impossible. Yet, it is another of this solid dimensions axioms. Suffer eternally, or Change!

What kind of sadness? What kind of pain? Well for instance pain beyond endurance.

Pain unspeakable.

For instance, how unspeakable to see all the dogs in lonely pens. Waiting for a friend to take them home. Who may never come. Prisoners in cells-- humanbeings locked up because they cannot be trusted outside in humanity. Knowing this could all be so different.

Religious people speak of the Light within the Christ way, the way of Buddha. But look inside my own heart, on the left side of my chest is darkness, yet even in this darkness a faint light exudes. So my light is a dark light—a blue light—sufficient to guide the children of darkness along our subterranean paths so they will have a safer journey. We must all follow the ways of Creator the best we can, even we, the blind, and sad.

This Sunday at Grace the sacrosanct upholding an imperial staff sails forth like a figure head on a great spiritual ship, leading the clerical procession behind her, their long purple robes austere yet rich. An acolyte swings a golden incense burner baring sweet smelling holy smoke, a deacon's pudgy hands upon a silver encased bible, uphold The Word.

New, vicious changes! The recently installed female pastor gives a sermon on love & invokes the name of God the Mother! A ray of light aluminates cathedral!

Here we all congregate. The little ones strut and stomp to make themselves seem bigger, the big ones try to move with grace and appear undistinguishable from anybody else. We all have the same thing inside—the same hunger for the unnamable.

And somebody spoke of, The Road.

Therein in a burnished wooden pew @ Grace, I am given inspiration that to name each of these segments of JOURNEY. This current one, vol. 2, will be Infinite Love.

Which brings me to mind, the advertisement panel on the back of that wretched bus; bus of all pains and miseries, which just now departs from my mind—another trial of brokenness between human beings—this panel advertises the Coming of Mother Ama, an brown skinned woman from India called as a girlchild to the ministry, who has set up ashrams here in the United $tates and her homeland, to which friends of mine—those turned away from their native-born Christianity by its bigotry—have made regular pilgrimages. Ama specializes in Hugs! She hugs each person she meets and her goal is to hug every humanbeing on earth.

Infinite Love.

29.
> The notion that everything we do affects others and stands to be judged by them constitutes a concept of human community that is long lost. In this world, corporations say not one word of sorrow to the children of the land who will inherit the dry and eroded mountainsides on which the trees once grew. Bankers take profits that close businesses and say nothing to the people made homeless by the deal.
>
> Rules of Benedict—Joan Chittister 2006

Searching for our identity in the cosmetic section of Macys where Paris fashion runway models like emaciated skeletons of choice, jump and jerk down the aisles applying dabs of colored powders upon their wan faces to bring them to life. Or searching for life in the monasteries, churches, mosques, ashrams and shules of spiritual sanctuary?

Transman has made his choice. He enters the small chapel to the side of Grace's magnificent nave. And there is greeted by a wordless small congregation in silent prayer. Over the alter an elongated Christ shining, so light, so frail, hovers. Christ speaks to him, *'would you serve me?'*

Thin bark of a Cross, --- light as air, of the Benedictines.

Can hear this old ark of the church moaning & groaning, for it is a ship on a tempestuous sea of faith, and faith alone. Wind whips around this jewel carved on top of the hill. An ancient tapestry hangs on one wall. A thread-woven painting. Its curly head cherubic male children have horns growing out of their locks! What have I got myself into now?

AWW MAH GAWD! An antique painting graces this little chapel. On it's lower left hand corner a black slave naked, with ebony skin and nappy hair kneels before an affluent European aristocrat wearing embroidered clothes and fine boots! This to rival in political incorrectness (but 25 steps away) a life-like nativity display, —sans Mary! With male worshipers, wise men, shepherds, goatherds, nobles—Jesus—and not one single female in the setting of 20-odd characters—not even Mother Mary! Saint Mary! Well on this rock I will build my order! The Holy Order of Mary! —A new Order of Jesus Christ!

The Benedictines are an order of prayer. Each voice needs the Word of the Lord. Even devils listen to the Word from the hallway of the church—hoping for salvation!

Healing. Says the spirit of the Most High.

I greet you with sadness. Thinks Red.

I am too strong, Red, for you to see Me. Says the Most High.

Each voice needs God.

God, who has given us the spirit of Tikkun Olam—the spirit of Justice. A heavenly society of angels whisper in Gods ear:

Justice: Oh divine Being it's only fair to give this new generation of that fallen earth the chance to know You.

Creator: I will send prophets out in the New Age carrying My Word—under their arm. To speak of Me, of salvation in their own language, --in a tongue My fallen children will understand. The type of messenger the children will be drawn to.

Justice: Those who call on You and enter into your paradise, how will they be judged?

God: They will be judged by their trust. Their relationships & how much love passed between them.

In the common world so many people are on the threshold of belief—because a revolutionary figure like Jesus was, makes so much sense to them. In prison, that tomb of regret, the incarcerated with dead time to serve, wait, Bibles/ Korans/Torah's & Spiritual Meditations in hand, having found finally at the end of a sad journey that You are the last place to Who they can turn.

For so many decades my desire to love humanly and be loved was my persistent desire, my constant craving. Each night drove me out into the gay taverns on a relentless pursuit to meet a woman, take her home, fuck, then sleep cozily together in a warm embrace, and thus cement in the bonds of a permanent life together. I often wonder if Jasmin was a gift from God. For 16 years we were married, and still remain friends today. Up until that time, and sadly, after, my relationship life was pathetic. Pathetic! I could stand here and say it was pathetic dozens and dozens of times and not be exaggerating! I'd be saying it for all the lonely years, for all the times lovers left the following morning. My pathetic attempts to get lovers, to have marriages, relationship, family. The men in my life, I was not interested in for a relationship, maybe if I could have been, my love life would have been easier, for they weren't as illusive. So the few times I did achieve this nirvana called an *intimate relationship* approaching marriage with a woman it was so rare. Maybe this must be the groundwork of setting up a new Order. To love, on a different plane. Maybe this is the Great Show about to transpire in my life!

The damage will be undone, says the Lord.

Red spent his entire youth middle and older age so far as a working artist. Devoting hours per day over a 40-year working in the labor market life span of his now 63 years. Upon his first conversion, after being an atheist since ten (or 11?) At age 32 (or 33), he felt he must become the church deacon, the church janitor, the church newsletter editor, taking on this role and that in service. For he assumed all other things he had done before he'd encountered the Divine upon his life's role was to be put aside! He was wrong in part. Yes, everybody not serving God down here during their stay on earth is missing the boat. But don't get me wrong. If you find a talent for something— for instance one discovers they have the capacity to be a doctor, it would be wise to do that. An artist or a musician develops that skill— this is their gift; use it to serve the purpose of God. If one is in the process of developing a skill and is recently converted this does not mean to abandon that skill and devote themselves entirely to cleaning the church, bowing in prayer exclusively or some other pastoral duty, it means that God calls us not only for our souls sake but because our gift can be used in the ministry of Her Kingdom.

>You shall live! You shall live again!
>--God, 2007.

>*Youth, then decline.*
>*Death.*
>*Then Life!*

***

God led me to a valley. I saw it was filled with cows and bulls. Tens of thousands of heads of cattle.

They all have names! God, (The Forever Young), declares, with high enthusiasm.

I know all their names! God adds, even more fabulously.

Will I know their names? I ask.

Many of them! Says God... adding, *as many as you want!*

How can I ever remember all their names! I say. And the Spirit led me to know that in heaven all memory comes easy.

And I went into the heavenly field and greeted each animal by its name; they touched their wet noses to my face and hands, and love passed between us.

As we traveled day & night upon a road of infinite love towards home, towards God, towards the end of our stay, God appeared to us with her heavenly Word, clothed in an opaque cloud with just a hint of pastel rainbows; garmented in majesty.

>Eat from my table.

There's always plenty.
---God, to the Prophet, 2007.

Well anyway this thing about setting up a new Order, Journal 1, subtext found inside my Unity of Utopia trilogy introduces it, and the next journal, (3) will delineate it. Where as this volume, (2) Infinite Love, is the *reason,* Infinite Love!

***

The bark of the forlorn dogs at the Animal shelter, where he spends 2 hours holding lost dogs in his arms, still ring in his ears. Transman ponders: I'll set up these community houses, each unit must contain its share of unwanted dogs & cats, who must be loved by members of the Order. That is one of my rules.

Transman journeyed across the water to Oak-Town where he got his mail—turns key to the slender metal box, 2 book orders lay inside, plus a check from the Bancroft. Oakland people speaking with voices like barks. Day is warm, the fog has dried.

When he gets back to San Francisco it's a long walk up Market street from 1st and Mission to 8th, the Public Library Main, a 6 story tall glass and steel gem, hollow in its center, with not enough room for the actual books.

The homeless use this public facility for its toilets and sinks, and little else.

"Open up that door, I gotta drain my main vein." A miserable, unshaven bum in dirty rumpled clothing, a perpetual drunk, exclaims. "I had a bad night man." It was a fonky night down at the homeless shelter. "It's for shit." He adds, growling. "Amputees and blind men placed in the upper bunks."

Transman Red he has no time for this bullshit; his mind is affixed to higher things. Privately, Transman vows not to have any such characters involved in his Order, nor to service their needs for housing, food and counseling care. There is some other poverty-bound flock to whom he would minister! Who is it?

> *Eat from my table.*
> *There's always plenty.*

Hum, well maybe we'll set up some kind of outer ring of support help, outside the actual Order, and outside it's more informal Community. A work of something or other…(See *x below.)

While bent over a computer studying fervently under Convents, Monasteries, Religious Orders, he find this:

> These two movements, representing what Brenda Bolton has called the "Medieval Reformation," brought to the fore the most gender-ambiguous area in the Christian religion: the realm of the spirit. "In Christ Jesus," says the Scriptures, "there is no male nor female." Spiritual power may dwell in anyone who is in contact with the divine; God is no respecter of persons. In the supernatural world it is possible for any person, including a woman, to bypass the male-dominated ecclesiastical structure while remaining within the confines of orthodox doctrine. According to the church, direct contact with God could be attained through prayer, asceticism, visions, the Eucharist, or mystical contemplation; and prophesying—warning against evil, predicting the future, counseling, advising, criticizing leaders—was allowable for anyone who had received genuine revelations from God. For medieval women, who were excluded from the priesthood, the new reform movements, with their emphasis on prophecy and evangelism, opened a theologically permissive "space" wherein they had liberty to develop their spirituality.

Disembarking the bus, he crosses paths with a small band of heavenly missionaries. Young women in white robes, cowls, rosaries dangling from their necks. One upholds a picture of Christ in her arms. They are modest, non-speaking.

"What order are you?"

"Mother Teresa!" Replies the one holding Christ she is exuberant.

Is this a coincidence? It is not. Is this a sign that I am approaching God? A foretelling of my own religious involvement to a higher degree?

That day Transman scurries around upon his routes, and at night, when the streets are cold and emptying he wearily starts towards home. Here & there a bundle wrapped in a quilt, rectangular shape, about 2 feet high lays on the curb at night. It is a human, cocooned for the night against the cold. Isolated, dying, bitter. Uncared for by the human family.

It has been a long exhausting day of foraging. It is the 3rd time on this particular bus when he heard insults hurled by some rowdy black man at an aged senior citizen--some doddering old white man hobbling along with a cane. This is wrong-acting! This behavior is not justifiable, but it is explainable-- by years of the legacy of slavery at our beginning in this country, and neglect forever after.

Even the holy world is not exempt from strife. Scandal @ Grace! A female among the priests in charge has chopped off the head of one of the other priests—one who's been there over 10 years! Why? It makes for speculation. Is it sexism? Maybe she wants to take over his position! A power play for feminism? Maybe she lusts after his clean-shaven slender handsome body! Desires his slim hips riding between her thighs at night! Virtually everywhere on earth politics rears its ugly head, Grace is not exempt.

Transman was not exempt from The Hate. He thought: 'Fuck you white men! The upper class men of this church! They are bigger, and command all the attention and respect, while I am practically ignored! (Not the fags, not my friends, nor any people who have been friendly to me.) These privileged, favored ones will read my book and suck my dick!'

And of course, back at home—my own queer community, --- Transsexual woman asserting their female rights by using male privilege, which they once had and have not shed. I think of trying to start some kind of religious spiritual group with trannys and it makes me laugh. Impossible! As a group we are too damaged emotionally.

How do you manage a herd of crazy trannies? You need a tranny wrangler. Or so the saying goes.

What I saw over a period of months, 2 years, at the now-dead Trans Space, that spectacular failure, which made the gay newspaper reports and is documented in my diary PASSAGE, has made me change my mind about trying to set up any kind of work for trans people. It's fraught with great hell.

To make it short, my point is, that our human family dwells in A House of Contention, especially messed up is our transsexual/ transgendered house. Start a work of spirituality, which is aimed specifically at trannys, what a joke! Yet, All it takes is for one transgendered face to re-ignite that dream. She stands at an intersection, waits to cross, high cheekbones, bronze color face enhanced by cosmetics, sturdy, slender, just over 6'2', graceful, long colorful skirt, bosomy blouse over her packed bosom. Slender, strapless, shoes. Large & dainty; she is my sister. A transsexual woman. Thus again I fantasize my dream of Christian multi-faith outreach to tg/ts; especially queer poverty level people, ones who need help—a religious disciplined Order

Friday free food has come again. --- Waiting in the line at Saint Gregory's Episcopal church atop Portrero Hill with a sweeping view of SF downtown area. Today grey skies at distance. Rectangular skyscrapers. Hazy. On the hill sunshine & the wind blows. Here while at San Gregory's amid drone of shabby attired poor, mostly old rough Asian females, few whites, and almost no blacks. We all stand, idly waiting. Speaking of how long the other free food lines in town can be. Lethargically describe, with gnarled hands, about the contents of their small SRO hotel rooms, I overhear an inventory from the jumble of those dense small closets.

"What kind of place you got? A single room or a double?"

"You know that guy who use to be a tenant before he got kicked out? Who tried to break into my room? Put a ladder up in the hall, next to my door, he was gonna go in thru the transom. It didn't work. They didn't get nothing." —And the like.

Waiting in line, thoughts. As a point of reference for this growing idea of my own work let me speak more about the Order of St Benedict. Which is 1,980 years old. It begins with 15 minutes of silent prayer in the small chapel at Grace on the nave followed by another 15 minutes in prayer and song. (Song is prayer 2 times over. St. Augustine.) After which we repair across the church grounds to the dining hall for soup, bread, & fruit, while being read to by one of the Benedictian congregants. Then 20 minutes of talk in which any difficulties are raised. Then volunteers to provided duties for the next week's service are decided. 15 more minutes of prayer in song. Leaving service at 9. 3 hours of mind-cleansing communal prayer.

My idea of a religious order would help house the poor, feed the hungry, provide a religious center & discipline for the believers (Christian along with multi faith) which include living together in commune. Many houses set up in areas connected by regular singing and worship services with all the houses come together at a local church, synagogue or ashram which would include their congregations as well. Our religious houses would pray together, eat food together, brothers/sisters, sharing in their mutual vow of poverty which all must take—and provide order. Discipline to their lives. I am reminded of Saint Dorothy Day—a common day saint who set up her socialist communities in Christian houses all across America in the starving post-depression years of the 1930's. She insisted that religious love & stewardship of God, as well as social programs must go hand in hand. Unionizing, feeding the poor, day care for children of working mothers, printing & distribution their newspaper the Daily Worker etc. Periodically she'd go storming around the nation disbarring houses that had fallen into spiritual neglect! Must be remembered that my Order of Mary, A New Order of Jesus Christ must be just that—religious, God-based. (God by many Names.) I will not veer from this point. Maybe some secular homes will be set up as a work of the communes of the actual Order (see above x*)— for instance take over an SRO building, purchase, remodel, and rent the units out at low-low cost, a nominal amount $200 to $400 per month to homeless whose lifestyles are stabilized. These would live there in an individual fashion not be part of the Order. But would come under its jurisdiction. (Oust unruly inhabitants; those relapsed back into substance abuse or uncontrolled mental illness.)

An Order in which we will serve God daily thru prayer, thru deed, and have better lives for ourselves.

I'm setting up a new Order—and a new way. Says Jesus. *You will be married to each other.* I take this to mean not one-on-one monogamous. Or maybe this is only a mental thing.

A silent order that would go around doing justice--& not engage in politics but in good works:
> To help the old.
> Care for the sick.
> Befriend the lonely
> Accompany the fearful.
> Champion those unspoken for to justice.
> To struggle with the downtrodden.
> To aid the weak.

2 days later was speaking to life-long fellow Transman bud C. Who again is going back to his upcoming Vipassana. A Buddhist retreat. His mantra there will be to give up sweeteners and caffeine. And the next morning I awake and am inspired to give up sugar! Benedictian prayer intervention? For my physical salvation. (The body is the tabernacle of the spirit.)

In JOURNEY Volume 3, I must write down the rules for the Daughters Of Courage, a Holy Order of Mary a New Order of Jesus Christ (after Rules of St. Benedict who lived on earth circa 200 AD).

I feel God growing up thru my heart in the insisting urgency of spring & it's terrifying. Great. So awesome. I'm afire—like a flame that shoots up thru me out of the roots of my heart thru the soles of my feet thru my body, eyes, and rushes out of the top of my head…

Well like they say, you never know who you're gonna meet & you never know what the weathers gonna be like.

Saul kept on threatening to kill the Lord's followers. He even went to the high priest and asked for letters to their leaders in Damascus. He did this because he wanted to arrest and take to Jerusalem any man or woman who had accepted the Lords Way.

When Saul had almost reached Damascus, a bright light from heaven suddenly flashed around him. He fell to the ground and heard a voice that said, "Saul! Saul! Why are you so cruel to me?"

"Who are you?" Saul asked.

"I am Jesus." The Lord answered. "I am the one you are so cruel to. Now get up and go into the city, where you will be told what to do."

The men with Saul stood there speechless. They had heard the voice, but they had not seen anyone. Saul got up from the ground, and when he opened is eyes, he could not see a thing. Someone then led him by the hand to Damascus, and for three days he was blind and did not eat or drink.

Acts 9 1-7. Holy Bible.

30.
The processional to the alter is smoking, flames shoot up—spiritual flames! The minister intones from the pulpit, something feminist, a long suppressed document from 1st Samuel. Where his wife declares about him, 'When I was young and fell in love with a fool.'

Walk thru the vast arching overhanging lofty reaches of Grace Into A Great Silence. -- Past the parade of the sexist murals, now dusty, faded pastels. Only 1 girlchild, but many boys. The few 3rd world men are on their knees. Several women. It is predominantly men and boys, well dressed—and standing authorativly.

To walk into any Christian church, Jewish Temple, or Islamic Mosque is to venture into a great silence of a different kind. The absolute suppression of the female voice. But hold on! Before T. passes his severe judgment, at the nave of the Benedictines, there's Christ uplifted in a wood carving with pastel paints, done several hundred years ago, surrounded by human forms of 4, statuesque, with rounded hips and bosoms, head cloths and veils—traipsing of women! 4 women—all at once! Independent woman commanding their own boxes within the niche, they are serving our Savior by adulation, lyre, harp.

The Spirit moves me, speaking. *Do you think I have love in My heart? Infinite Love!* (Light shines behind the high stained glass windows, majestic.

If the human race can be looked upon as something evolving under God to a higher dimension—then one great hindrance to the human progress in the world is the ill treatment of women & not until this very great injustice is defeated will we move on. The quality of women's lives, the robbing of their power, the suppression of their self-fulfillment is one of humankind's greatest faults and subsequently holds everybody back and will do so until this fault is a righted.

> *Help us God. It is so hard—being human. Knowing we have to die. Seeing the pain of others, and knowing the pain of ourselves.*

The Gospels compelling ministry is not only Jesus' love—but also her-his intelligence. Aren't we suppose to be likewise? See the woman helper-furrowed face, her hunched shoulders, as she goes about her duties serving the church. Beneath the ladylike cosmetics there is a terrible rigor; great cloudy brows set into the stone of her spiritual face, a frozen expression trembling in perpetual rage. Not only do I love her, but I understand the reasons for her pain. Denied as a woman. A long 70-year lifetime of being shunted back to second class, then again to third class after 2nd class men of color are finally given their rights; pushed down, no matter how hard she tries to climb up. A portrait of her should decorate this dining hall! She should be Dean! She should be Chancellor! Remember, women don't want violence, nor chance the possibility of annihilation. So they capitulate to men, but it does not mean man has won. Women withdraw and from that point take the fight to a higher level-- & save the battle for a different day. A day, when they are assured of victory. Victory by means other then brute violence---by trickery, by the changing of dynasties due to some other natural occurrence. Trickery, this means the generation-unto-generation of women's secret practices of witchcraft. This means the withdrawal of her true love from her husband, even from her children. Denying them her secret gifts and powers, just as she has been denied power in the larger male-dominated world. This means so much loss for her, for her family, for community, for the whole earth.

More evidence of pain: The pretty unattainable faggots of the church. Who care for no one but their own gay kind. (And cute ones only my dear.)

The lovely *Brotherhood* Of Man Commemorative plaque stationed in a stone niche upon first entering the cathedral. All the male—wording, indicative of greater injustices, and favoritism, especially brute force.

The dining room desecrated by 7 large portraits of Bishops and Deans from yesteryear, nearly all of them male. Only 1 female. None a person of color.

Rule of the Daughters of Courage. Uphold the prominence of women in the Order.

Oh by the way—here's how to pray:
>Our Creator who lives in heaven
>Your name is Holy.
>Your paradise, come.
>Your will be done
>On earth as it is in heaven.
>Give us this day our daily bread
>And forgive us our trespasses,
>As we forgive those who trespass against us.
>Lead us not into temptation,
>And deliver us from evil.
>For Your's is paradise, the power,
>And the glory, forever.
>So be it.

You see I have 'de-sexed' the common text. That is removed all patriarchal 'fathers', 'he's' and 'kingdoms' which are offensive to the female-center.

A woman is abducted. Held down and raped in succession by 4 men. Continuing to imprison her afterwards, a sadist among them suggests they should cut off her breasts—and cut out her vagina, which they have just used—while she is still alive. A more humane of the vicious thugs demurs, the other 2 agree and the 3 prevent him. This scenario--but carried out to the fullest mayhem--- is actually going on in parts of South America today, 2007, in the constant war between roaming bands of hoodlums and native tribes people. The most horrific practices of mutilation and dismemberment of Chinese women was used by invading Japanese soldiers against Chinese in their capitol city of Nanking. It is the ace card played against women—targeting their sexuality, their gender. And it is against this that the great tide of women must be vigilant and fight eternally.

    ***

This day and age when people pay God no attention on the one hand, to the worshiping and paying too much attention to persecuting others by using Gods name on the other, in this day & age I must set up my Order.

It will be a frugal Order. Account for every penny. Practice good stewardship for God, in careful budget with no extravagance. Pick pennies up off the street. Waste no one, including people.

My work is valuable. Because God's calling to everybody, not just to those who sacrifice in a monastic discipline. Common people relate to a common life, such as what I am delineating here in my diary JOURNEY.

Those who truly worship and seek God and are of a spiritual mind, who upholding the goal of good and to carry the Light for humankind will be admitted, not only those who practice Christianity.

There are those who practice their religion that's mysticism. There are those who are shriveled & small. There are those who have no practice at all. There are 'normals'. They are transsexuals. They are a regular sort. They are wild artists.

We are all apples on the same tree.

      ***

My friend I call 'cousin' Carlos comes to town to visit. He tells me of his adventures one day, in the Mission district: "When I was in the Mission 3 women propositioned me, one of them even had teeth. They were the ugliest foulest prostitutes I've ever seen. They ain't wasten' your cash on soap, that's for sure."

Carlos and I have many a laugh as we journey around town sightseeing & eating & sitting in coffeeshops. I try to tell him about Grace, just to confront a stonewall as strong as the fortress of any cathedral on earth. It is difficult to lead them to The Canterbury Way, impossible even to speak about my experience there. So many of my friend's outlook on God—which is interchangeable to them with religion--- their outlook on God is a shut door. Complete, angry, rejection.

At table with Carlos and C. who is staring across the table at me, me drinking a decaf coffee with cream no sugar in hand. His nearly bald close cropped head, shoe button eyes, red Van Gogh beard; he informs me: "Red, when you die you don't want all the proceeds from your books and those paintings to go to the *State,* or to any of your relatives! Do you?" (My numerous relatives whom I haven't seen for 50 years.) "Just think of it! All your hard years of writing and painting—and it all goes to the *State!* The *State* can take over the profits from it if you don't have a Will!" Then I better make out a will! So here it is!

Thus again I repeat my last will and testament; there is a precursor of this document in AUTUMN CHANGES, The Epilogue, (Vol. 5) I believe. My estate means all my writings, copyrights for them, and all my paintings. This body, the estate, will be referred to as my art.

My sole heir is to be ------ Jasmin ------ with the Bancroft Library's help, —this prestigious UC Berkeley acquisitions Library, in which a copy of all my books, and some of my papers is already archived. The idea is to protect the integrity & availability of my work. & no one can act as censor of it, nor change any words of it.—Under the guise of 'editing'. I hereby appoint a commission of my friends to monitor what happens to my art, upon my death, or great incapacitation. All the money proceeds should go to Jasmin.

If Jasmin should die before I do her share or control of my art should not be transferable to any person, but revert to the Bancroft Library.

The members of the commission are --------, --------, -------. -------. And -------.

31.
        A cat's job is simply to:
        Catch mice,
        Procreate,
        Find a spot in the sun and sleep,
        And be a friend to the people.

Each house of the Order will have its proper share of cats & dogs, plus other small animals, and no one with compromising allergies to animals shall join this Order! Living spaces can accommodate the allergy-prone by removal of all rugs and upholstered furniture (which hold dust, pollutants) and thorough sweeping and wet mopping of floors regularly.

Drink from the wellspring, which is God.

Daughters' Of Courage is for those who desire to carry their spiritual search to a higher level, a deeper degree.

So here I wish to start my Order—in SF, this city of greed, and acquisition for profit over people. Where one can overhear tourist's stories: "these rents! How can they all survive? They all can't be making that much!"

I hope that mine will prove to be more then just a historical document… But like the Rules of Saint Benedict also inspire faith. Not merely a glimpse into 300 AD monastic life cloistered inside a grey rock-built fortress.

Did I mention persons of all sexes & genders can be in the Order? It is not a nun's-only convent, nor a monk's monastery which bars everyone but the male sex. So there will be male and male-born 'DOC's, (XY) in addition to those female-born (XX). * About de-sexing of liturgy. After the he's are turned into she's, the mothers added to the fathers, it's different. But the same.

* There will be a clarification on these points delineated in my sequential volume of Journey, number 3, Daughters Of Courage, A New Order Of Jesus Christ, under the heading of Clarification On The Points.

This Order shall be dedicated for the glory of God & the good of humanity.

Members of the Order will pray together, and pray often and at regular times! They will frequently be in intercessory prayer for the planet. More & more in times like these my prayer is—God don't put an end to it, this world—your grand experiment!

Oh, all who join the Order of the DOC must take this vow:
    Q. Do you renounce Satan and all the spiritual forces of wickedness that rebel against God?

A. I renounce them.

Q: Do you renounce the evil powers of this world, which corrupt and destroy the creatures of God?

A. I renounce them.

Q. Do you renounce all sinful desires that draw you from the love of God?

A. I renounce them.

In addition, the following vow must be taken by all who are Christ centered; searching Creator thru Jesus Christ:

Q. Do you turn to Jesus Christ and accept her-him as your Savior?

A. I do.

Q. Do you put your whole trust in her-his grace and love?
A. I do.

Q. Do you promise to follow and obey her-him as your Lord?

A. I do.

God's greatest sadism towards the human race is giving us our own free will. Because by following our own desires, time and time again we fall into traps and are stuck there to our sorrow. God tells me our goal should be to shepherd the sheep. To urge them onto the correct paths. We all want the same things, ultimately. Peace, joy, food, community, safety, warmth. To be validated for our works and for who we are. —Something I've had too little of!

The Closure is a metal scepter carried by an acolyte holding it aloft as they walk in front of the Holy Procession, —symbolic of being willing to go where the gospel sends us.

My instructions are--- to persevere. You will serve any good, well. Go Higher!

The crippled lame and halt will come first to see God.

Am sick of the quasi mystics, these gurus of the world—without those disciplines of a religious life--- who, in a parasitical fashion use all the good gifts of the church from God for themselves, and impress common people with this knowledge in the guise of philosophy, but neglect to reference from which their enlightenment originated. Thus the children are left blind, and unable to find the wellspring on their own. So here and now, I am telling you—all my enlightenments, all my prophecies, and my ideas, they come from my pursuit of God during my stay in various churches/synagogues and other Holy places. My enlightenments do not originate in me but are from the Creator, via the Holy Spirit, which She has given me and can give you too, if you ask! She will alight upon you as a dove!

Another of my gripes are those who live as if $ money is their God, they get less from life, give less to life and have less use by humankind. First, because of the evil they are doing in the progress of obtaining riches. Second their energies could be devoted to the good of all humankind instead of just their own aggrandizement. In the time they spend, miserly counting gold in dark vaults, they could discover ways to change this societal structure to one where all are accountable for their actions on earth. Time stolen, time wasted!

Those who join the Order will receive basic training in the spiritual, just like a soldier learns maneuvers at boot camp. *Joining a religious order can discipline the immature soul as to those things worthy of life.*

2.2 billion of words population don't have access to water. India, Bangladesh, Africa, Palestine, Gaza strip, Left Bank. We can make the goal of our various houses within the Order, to work on ending lack of potable water, and world hunger!

***

WOW! Today @ Chinatown public library read what belonging to a Benedictine order really involves. Its severity, strictness. My Order---- by comparison--- would be more easygoing. Here are some rules of

Saint Benedict. No monk shall be allowed to own anything. Not a book, not paper, not a pen. Each monk lives alone in a private cell. No speaking to anyone, not even other monks but upon the once-per-week stroll thru the woods. Monks communicate with one another at daily services—tho not in direct speech, but only thru recital of scripture. Thus, their order is a severe closeness. One enclosing yet held apart from all, which humans cherish on the animal level. To live out ones life in such an order is a very long silence.

Well this text brings us to a very delicate subject—love, sex, companionship, personal love between two individuals. As well documented over my 40-year span written about, my love life has been abysmal. Adventuresome, yes, but way too much evil loneliness eating away at the edges in those long-in-betweens, when there was no lover, no friends. My best years were a 16-year marriage to a woman, in which I was happy, tho lacking in community. All the while we were together, warm and cozy in our bed, still, part of me was missing community. Now, alone in my room at night, I venture out daily and have reached out to scores of people. Am building community. Go to Grace Sunday go to Shar za'hav Friday. Attend support groups. Lead my own drop-in Wednesday coffee gathering.

The nuns and monks have taken the vow of celibacy. They renounce human marriage between two people, in favor of marring Jesus Christ.

It is my personal belief that one cannot fully serve God and serve their sisters/brothers in community as a married person—whose vows and dedication is, number one, to their spouse, and immediate family. They will always put their loved ones first when faced with a trying situation. How can they then fully give themselves to Jesus and to the service of Her/His ministry? How can they put the common person above their own mate? They cannot! If the lonely beg for their companionship over coffee and sister/brotherhood in daily pursuits but the monk or nun would prefer to rush home to hop in bed with their beloved, how can they be of great service? If they don't truly need others, *and God*—being so enriched by a happy personal love life, how effectively will they reach out, and how dedicated will they be to building a greater community? A married twosome living in the Order of DOC, would it be a benefit or a liability? Would the other sisters/brothers feel overwhelmed by the formidable forces of a twosome in their midst?

Which in turn brings us home to the crux—Infinite Love, and what does that entail? Can all the rules of Saint Benedict approach it's meaning? Are these disciplines the ladder by which we attain the Eternal? Is it the Long Silence, which is needed? Can a lengthy life of lonely pain suffering as a common person who seeks out common love in diverse meeting places and watering holes of human habitat, be transformed to one holistic in serving Christ, and married to Her-Him alone?

Those who would join this Order are they searching for 'the love of their life' when they could be searching for the love which surpasses understanding, the love of God?

The Spirit guided my right hand to touch the ring finger of my left—and asked me, *would you marry Jesus?*

I would. I replied.

32.
A Little Homily On Race:

>Light Bright and Almost White
>
>Light Voice: Well then there was this one Negro, fair, pretty wavy hair, a lighter brown skin then the other common Negroes. He was a case.
>
>Black Voice: Yeah, my momma always told me, there's these folks, Negroes just like us, but who thinks they white—cause they bright. Fair colored yuh know. Don't agitate 'em when yuh see 'em walken' nose in the air. They won't speak to nobody darker then them, thinking they white, thinking they in a different world, and believing this--- just on account of the color they sees in the mirror and nothing else. They don't know nothing about no whites. Don't know no whites. Never lived up north with no whities.

Light Voice: Well there was this one case, he'd walk by, nose in the air, just like you said. He'd stop and talk to me of course…

Black Voice: *Of Course!*

Light Voice: Cause I'm bright myself…

Black Voice: *Humpth.*

Light Voice: Anyway, poor Ronald. He was a Hawaiian one month, next time you seen him he didn't remember what he'd said before so now he was from Martinique, or some Caribbean island. Next time, he a Japanese or from South America. And he'd never let you forget it. He'd always manage to bring that up during the course of the conversation. He'd lie. He'd lie big time, oh yeah.

Black: I'm acquainted with the lad. Yes. Most people I know wondered why Ronald just didn't go and be white—pack up his suitcase get on the subway and go over to another section of the city and introduce himself as Joe Smith or somebody and start all over as white.

Light: They didn't realize that although blacks might have assumed Ronald looked white—in comparison to them he was white--- but to a real white person Ronald wasn't white. They might have guessed he was Negro. They might not have. But they knew he wasn't pure white. And therein lay the problem.

I just threw this little sermon in to describe some of my relatives, and my peculiar particular predicament—one that estranges people from each other. There are many predicaments which estrange people from each other—and thus, if struggling to rise up out of our burdens in a Herculean effort to survive, we give up what we wallowed in for so long; the abysmal alcoholism, drugs, morbidly entertaining our misery—throw off those yokes and seek the Light, and in so doing we stumble into religion, then consequently after a few years of sitting in pews, or chanting on mats we begin to seek community. Religious community. Among our chosen group of likeminded people, in which we hope all broken parts of our lives will be repaired, and all broken family members will be united into a whole. In the case of DOC it would be inclusion into the full body of the Savior. One sister/brotherhood inside Christ Jesus, each member no longer alone, no longer defeated, and no longer invalidated.

Such is the motivation for my Order on the common level.

The divine motivation is the seeking of Creator, and for the glory of God.

Both are essential!

More & more the last sleeping places of the cities homeless are beginning to look like the funeral bier of a pall-born corpse. Mummies, covered by shrouds of blankets tucked neatly under both head and foot in the reposition of the dead.

Inside, wraithlike, their spirits are lost to any further human interaction. There is no hope.

To most of us who currently live a bare life, we may feel a frightening similarity to these so far gone. Seeing these fellow humans dying by degrees over the years outside on the cold concrete is a dire warning to what we too could become if we slip up too badly. If we make financial mistakes also socially/emotional missteps. ---If we somehow over the processes of time & fickle fate allow ourselves to retreat into a shell and become hermits, or isolated loners with no one to care about us.

For many years I dreamed of a romance, which would outlast time. A happy home,-- in the singlular sense. This would protect me from the cold heartedness of society. This would be my refuge and my warm blanket. My security. Everywhere this ideal is fostered by the media, by advertising, suggesting it to us thru every orifice of our brains. A personalized license plate number, a song, a phrase conjuring up the

'Love Energy'. It is the common love. Common love is what they all are speaking about. Signs of this are all over the place & how long does it last? Eternal Love, Infinite Love, outlasts time.

Don't have to mention all the billboards & posters around town baring the 'Dare To Be Happy' or 'Now You Too Can Be A Star' advertisements selling some product or another—which equate happiness with material goods.

In Union Square Park, couples lay in each other's arms, talking softly. I would lay with the flock around our Shepherd.

Well, I don't know the answer to this perplexity. Am only raising the questions. Time will reveal God's intent, for those who earnestly seek!

If God's coming to set up a new dispensation on earth it stands to reason S/He is not going to do it thru a conventional church, a church which does its business as usual—in fact perhaps not thru any actual church structure at all. That's part of the problem—business as usual churches. Mother Teresa was a saint, and inspired the continuation of a traditional order in a traditional church. Mother Teresa's order is a miraculous development, and she and her Sisters inspire faith anew in great waves over the earth. Her order is not a breakthrough in its fundamental ideas. *(Women's liberation, women as priests, acceptance of glbt people, interfaith worship of many different kinds of beliefs together, as sisters and brothers under the Creator are some examples of new ideas.)

Our Holy Order Of Mary, the DOC, will not be a business as usual organization! Nor will it be connected to any great extant church!

Care for the elderly in the Order: the elderly must by no means be tossed out of the Order upon their incapacitation due to infirmity of old age. If an individual cannot be cared for under the roof of the Order, they must be visited all visiting hours available in the facility in which they are housed. (IE, if a hospital/nursing home's visiting hours are 9am to 9pm daily & nightly, there must be a member of the Order right by their bedside during all this time! --We're family!)

As the Order grows into many separated Houses, all united in regular gatherings, large duties like the one aforementioned may be shared among many different Houses.

33.
Most people if they saw the devil standing there they'd run in the opposite direction. But that's not how he comes to you. To send beautiful people, is often his style. People who seem to promise much. Offering sex. Love. Fun. Joy. Friendship, popularity in a social group. See the hand of Satan and have nothing to do with it. Recognize him. We see just the surface gifts, which are tempting, but that is an illusion. *My Will is that you be gentle as doves and wise as serpents.* Says our Savior.

Remember Dear Children, don't be fooled, Satan is powerful and he is cunning, because the stakes are high. He has a whole army which can be amassed anywhere at any time. He has the best women, the best men. They come to you offering much. For example, your interest is sparked by the announcement of a beautiful choir to be singing somewhere. Don't forget, the best singers of gospel songs can be his. You prefer the church with beautiful singing, but this one just happens to be corrupt thru and thru, where as the church of tiny voices, which are not so talented, is more innocent. You wish to hear the beautiful music of God, but it is in a Satan-run church, which took it over long ago! Many innocents are trapped inside this church, in its pews, in its choir, even the lead singers—still not realizing where they are! This is why God Almighty has given us the Holy Sprit, who gives us the power of discernment. She gives us inner sight of people as they really are, as God knows they are, so pay heed!

Further I must repeat as said elsewhere, that I don't like talking about evil, nor these negative things and tricks of the underworld, but when the Spirit puts it on my heart to reveal them to you thru these writings, I obey. It is an unpleasant task, a bad subject.

Prayer is vital in fighting negative forces. Prayer in concert with others can encourage those who don't pray much on their own. Somehow we seem stronger together, our prayers summoning up the Holy Ghost who smokes like silent fire! We must pray always for the good, Dear Children! We must pray often, from within a forgiving spirit, and bowing low to the Great Being Who has made us all!

34.
Who ever will set up a new religious Order will be an engineer of big things.

One might say, well there's already too many religious sects! There probably are. But the seeker needs something more! If one finds there is no extant body of worship practicing locally which is in tune with their private view of scripture and of life, but upon searching do find bits and pieces of what they need here and there, some of it said by one religious body, others performed in another holy gathering, thus validating their own mind stance, the seeker should take confidence. Being unsatisfied for so long, they may just want to go off on their own, putting all the fragments together and Vollia! A new Order begins to arise. Those likeminded individuals are drawn to it even before its inception, some gathered from the many houses of worship where the seeker has tarried and gotten to know them, while presenting her/his radical ideas after the service at Hospitality/Oneg Coffee hour, other stumbled on across life's path just in daily living, still others informed by the first brothers & sisters to be drawn close, and them all deciding to give this new Order a try. The religious institutions from which the members of the fledgling Order are drawn have failed to hold their members. They are too conservative. They are too earth-bound. They are too preoccupied with worldly things—tithes, memberships, monies, pageants, bake sales, and other miscellaneous fundraisers, --- they relish their programs, savoring them, rubbing their hands together in glee and are not fervently focused on the spiritual. They are prejudiced and back-biting as a congregation. Pounding their bibles in hate. They are exclusionary and turn cold shoulders in their onegs, speak foreign languages and exclude the stranger at their social hours. They do not practice a religion sufficiently aesthetic to woo the driven seekers. Concerning themselves with form & fashion of a church/synagogue, not delving to the heart of God's urgent message. They believe in man over woman, rich better then poor, no interracial nor interfaith mixing, and no queers! You would think they would have learned—but no---time marches on but the fools are standing still!

You See! Says the Lord. Yes I do See, and must act upon my vision.

I've been down, down in the pits. Depths of depression, the blues—so mentally sick I couldn't talk and make sense.

And am returning to you to tell you what I've seen there. A wasteland. In the extending slum rows of despair, sickness of mind & body of inhabitants barely alive. Such great desolation —all of it able to be undone by real human sharing.

People need security, peace for community to flower! They need safety in which to build & tend their gardens of abundance!

Inhabitants of this wasteland, the poor, should rejoice because they are closest to God-- why don't they recognize this? Why aren't they dancing with joy in the Palm of God's Hand? Because they aren't organized. Organized and empowered---by the vehicle of The Word, which can deliver them—but has instead snatched away all powers for itself—what vehicle is this? That great garrulous beast—Organized Religion.

For Houses to live communally would prevent homelessness. Our nation is slipping from its economic pinnacle of generations ago, and few will be ready for the consequences. Budget cuts will devastate the poor living partially on largess of a once-affluent economy. The poor and the class directly above it who in part serve the poor as health care workers, administrators, case workers, educators, technicians, will see budget cuts/lay-offs at their own organizations & increasingly the poor population who they serve will become more difficult to work with, and more criminal being driven to the absolute end of their strength. For a single individual to pay gargantuan rent is foolish. If a House full of like-minded, religious centered persons can share resources, rents, kitchen, bathroom, living areas, yards; also sharing food, transportation, they will be better off.

So by living communally we can survive & within a situation which is harmonious, orderly, with others. Keep off of the streets and not be homeless. Nor friendless.

***

Here are some interesting notes lifted from my fiction novel Daughters Of Courage. A precursor to the Order. Which at its time of creation was more political and less religious. Done with a more dike-feminist slant. You may find them interesting and instructive.

The DOC written in 1996, after escaping from a foreclosed house to a warehouse space from which we were later evicted, has as its Appendix, the following skeleton which was in due course suppose to be turned into 'The Manifesto' of the Daughters of Courage—in that novel—I quote:

ARTICLES OF THE MANIFESTO OF THE DAUGHTERS OF COURAGE:
I. Sex
II. Food/Basic Needs
III. Housing
IV. Money
V. Fun
VI. Protection/Self Defense
VII. Spirituality
VIII. The Place Of Men In DOC
IX. Health
X. Learning/Education
XI. Careers
XII. Children
XIII. Appreciation & Pride/recognition Of Dykes
XIV. Production Of Food/Protection Of Animals.
XV. Old Age Homes/Care Of Antique Dykes
XVI. Arts/Music—Inspiration Of The Soul Thru Music, Dance, Painting, Spoken Word, Film, Literature, Etc.
XVII. Women In institutions, Mental Health, Prisons, Day Care, Schools, Universities, Etc.

These are the points, which must be discussed about the Order.

I think differently now, after transition. That book was one of the last I wrote before my new dispensation as a Transsexual man. Which came about one & one-half years later. With new hormones coursing thru my body, a new bearded, stockier presentation to the public, a new lifestyle. And subsequently a new interest in the male-born race and a partial identification with it. The following lifted directly from that book I've left as it was written, with fictionalized references. There is an occasional 3rd person reference to the hero of the tale, a dyke preacher named Valiant. Here are some notes from that original. (By the way, used dyke instead of the old, original, streetlife dike, in trying to clean up the book and make it more salable to idiotic dyke feminist white middleclass publishers, an idea that failed miserably to bring results):

>Manifesto of the DAUGHTERS—A new Order of Jesus Christ.

>Article I. Sex.
>Women will e allowed to have sex in the houses. ---If it is the purpose of that house. Some houses will be for celibates and have no sex. Others will be free love among the women. No one should be left out. Sex for everybody-- even the not beautiful, the old. —It will be the duty of those women who choose to live in a sex house that they give all women in need who dwell in that house, sex. (Tho the idea was based loosely on a convent or Christian nunnery, the idea of celibacy was not a feature she chose to continue—unless the members did.)

>Those who wish celibacy, --this can be their calling. They'll set up in a separate house within the Order.

>But most houses should promote bonding, group bonding, including sex.

>Sex must be done disciplined. —Not wild orgies every day. —Nor dragging in strange women out of the night. —The sex should be among members only, or the whole thing will fall apart.

>Much of the Daughters facilities will be in design like the old nunneries of medieval times.

To set up a series of connected centers across the USA and eventually the world. —Hostels for females, which will be dyke centered & administered by dykes; housing, information centers, support centers; encamping in the doctrine of female liberation, evolved with a theology of female Christianity—a female God, a female Jesus, and an androgynous Holy Spirit; --and featuring all the female Saints. The Godmother.

The hostel would include all women, even FTM's, and transgendered—postoperative transsexuals. Maybe they would have houses of their own with them alone, or including the biological females who will accept them.

Some males will definitely be connected to the Order.

Article III. Housing. —The Model House: The house: The house should have land, at least 3 rooms, and 2 bathrooms. Women can tent out on the land. —It should have a lot of land—for this purpose & for the purpose of growing some vegetables and sheltering some animals. And most definitely for a fortress. —This housing in the city. In the country, acreage should be obtained. A woman's fortress in the country where food will be grown & livestock raised to augment our diets with some level of self-sufficiency.

The groups will be multi-racial, multi-cultural, women of all ages, women from all classes.

The houses/convents (or forts) should be set up in mixed racial neighborhoods so it will be safe for all kinds & colors of women to attend.

--Safe retreat areas. —Country property away from city violence. —Must be safe from rednecks, neo-nazis, reactionary mountain men, drug growers, and other wrong doers. A quiet place, a saving place for shell-shocked women and abandoned animals.

Article II. —Food.

To have big parties with food. From banquets of catered foods—donated by dyke businesses-- down to simple potlucks where each dyke brings a dish to share with the group.

Article V. Fun.
I'd like to see more women out in the street. —A dyke street presence... In SF... Not just a dyke march once a year—or a Take Back The Night March—or a street fair on Folsom street or Castro; but hanging out... milling about... a sea of dykes!

Article IX. Health.

Article XII. Children.
She'd forgot a most significant and worthy Article for the list. —Children. One last addition, an oversight on the part of a dyke, to whom children were but an afterthought. So she wrote it into the Manifesto while she itemized that days events.

Article XVI. Women In Institutions.
--Mental health, prison, daycare, board & care, retirement homes, halfway house facilities.

Article VIII. The Place Of Males In DOC.
Faggots, fairies, fathers, friends & other miscellaneous men. —The Men's Auxiliary. (Add Transsexuals—FTM's.)

Article XVI. Appreciation & Pride/ Recognition of Dykes.
There is a need for recognition of dykes & dyke works & dykedom. Lesbians need to be celebrated. So long hiding themselves under rocks as protection—so long shunted away by embarrassed families, and ignored in their church, schools and work places—getting no glory. LESBIAN PRIDE!

Article XV. Old Age/Homes, Care of Antique Dykes:
We will build places for old dykes to live and be treated in their dying years the way they tried to make their lives when they were autonomous. Without stupid, callous, underpaid nurse's aids storming in and forcing them to dress in lady

clothes when they've lived as butches 50 years; nor for our tranny member's, men's clothes.

Their lesbian couples will be respected and acknowledged. Dyke marriages will be honored in these institutions.

Article VII. —Spirituality.
Stupidity. —One of Satan's tools. No dykes care to investigate the true & real power of God the Mother and Her only daughter Jesus Christ. Because of being brainwashed by the patriarchy into thinking She is a male god. It is a lie.

In addition to telling people about God The Mother, and to warn them of the devils lies—which is the Kristian church & the fascist Religious Right, there should be a person in the front entrance. Her duties will be to S. To greet newcomers, direct them to the proper workshop areas, etc. She will be paid $4 per hour.

Note: Definition: S. —To S means reading thru the bible and putting a big S in front of all the he's, --turning them into She's.—In red letters, until the bible is thoroughly marked up with the truth.—And in red letters.

(Later The Revolutionary went back over the Manifesto and drew a line thru the part which stated: 'She will be paid $$' Removing it. Substituted: 'No money, but barter for goods, or room & board'.

Article VI. Protection/Self Defense:
One of the main rules of DAUGHTERS OF COURAGE is self-defense. (For women especially.)

Women must master every aspect of this—either by using their own hands and feet as weapons--or by weaponry; guns, knives, etc., --or by enforcing zealously a law keeping body; police, guards, prisons, retaining facilities for criminals, etc.

We must have a safe place, an impenetrable refuge, a haven for ourselves, our children, for the sick, feeble, and old people.

Editors note: Here is a portrait. A young slim dike, a bisexual butch trepiditiously walks thru her neighborhood in great fear of loitering gangs of male thugs. Evil corrupted men who have lost their souls to alcohol, drugs; crime, and have a rapacious nature. (See page in INFINITE LOVE.) In her small cheep lodgings she has 2 pets—which prevents her from moving out into a homeless shelter in a safer neighborhood. She is afraid coming & afraid going. She dares not be out after nightfall, in which vicious mayhem happens without witnesses. And the few witnesses too terrified of repercussion of the gangs, to speak. Her gender is suspicious to the ignorant lowlife gang members. She would be taken in by DOC, into the Order if she chose and could meet their requirements, and if she couldn't or didn't want to take on the yoke of a religious order, she would be housed by the Order in one of its safe units, under its jurisdiction.

>Article IV. Money:
>This money system is dead. It's a dry branch. It's withered, and it's going to burn up—on a hellish bonfire.

>Article XIV. Production Of Food/Protection Of Animals:
>A commune, or shared farm shall be set up outside of town/city, on a wide acreage. Here shall be cared for abandon animals (pet cats, dogs, birds & others). And we will grow our own vegetables, and raise our own livestock in a humane fashion, which will be allowed to live to a mature age & slaughtered for food.

>Houses of the Order, and safe units under jurisdiction of DOC will be a peaceful retreat for shell-shocked sickened city dykes and their animal pals.

>The goal shall be to purchase this acreage, in order to be more autonomous. With no greedy landlord to answer to.---A working farm that no one of us alone would be able to own, but we can own collectively.

>Article XVI.

A small 12 key tiny toy piano can be taken to anywhere we gather. I'm going to get one next GA (welfare) check. —if the bank don't swallow it up first.

In song, musical notes—even just a few notes, will remind them of the unceasing love of God, and that paradise is not far—but a breath away—beyond this curtain of flesh and veil of tears.

--As music is strictly the language of the soul, not tarnished by human interpretation and lies. It has not pictures or words. Visual resemblances to be guessed about and fought over, or meaning. ---Just on the subconscious level. Song! Music! Notes!

These points & commentary are of interest, hope you will find them instructive, as to part of the true purpose of DOC.

35.
There's things people learn when they're poor which they can't learn when they're rich. They may intellectually grasp the idea of what it means to be homeless, but not really understand it with their whole being. Take it in deeper down into the cellular level of each muscle, fiber of what it means to have a living, animal existence. If you go walking down the street you will see it. It. *That desolation which surpasses all understanding,* wrapped up in a single soul; the terrible sight of a humanbeing, homeless, & think, 'how sad, how horrible for them.' But what a world of difference it makes if you find yourself ambling down some street and catch a glimpse of your reflection, haggard, gaunt, thru vision blurred by days of sleepless, ill-fed, with no place safe to lay down and rest; unable to walk a straight line, come to face with this terrible image in a shop window, you see 'God this is me! This is what I've become!'

General Hospital. Public bus. Minorities with children, brown skin, surrounded by much family, spouses, a pack of small children. Their pressing need crowds out smaller, older single individuals from the city's dwindling resources. The immigrants of this country increasingly hate us. And I hate them! Hate them for their religious prejudice towards me! For their language-bound clans and favoritism. Minorities will always help others who they perceive as their own… And who is the tribe of Nobody's People?

God has kept me above the public mass---just dangling my feet in it from time to time as a reminder. So I would *know*.

When young transboy was raised, a Colored child on Chicago's black South Side, he was kept apart from those razor-brawling drinking black Negroes in the slums, the ghetto's worst part. When, a bluejean scowling face dike he ventured into white skid row, drinking among alky rummy bums of Clark street, when he inhabited haunts of the beatniks, the hippies, precariously near substance abuse's downward spiral, he managed not to go down into dissolution, but fell far enough to *see*. Then he'd bob back up to the surface with his pens and papers. His canvases and brushes & paints; upon his head sat the inspiration of a dove.

We the people do need a safe place, those of us who don't fit in with the common herd. Who have no families, or too-small families. Who are artists. Who are not of a traditional mind. We need to band together like any other flock! With the Divine at our helm!

Social conditions bring the knee-jerk reaction of radicalism—either to the far left, or the far right. In respect to politics, and this current state of Am-Erica, here's an excerpt from AUTUMN CHANGES (My Semi-Unofficial Autobiography). I refer to chapter 420, page 1584:

I do not take these words lightly, that I have said, previously.
As you see by my diary I was once bourgeoisie, middle-class, proper
acting and raised to respect authority; but in the course of my living
I've seen much of so-called 'authority' is corrupt.

I've prayed about this, and thought about it. —People who read this
may not rise up and do a damn thing! And my book may just serve as
a warning for those in power—that if they don't do the right thing by
people, animals, and everyone on earth—eventually they will have to
pay, and the price will be high indeed.

Yes, maybe that's all this will lead to—being a warning written down on stolen sheets of paper, on borrowed time…

Whereas in former documents, violent overthrow of the corrupt state which has seized our Democracy by the throat was preached, INFINITE LOVE suggests a different alternative. A way to live. A simple life. A revolution by peaceful means.

Dear Children, I have just presented a strategy of survival for this terrible age to come. We will set up the Order, a religion-centered commune. As family, in God. We will live so close we can smell each other's farts.

We will be each other's clan—of many different races. We will have a people at last! We will have the tribe to whom we must be committed!

As for The Red Jordan Reading Societies referenced slightly in AC, as the old under-funded, Transman's dream for his nebulous future--- then fleshed out in the sci-fi trilogy of his Unity Of Utopia series, (EMPIRE!, Man Gone/Starvax, Acts Against The Powers Of Authority.) Whatever will become of them shall be. They are thrown onto the winds like a seed! Wherever they sprout and whatever plants shall grow from them is now out of my hands and for the future, for life to decide.

Here is another prophecy also taken from AC.

> Mine is a kingdom expanding faster then
> the speed of light. I Am in a universe
> which is being built right now out of the
> rafters of permanence.
>
> Within the Almighty are Christian, Islam,
> Judaism, Wicca, Native, and many more. You ask why all these?
> And I answer, Well, would you have it that they be left behind?
>
> And who are My Saints? My special ones? A most highly powerful human—selected and sorted out from many genetic codes, thru many generations.

You have been created 2-Spirit, so that you will know more.
The Lord(ess) came & reasoned with me in my own language. Instructions for The New Age, at the end of the old world. For its last primitive civilizations—its fierce Atom bomb warriors of armor & Viking-horned helmets, it's barbaric hoards, clashing, bloody, are quickly passing away along the ultra modern silver highway of a fantastic sci-fi futuristic progress: they are disappearing, and behold a new world is rising up.

A prophecy given to Red Jordan Arobateau;
--July 2004.

***

Who is scarier to God? The weak and vulnerable, or the rich & powerful?

Arthritis, aches, and pains not yet 64 years of age, the black clad older man tugged his cart along behind him, walking the city streets. On any given day might be in the library at free computer using its hour limit, in Chinatown purchasing cheap meat & greens. At Grace Senior program, at the animal shelter holding dogs in his arms, at his support group, which he led, recycling aluminum cans on route home. He was certainly glad he took retirement at age 57 after being unjustly fired after 6 years on a job. WOW, what amount of work he'd done in that time! Instead of waiting until age 65, by government mandate. --- Social Security having pushed up the date to 66. Would not have the stamina he had just a few years back. Yet all of society urged him to work until he'd passed the 65-year mark—for higher benefits. For a crappy $30 or $40 more per month added to his lifelong monthly social security check, but he never would have been able to finish AUTUMN CHANGES so rapidly, nor his great show biz novel STAGE DOOR. How about CHINA GIRL, his beloved transsexual woman novel set in the decrepit yellow ghetto of Chinatown? How about the painful 9-month rewriting and entering onto disc 7 of his books from 30 years past and putting them up on internet Print On Demand! Then, there was PASSAGE, 1 thru 9; now JOURNEY! All, because he did not capitulate to society.

Remember they are lying to you Dear Children! Don't fall for it!

Red wanted to learn something—he picks up the white mans book about Zen Buddhism. —First thing he reads, on the front page is how this man, just like Transman himself, went to Korporate Kapitalist Kinko's with the idea of printing out his book then distributing it here and there in petty little consignments. —Also like Red, he first sent it around to publishers—like the Transman he was rejected by most, but there the comparison stops. Unlike Red after 5 or 6 rejections a publisher accepts him. Accepted! He then 'decided to take a chance on it.' The old Transman drops his book to the floor in disdain. He'd learned a lesson more valuable then all the Zen Buddhist interpretations packed inside its covers. It is, the white man gets published, —you don't! You not a born man, you colored, you can't get no job but minimum wage! And you crazy! You crazy mo-fo!

You're always going to be angry at the white man, always—because he got there first & grabbed all the good stuff for himself. The advent of modern civilization as we know it, industry, science, medicine, arts communication are built on discoveries of foundation of ancient civilizations—non white civilizations--- now are his domain. Instead of being of a charitable nature, and ordering the distribution of gifts in an equitable fashion among all on earth, thus raising up the civilization of the planets en toto, he has taken the easy route out—creating inadvertently, thru the process of neglect over time, class divisions, slavery, wage slavery, and the disfranchisement of all colored, female, and other non acceptable human beings—alien to his fraternity of good old boys.

Transman had been thru two decades of bible studies, and now onto torah. He was after a long beginning as an atheist, at last, upon the Path, the Road. Had tried to submerge his hurts & complaints, to forgive others, so he could progress, grow past the stuck places and move on with his life; living in a humble state, up to this very year, so far, of our Lordess, 2007.

See the evidence of earth societies if you are in doubt!

All the sad animals mal-formed because of human neglect.

Behind those voices of tin, what is it? Listen!

There are the raw elements, which are uplifted, wind, fire, air.

Next are the leafy airy things, light, vegetable leaves, growing plants.

Then are the creeping creatures; snails, slugs, snakes frogs, toads, tadpoles; slimy slithering crawling; gnarled roots clutching.

Then are the rich earth rocks and minerals.

This is how planet earth evolves & devolves. You are part of this scheme of things. Listen to the earth beneath your feet! Hunger for the Voice of God. Become Spirit-centered. Do not listen to the voices of tin. Do not trust the judgment of the superficial ones. —But forgive them, they don't know what they're doing!

Remember they are lying to you Dear Children! Don't fall for it!

36.
Poor psychic Sylvia, prostituting on national TV, reduced to fortune telling. Whenever the fine arts are filtered down into the common mass their authenticity is bound to suffer. How much of her genuine gift is polluted by having to crank out prophecy after prophecy in one or two sentences in a 15-minute segment framed on commercial Television on the Montel Williams show? *(A handsome, strong & intelligent, and very decent Black Brother.) Of course most people who go to see Sylvia are concerned with issues personal to them. And forgo her greater seeing. Those snap-shot visions given to her of heaven. Related revelations, which are far the greater gift.

Yes Dear Children there is a Paradise—for I myself have seen it! Glimpses and fragments. Just as my works purport to reveal secrets to you, in these scraps of information shot out of the cannon of free thought, by free association. So the Creator is giving me glimpses of our eternal resting home. Little flashes of the sight of it. And it is beautiful! Marvelous! Beyond description! Every joy is there, and peace reigns everywhere. You will do many of the old things you once did on the mortal earth, but now, in a new way. Peace covers all and blankets all. All violence has been withdrawn. I cannot stress this enough. This is the glimpse of heaven given to me. And it is thru my own experiences with the beyond that I can validate many of the things this Psychic Sylvia is saying, for I have had the identical experience--- before I even heard of her!

Yes that psychic Sylvia does indeed know what she is talking about. For one, the part about heaven being another dimension just beyond our own realm, on a level slightly above us. When I held one of my cats, Angel in my arms 20 years ago, as he was dying, in one of my first mystic experiences I saw his spirit ascend—rising at a diagonal up towards that zone.

***

There sat earth stopped in surrender before the sun who marks her days; time evenly & eternally moving on.

A black gangly crow legs sprawling flies against the wind.

SF Castro/Market Street District. This vicinity is like a little city to itself. Every 3rd person you see rushing about is gay all the way, or some kind of queer, and you know them from somewhere past or present… How we have changed! We all look older. A few, suffering from worsening physical disabilities. No longer beautiful young things worshiping frivolity. Now we too *See*. What before we missed. Reality. The party is over. The show done and the houselights are up. We have both stepped down from our pedestals. We greet facing, age-blurry eyes staring into old eyes that twinkle looking back from a face with wrinkled skin. Maybe we were enemies back in the day. Time has washed that aside. Maybe you were the belle of the ball once, while me, the wallflower. Today you look like you could use a friend. You know what they say, yesterdays hustler, tomorrows trick. This has become their song: *'no peace I feel, only sorrow do I find.'* They are sick to their soul. They are turning green. Green. You know what that means, when something turns green? Corrosive, rotten. The solution is to give up the old ways upon which we are going and begin on a new path.

I know 5 transmale sex-hustlers. Just brushed past one moments ago, me on a mad dash to get to a free computer, him accompanying a trick, a bigger beefier bio guy. This small bearded T-guy reminds me of the other's, 4 sex workers—dick servers. They are loners. Strays, who stay well outside of the trans brotherhood. Out of guilty pleasure, false pride, or shame? They self segregate. How many dicks have they sucked? How many balls have they squeezed? How many inches of hot dick meat taken into their cunts? Transman recalls the 1,000 pussies he fucked, sucked, and rode in his long days on earth. Maybe I will write a raunchy sex scene, during which I will turn myself on to a hot golden glow by increments as the words skip out into sentences off of my flying fingers onto pages and use the final document to jerk off... A sex vignette in which a lithe transman services a hairy masculine bio male fag pumping a fat peter, and is treated to a good fuck in his pussyhole. & now, for the finale of JOURNEY Vol. 2, INFINITE LOVE. For this end I must convey to you something spectacular about DOC. I sit here before my computer with two parrots, green & white, one on each shoulder & wait for the message. I am preparing for a bird of a different sort. I wait for Creator's Holy Spirit to alight on me like a Dove! & God has said—for the information I want to, *Go inward...*

Wonderful high energy at schule tonight. Friday, opening evening of the 2-day Shabbat. We sang and music played, some from the congregation skipped around the bema in a serpentine circle, holding hands, that wove thru the pews. As two T-men struck a match to light the holy candles one read a short commentary from a Jewish poet Hannah somebody, whose name escapes me---about how a match must be lit to start the fire, and in so being lit, dies, looses itself for the sake of the flame. Then all might appreciate the fire. So must I too die? Loose myself into infinity to free up my work so that it can fly out to the world, and be heard? Sobering thoughts. The doors of the ark are open... the bread is broken... Pray Dear Children! Pray and pray often!

> *Pray that:*
> *the Eternal One might comfort you,*
> *That the Eternal One might defend you.*
> *That the Eternal One might enlighten you.*

That the Eternal One might uplift you.
That the Eternal One might give you
the desires of your heart.

37.
I think it may be extremely difficult for the religious to understand, that anybody who truly loves God and tries to have faith in God, will probably go to heaven, no matter by what Name they call upon this God. There are those have a vested interest for people to choose one side or another, but it is false. All that call upon the Most High, will see Her, eventually. And will be taken back into Her fold with extreme love—after all, She has created all of us. Some religions, --- called the higher ones—have evolved a greater understanding of Creator, Her ways and works, how She operates, what She wants from each of us, ect., but it doesn't make them better then those who worship in simple ways by a primitive faith. Even those who just look up to the sun, fall down on their knees and let their hearts melt in forgiveness; so what I am going to say now must be seen in that light. Your love of The Eternal One, searching of Her, your giving spirit to other children of Creator, and hard work to do the right thing is a righteous road so lets not quibble about religious practices, beliefs or dogmas. The world is at war because of it, and this is not what She wants! Amein.

God calls! And all must answer. All!

The Daughters of Courage must uphold the idea that those who truly Seek Gods Face, and cry out to be held in Her arms, will be eligible for membership in the Order, no matter what their religious practices—(of a good nature, but no workers of evil). --- So Christian, Jew, Muslim, those who see God in an entirely Female sense, Buddhist, Hindu, Native Practices, and other worshipers must tolerate each others ways side by side in doing Good, and performing Good Service for Humankind.

The sight of God is too great for human vision—they've been told, and me too, even before I was a believer—even wrote a book with that in it's dedication page. WESTPOINT OF THE UNIVERSE. Can't find that page now,* but its probably at the Bancroft; its handwritten by that crazy, loveable Irish woman, a socially polite drunk Leo the Lion, on pink notepaper with blue ink, rosebuds decorating the border, and used as a preface for one of the books in that huge novel. It ends, something about so great is our joy upon seeing the Face of Creator, that 'we'd surely see God, and die.' Die on the spot!

*Is It True?

Is it true, o Christ in heaven
That the highest suffer most?
That the strongest wander furthest,
And more helplessly are lost?
That the mark of rank in nature
Is capacity for pain?
And the anguish of the singer
Makes the sweetness of the strain?
Is it true o Christ in heaven,
That whichever way we go
Walls of darkness must surround
Us, things we would but
Cannot know? That the infinite
Must bound us. Like a
Temple veil unrent, whilst
The finite ever wearies,
So that none therein's content?
Is it true, o Christ in heaven
That the fullness yet to come
Is so glorious and so perfect
That to know would strike
Us dumb? That if ever for
A moment, we could peer
Beyond the sky with these
Poor dim eyes of mortals,
We would just see God
And die?

Saturday Shabbat service. Now I'm on the bema. I'm wearing the traditional black and white male prayer shawl draped over my shoulders by a transwoman friend. The ark is open. The dressed scrolls—Torah, the Jewish Holy book-- is taken down out of the ark to the alter. See instantaneously, the pageant. Moses coming down off the peek of the mountain, shrouded in clouds; am connected back

2,000 years ago to see The Word given to the Jewish people, hence to all people of the world, there at the foot of Mt. Sinai, after being written in tablets of stone by the fiery Hand of the Almighty. The magnificent scroll; it's a small piece of the Creator's flame condensed into a small rolled up parchment. It's a part of God! And I want to touch it! I do! I touched the wooden handle of the scroll, as we assembled prayed for healing.

Ve ahav ta Adoni. You shall love God.

This book is entitled JOURNEY. I'm on my way. On The Road by Jack Kerouak. La Strada. Don Quixote on his pilgrimage of Christendom.

After today's service got an idea of how terrible & huge God is after a Torah scholar's analysis of scripture: *Breishit bara Elohim et ha-shamayim v'et ha-aretz.* In the beginning God created the heavens and the earth. How the letters of this piece of scripture indicate all the 'time' or 'space', which lays *before creation itself!*

Well over this long Holy Weekend, I do experience something of a more worldly matter.

See at once how earth-changing the coming of Christ as the long-awaited, long prophesized Messiah was for the Hebrew People. The traditional Jew has many laws, which Jesus discarded with a simple statement:

> *Love God first, and Love each other as you would yourselves.*
> *–Upon this hang all the law and prophets.*

After sundown at the beginning of Shabbat, on Friday, until sundown Saturday, a traditional Jew must not ride on motorbuses nor get to synagogue by car, but must walk. They must not do work of any kind. He or she must not carry anything---including their housekeys, which thus must be worn around the neck on a string. They must not ring doorbells, or they would be breaking the law. For a latecomer to this reform synagogue I attend, the door will be locked for security purposes and entry impossible without summoning the congregation by ringing a doorbell. Often there is a traditional (Orthodox) member who arrives late who must stand outside the door waiting by chance for someone to exit or see them outside & open it. For those Orthodox Jews not wanting to break the law, there is the ataxias, allowances for those who lived within the 4-walled city of Jerusalem; they were exempt from the law. So today, modern day Orthodox Jews have created a spiritual ataxias in NYC, framed by the Hudson River and the East river, with the sides of Manhattan serving as the other 4 walls!

This new law that upstart Messiah gave was earthshaking, for it thus simplified and streamlined daily routine! On one hand if this is all that binds a people together, it is necessary. On the other, it is time consuming, time better spent on something more progressive. My bud, a doctor, says that it's perfect for people with compulsive disorders—they can spend all Shabbat worrying about if they've broken any laws!

    ***

    From the beginning
    I was with the Lord.
    I was there before She began
    to create the earth.
    At the very first
    the Lord gave life to me.
    When I was born,
    there were no oceans
    or springs of water.
    My birth was before
    mountains were formed
    or hills were put in place.
    It happened long before God
    had made the earth
    or any of its fields
    or even the dust.

    I was there when the Lord put the heavens in place
    and stretched the sky
    over the surface of the sea.
    I was with Her when She placed
    the clouds in the sky
    and created the springs

that fill the ocean.
I was there when She set
boundaries for the sea
to make it obey Her
and when She laid foundations
to support the earth.

I was right beside the Lord
helping Her plan and build.
I made Her happy each day
and I was happy at Her side.
I was pleased with Her world
and pleased with its people.

Pay attention, my children!
Follow my advice,
 And you will be happy.
Listen carefully
to my instructions,
and you will be wise.

Come to my home each day
and listen to me.
You will find happiness.
By finding me, you find life.
And the Lord will be pleased
with you.
But if you don't find me,
you hurt only yourself,
and if you hate me,
you are in love with death.

About creation of the Holy Spirit; from
Proverbs 8:22-36. Holy Bible.

***

Let speak rite-now about the nature of God. God is like your parakeet. Yes. You have a parakeet. You have a cat, a dog. They are part of your family. You have a human family as well, sisters, brothers, children, a spouse. Maybe a friend or two. God is part of your family, just like that parakeet. A vital, irreplaceable part of your family. God does not look like a cat or parakeet or dog. We are instructed that we are made in the image of God, thus God looks like us. There is only one of this God, where as there are countless dogs, cats, parakeets, and other humans—7 billion count on the last human census. However all can share in having this God, simultaneously, for God is Great. So, your family is complete with friends a spouse, children, siblings, a cat and dog—and GOD!!!!!!!

If you are sailing on the Titanic and it begins to sink, you grab your birdcage with the parakeet, your cat & dog, your spouse, your children, your sisters and brothers and your friends and head for the upper deck and get in the lifeboat---Don't forget about God! DON'T LEAVE GOD BEHIND! You will need God even more then ever if the great ship is sinking! And this messed up world may be sinking soon, just like the mighty Titanic! God luckily does not sink! God is Eternal—and this is Good. God is Good children!

38.
Go inside the dark confining places &
You will fit.
Take Jesus away with you
And begin his ministry in your home.

We have worried about such mean stuff! Some mean person who has committed atrocities. *I'll avenge this in my Own time.* Says the Spirit of God. God sets loose a slow-walking devil on his trail it may take 20 or 30 years but one day the person will hear him come tapping along with one iron hoof as a giveaway so he won't sneak up on them and catch them unawares. If you done something very wrong, an atrocity, fall down on your knees before God, plead the Blood of Christ given in sacrifice for us all, and you will be absolved of your mistakes. Then begin to make restitution to your victims. If that is impossible then begin a dedicated life of unselfish service for no or little pay in the works of God. I'd like to think I've paid for my damage. Maybe God still has to kick me around for another 10 years or so. Then employ me in the service of human kind. If so, then so be it.

God has waked me into a frenzy of God-ness. Went down the hill got onto the J Church line, rode to 16th and Dolores, Sha'ar Zahav

Temple; Friday night past and Saturday morning. Climbed up the hill to Grace 2 times this Sunday.

Like I said before: *I feel God growing up thru my heart in the insisting urgency of spring & it's terrifying. Great. So awesome. I'm afire—like a flame that shoots up thru me out of the roots of my heart thru the soles of my feet thru my body, eyes, and rushes out of the top of my head...*

39.
Saw the headline first: 27 DEAD! The one who'd caused the trouble was shot; maybe is killed. I'd stabbed a few myself.

Well this is how it all started, I was on the subway train back in Oak town, the black ghetto, and these 5 thugs were on it, and as the train got near the exit I thought, 'there's trouble coming'. I had been on it earlier and they had caused trouble, especially one, with reddish blackfolks hair. Well here it was late at night, and here they were back.

The worst one, with red-brown nappy hair and a wild loose alcoholic/drug face, crossed with hate, he saw me wrapping my hand around my leather shoulder bag, because the next stop was the highway freeway (you know how dreams are confused and conglomerated one stacked upon the other), and I think; 'these evil bastards are going to do a robbery—snatch and grab—it might be now where they'd have better odds of escaping. In an instant they'll snatch peoples stuff off their arms; watches and shoulder bags and stuff, then dash thorough the train doors the minute they open; run out of the station, and zoom away off on the freeway which intersects here.' The evil ringleader had been eyeing me; suddenly he stood up and said "IT'S ONE OF THOSE FREAKS! IT'S GOT THE BODY OF A WOMAN! SEE I TOLD YOU!" And then they were after me and after my friend, my opposite, who looked like a male-born-female, which is what she was; she, dressed up in lady clothes. They were after us, we began to fight. The whole train was in an uproar. Hell broke loose.

Then, you know how dreams are, the fight dissolved; I was with my ex-wife Jasmin, a biological female who dresses like a bellydancer which she is; and we were on the other side of town, the quiet, wee-small-hours of night. It had got so late the busses had almost stopped running, we left this store and raced across the street to try to catch the last bus. We stood on the curb on the opposite side waving our arms for the bus to stop, me frantically, yelling, her sedately waving her arms, ladylike. This dream personifying all the worries and fears of a queer who must travel great distances to socialize with their own kind, in distant gay watering holes….

You see it's always the violence. The violence of this earth. The violence that nailed Jesus to the cross. The violence, which suppressed women. The violence, which eventually arrests information, the free spread of ideas, of sciences, of the truth. It is always the violence, which is, ultimately leveled against us, to stop us too.

And us gays, it has been this thing since our very beginnings as tiny children. We were hushed. We knew not to talk about anything queer. As Coloreds, since white hooded anonymous Klu Kluk Klan riders of the 1900rds, afraid to show their faces, rode down into the black sector setting cabins of Negro families afire. The same as the gay bar raids of the 1950's when we were persecuted by howling thugs in fast cars who'd drive by our only places of assembly, the gay bars, baseball bats in their hands, to bash queers. The hatred, and then swift follow the jeers, fists, boots, blows, guns fired, death, coffins.

My Order is called Daughters of Courage. Courage. What a hard word. It means we must have it, uphold it, use it as our shield, our energy to maintain our good works, to keep standing in a hostile brutal and bloody world. An Order of People of Courage.

I always tried to be so big. —To lift myself up above others & also tell my message that I was on fire to say. But I guess when you get down to it; I always wanted the same thing as everybody else. To run like the wind with my beloved at my side. To have a home with someone. To be with them, safe and warm and have safety, food, joy, shelter, fun, laughter, friends, good times on-going. Good fun under the sun.

I don't know if these things will ever be given to me. Already I am old, much already has been taken away. Awake in the morning, half asleep over-hear myself ask God; 'do I have to keep going?'

And God answers, Y*es, you must. I Am all you need.*

Red: Even in situations, one like that? With the murderous thugs on the subway car?

God: *Yes. I Am all you need.*

Well furthermore, beside all my own struggles, there's this compassion for others. Like older gay women. The type who were the love of my life, my passion as a youth. I know many attractive older femme women, earrings, cosmetic attractive, wardrobes and nice hairdos, time & the flesh are marching against her; femme women who are loosing the fight against this world—which is wearing their hearts down, tho they manage to keep body & soul intact. So many of my sisters have a profound disgust with this world. They are only living out their days hoping to have safety warmth, a decent living quarters, and some community into old age. Having abandon the thought of a relationship, prosperity or success, or being part of a vibrant, healthy and supportive outer world.

Now these, all these women, and a few men like her, would be taken into the Order and sheltered, in exchange their helping hands much needed!

Alan Ginsberg said 'I have seen the finest minds of my generation nodding, spaced out in doorways like junky angles'. I myself have seen the finest minds of my generation unbelieving of You, Almighty Creator, spread out throughout all the cities of great influence of this world. Many of this age are being converted to You in all seriousness. The fearful ones. The desperate. But the strong-minded, the intelligent, those who think for themselves and make decisions, who create, who venture out as pioneers, the bold don't know You!

A radical love band of Costa Ricans are going around the globe stopping in at all venues of intelligent and compassionate minds carrying their global message, which is *to make everybody on earth responsible for everybody else.* Kay, the nun, and Co-host at the Faithful Fools tells me. She told them everything she knew about local radical love groups & Save-the-Earth folks, as a resource. It took her 5 hours to completely download the contents of her brain into theirs, consequently when I arrive for the monthly potluck she is mightily tired. A delicious repast of baked chicken, peas & corn, gravy & mashed potatoes & bread. I dine, while pursuing a book on Buddhism. Listening to conversation on many sides of the gathered circle. Drank their good strong coffee, which is what's keeping me going tonight as I finish up INFINITE LOVE.

'Society tells you to be a man, but you're scared. I won't kid you, you're so scared you want to shit on yourself, the army gives you a gun, —you are a killing machine. But you got a conscious. Some guys are killers. I am a man of peace.' Somebody states.

Muscles & killing. Macho posturing. This is not The Path.

Sunlit. The tired, hot sunbaked road.

I feel I'm harnessed into The Path. Locked into the universal turning wheels of The Way. For 16 years in a relationship I was practicing maintenance religion. Biding time, like most people. Worshiping regularly at church, but satisfied basically. Never searching beyond. —Before that marriage I was searching. Groping for the Path, the spiritual way. Attending 2 churches, one black, one white, and bible study and prayer groups, wearing out my bible with blue inked notes. Fasting, praying and seeking to get a hold of the Divine. Before that point of my conversion to God, I was howling, lost in spiritual darkness. Sad, hungry for a relationship, a family, and poorer then I am now.

I am still searching for something unnamable. Unspeakable. Unfathomable. Unknowable. Something Eternal—and beyond.

The Lord has given me a very precious gift. Did all I could to protect it by remaining clean and sober. To stay uplifted above the gnawing razor teeth of depression, those blues, which can make you commit suicide. I gave each last penny I worked for to stay housed. (Hence a storage for my works.)

The art of writing is a major gift on the lower rung of spiritual hierarchy. Faith, hope, & charity, (love) — all these in God --- being higher & love being the highest of all.

I always thought I was called to do great things. God give me one or 2 chores to do—gifts. My writing, my art. I've done it. Done it very well. For over 40 years. If there's anything else to do, the Spirit must lead me.

Well it's all up to You now God, if I am going to save the world, or go gently into that good night, my rage, rage, being by words only, by beauty in fine arts, paintings of many colors, blue, yellow, red, gold, magnificent purple, but by very few deeds. I will not lead the people! I will not be Kevin Buckminster of Man Gone/Starvax, on the podium, rallying the masses of citizens, running from the Unity of Utopia's secret police!

If God calls me out of dry-dock & has need of me, here I am.

Despite all my dising of unruly black people—which was once my race before evolving into the colorless spectrum of a global identity-- I have created the black hero Univak Ruth Global, in EMPIRE! Man Gone/Starvax, and Acts Against The Powers of Authority.

We sit here with our crystal ball, attempting to see the future—but if the Spirit doesn't reveal it, we will have to wait and find out the outcome of our lives in due time.

Sometime you see history unfold and you fear it's going to bring your life to an end by some eventual re-arrangement of world disarray, politics catching you up in mass confusion. The end of resources, a prejudicial fascist pogrom, a natural catastrophe of horrendous proportions, a global epidemic, economic upheaval, whatever...

Allah Most Compassionate, please do not let us destroy our beautiful earth! Mohammed—Most Compassionate, please take us in Your arms and shield us from the coming storm!

My old male cat sometimes sings in a high-pitched squeak along with his purrs. Mother cats sing and purr, a tiny high single notes to her brood of little kits slumbering peacefully in the fur of her belly, little bundles of fur with tiny furry ears, pink noses & yet unused utterly smooth pink of black pad paws. Mother cats have such love for their tiny little ones. Mother and child exchange the flow of that love, that life force. My own mother loved me so much as a tiny child—but things fell apart. Her mental illness. Those segregation days which held our race down back in the 1930's, 40's; incest on the part of her father, my grandfather—these sins which arise out of outer world, and the inner self. The pressures, which cut off the flow of that love.

So let the circle of violence be broken. —May I raise myself up out of it. May I not pass it on to others.

You see… that all the stuff of the past laments; injustices done to you, injustices we have done, stuff hard to get past, you will not have to go over it diary page by diary page repenting each last detail to God, each mistake—God is ready for you to move on! To take a giant leap forward—you see! Already you see The Road, & in your heart of hearts you sense The Path, all your fragments of Teachings connect, you see….

Open your eyes!

Red Jordan Arobateau
June 5, 2007
3:30 AM   Pacific Standard Time
San Francisco, CA
USA

DAUGHTERS OF COURAGE
A NEW ORDER OF JESUS CHRIST

Journey 3

Handbook for The Daughters Of Courage, Holy Order of Mary, a New Order of Jesus Christ. (After Rules of Saint Benedict, 300 AD, et al.)

You shall love God.

Ve' ahavta Adonai

TABLE OF CONTENTS:

1. Rules of The Order
Rules for belonging to the Order of Daughters Of Courage. Complete with additional comments by The Holy Spirit of God, both from the Bible, and those given directly to myself, the Prophet.

2. Clarification of the Points
Further explanation & discussion of points to be made & rules of Daughters Of Courage. (Hereafter in this document to be referred to as 'The Order' or DOC). & **Further Notes.**

3. JOURNEY Vol. 3.
Continuation of the theme JOURNEY, my daily diary, in which further personal insights, religious poetry & revelations from the Holy Spirit, relevant to the evolution of The Order, are given. Plus **FURTHER ADDITIONS** including pertinent excerpts from JOURNEY Vol. 1, and 2.

40.
> *A tall order Red Jordan.*
>
> ***

So far we have these rules as haphazardly first delineated in Journey Vol. 2, INFINITE LOVE:

The Daughters of Courage must uphold the idea that those who truly Seek Gods Face, and cry out to be held in Her arms, will be eligible for consideration for membership in the Order, no matter what their religious practices—of a good nature, but no workers of evil. --- So Christian, Jew, Muslim, those who see God in an entirely Female sense, Buddhist, Hindu, Native, and other worshipers must tolerate each others ways side by side in doing Good, and Good Service for Humankind, while in the Order and in her greater Community.

Obviously the majority of applicants will be unsuitable for even this, the most rudimentary of monastic life, and so will be added, when at all possible, to the Community, which will surround DOC.

> The Holy Spirit informs the birds when to migrate,
> The cats where to seclude their family's.
> The matriarchs when to sew their corn.
> The beginning & end of seasons
> before they were known.
> When to go to the hills.
> When it was safe to travel and where.
> The Holy Spirit of God knows all things
> and is here to help educate the world.
>
> Poetic utterances from the Spirit to the Prophet Red—2007. (These will not be annotated further in this document.)

I am turning to the Holy Spirit to guide this work.

There's a new dispensation in God coming along, & I'm setting up my part of it. —A work greater then Christ? That's like saying Christ was greater then God! Christ is the greater unfolding of God's Self to the people. This new dispensation is an even newer great unfolding of God's Self-in-Christ to the people. We are the servants of God-in-

Christ, Creator by many different Names; we are doing the work for God's Glory and to our great joy.

(Incidentally, at some point the Creator will; through Her/His humanbeings *create a Compassionate City of Help.* Hopefully partially thru DOC & Community.)

Further more let it be clear I'm not trying to set up a multi-faith Order. I'm setting up an Order of Jesus Christ which includes multi faiths—of believers in the Creator, a few of them or many of them Christians. –It's long overdue. After the purist tyranny during the medieval ages in which Catholic priests searched birth records of a prospective novices lineage back to the 3rd generation in order to unearth possible Jewish blood and expunged them from the church— just as Adolph Hitler by his murderous instruction to the nazis was to do 200 years later, right down to the anti-Semitism of small rural churches today. There will be Jews in DOC both converted and unconverted to Christ, as well as a multitude of other Beliefs.

Section 1.
RULES OF THE ORDER

Rule of Belief:
All members of the Order must believe in God/Goddess/ Creator/Allah/Great Spirit, in short, a Divine Creator by different Names.

Rule of Feminism:
Uphold the prominence of women in the Order.

Vow of Service:
It is mandated that the Order go out and do good works throughout all of humanity & animal & environmental kind. Service to the planet!

Vow of Poverty:
Many things will connect us. One being all delight in taking the vow of poverty.

Vow of Discipline in The Order:
All will obey the rules, instructions of the house, which are vows, rules of the Order.

Rule of Prayer:
We will take on the Islamic tradition of prayer no less then 3 times per day while assembled together, preferably 5 times per day.

Rule of Loyalty To a House of The Order:
All will remain loyal to the end in support of the House within the Order of their choosing.

> *All.* Says the Spirit of the Lord. *All, all & all. I love all of you. All is Mine. All will come to Me.*

Rule of Relationships:
As it says in the Bible, neither shall they marry or be given in marriage in heaven.

Rule of Corporal Discipline:
There will be law & order in the DOC & her Communities.

Rule of Leading a Religious Life:
We serve Creator; it is our mainstay, doctrine & practice above all others.

Rule of Animals:
Each House of the Order will have its proper share of cats & dogs, plus other small animals.

Rule of Abstinence:
No alcohol will be used for any purposes in ritual or daily living within this Order or the Community, in accordance with Islam. No smoking of any kind. No non-prescription drug use or substance abuse of any kind.

Rule of Fun:
The Order will have grand clean religious fun, outings, vacations, picnics, voyages to domestic & foreign lands.

Section 2.
CLARIFICATION OF THE POINTS

Vow of Poverty.
What does that mean? Renouncing worldly things. The Order has agreed it will renounce materialism, wealth, and gain. (The vow of poverty.)

Vow of poverty & semi poverty which will allow for instance a person to take the vow of poverty on a temporary basis without giving up home ownership nor cashing out their stock portfolios. But they must act as if they did not have any of this wealth during the duration of their vow of semi poverty, while they remain within the Order. Nor can they sneak out funds by which to live extravagantly. At the end of a measured amount of time they must decide wither or not to take the complete vow of poverty by renouncing the excess of their material wealth, or by some manner legally divorce themselves from this wealth, as it will always be a financial leverage of power over other Sisters & Brothers.

Rule of Loyalty to a House of the Order.
The Order will be composed of as many Houses as necessary to shelter the members. The Sisters & Brothers of a House must loyally defend their House from disillusionment arising from both in, and outside its walls. They will not be fickle, traveling from House to House to take up residence here & there on a whim, but after careful selection, trial, interview and due process settle upon a House and remain there for their stay in the Order.

DOC will lead church/religious services and speak to the common people who may gather in Community around the Houses of the Order in various locals. They will prey, lead rudimentary services with group singing, and give communion. (All will share in the bread & grape juice of Community Oneness—but those who can, will take it as The Eucharist). The goal of DOC is not setting up churches, and so these churches will not be elaborate, only rudimentary, sustenance level.

DOC will have female only and male Houses, and mixed Houses. Houses for those who choose celibacy, and those who don't. No sex in the Houses of abstinence! Any sexual overtures made must be reported instantaneously to the House Prioress!

The Houses of the Order will be Sisters only, Brothers only, Sisters & Brothers together. Houses in which celibacy is practiced, Houses where it is not. No non-ordained members will ever live in the Houses, but in DOC supervised Community houses. Everyone will have their own room within the House.

Rule of Relationships.
Special friends within the Order. As it says in the Bible, neither shall they marry or be given in marriage in heaven. That was Jesus' description of Paradise, and a direct order from S/He who was half God/half human. There will be special friends within DOC serving Christ together, married together in the service of Christ, but not a twosome as in a complete unit together, nor married in the worldly sense, —thus freeing them to share their individual presence with the others among the Houses of the Order.

This exclusively of a 2-person marriage/relationship shall not be found in the Order of the Daughters Of Courage, a New Order of Jesus Christ. Nor will there be found human aloneness, nor human separation. Sisters & Brothers who live in the Houses of the Order always will be together, maybe ten or twenty going out to worship somewhere en masse, or maybe just 3, off on some mission of practical necessity (grocery shopping, etc.) or of minor religious mercy (bringing clean laundry to a sick Community member). There will be no single ventures, and few coupled ventures out of the Houses.

Rule of Corporal Discipline.
There will be law & order in the DOC. There will be no drunkenness, violence, brawling, bad behavior with physical intimidation, no abusive behavior of any kind in any of the Houses of the Order, nor in it's greater Community, nor in any of the units under its supervision in the common realm. None will be allowed & acts, which break this rule, will be punished—by suspension, disbarment from the Order, and/or from the House in which they are living, or by lawful

prosecution, depending on the severity of the violation(s). There will be zero tolerance of these behaviors in any House or supervised facility of the Order of DOC.

Abstinence.
No smoking of any kind. No cigarettes, cigars, pipes, nor marijuana, except medicinal marijuana by doctor's orders, and this under permission of others in the House. No non-prescription drugs of any kind including no psychedelic drugs, LSD etc. peyote etc.
Native American worshipers must substitute some kind of non-narcotic substance instead of peyote—just as the Christian-Judaic communion, & motze in many facilities is grape juice, and no longer wine.

Rule of Leading a Religious Life.
I am reminded of Saint Dorothy Day—a common day saint who set up her socialist communities in Christian houses all across America in the starving post-depression years of the 1930's. She insisted that religious love & stewardship of God, as well as social programs must go hand in hand. Programs which included unionizing, feeding the poor, day care for children of working mothers, printing & distribution of their radical newspaper the Daily Worker etc. Periodically she'd go storming around the nation disbarring houses that had fallen into spiritual neglect! Must be remembered that my Order of Mary, A New Order of Jesus Christ must be just that—religious, God-based. (God by many Names.) I will not veer from this point. Some secular homes will be set up as a work of the communes of the actual Order, this is a supervised facility—for instance take over an SRO building, purchase, remodel, and rent the units out at low low cost, (a nominal amount $100 to $400 per month) to homeless whose lifestyles are stabilized. These would live there in an individual fashion not being part of the Order. But would come under its jurisdiction. (Oust unruly inhabitants; those relapsed back into substance abuse or uncontrollable mental illness, because of refusal to take prescribed pills.)

All works of charity (love) & service must be in accordance and obedience with the words, scriptures, & laws of God as spoken in the Ten Commandments of God as given to the Hebrews at Mount Sinai.

Service—Works.
There are so many works it's limitless. As an example, there are so many poverty level old people suffering with limited range of motion & energy who can't afford to pay someone to help them in their twilight years. The DOC would also be ready & mobilized to do good protest. For instance march to end the rape of women in Darfur, or the escalation of US militarism in the middle-east. Mobilized at a moments notice.

Prayer.
We will gather together daily at minimum per day 3 times for prayer, worship, and community. All liturgy, all styles, Christian, Judaism, Islamic. And we will meditate. The meditation is regularly every day using Buddhist techniques.

There is no time or space with God. We (as an Order) will pray for people across the world both now, those who have lived long ago, and those to come, who we don't know their names or nations, only hear in spirit their lone voice whispering 'Help Me'.

Rule of Animals.
Each house of the Order will have its proper share of cats & dogs, plus other small animals, and no one with compromising allergies to animals shall join this Order! Great animals, such as unwanted circus elephants, injured livestock, experimental monkeys, etc., may be housed in one of our Houses & lands as a refuge for them in rural areas where local zoning codes allow.

Further Notes:

DOC may prove to be a minor work. God may be beginning to do something else & needs DOC as a stepping-stone to get there to that place. A brief transitional point. This tiny Order may thus disappear, engulfed by the evolution of time—a necessary point used & long abandon and all but forgotten.

DOC may live out its life confined to these pages alone.

Be ready for something completely different. Be ready for something new. Based on ways to live.

> The Prophet (Red): You said You're setting up a New Order God, why?
>
> Creator: Because I want it.
>
> Prophet: Why?
>
> Creator: Because I'm coming back.
>
> God to the Prophet (for herefrouth in this document the Prophet referred to is Red Jordan Arobateau (born 1943 in America)) unless otherwise specified by name i.e. the Prophet Isaiah, the Prophet Elijah, etc.
>
> I want God! I must have God! I must have God right now!

Amazingly results come thru the forces of prayer and supplication.

Prayer, intercessory prayer, is vital to this Order! We pray for our loved ones, for humanity stumbling and earth-bound. We pray for the whole earth.

Prayer is mandatory & Orders of Prayer are needed because the world has gone astray—severely astray. Intercessory prayer breaks thru time & space to beseech the Ear of Creator to counter-act severe events, which have gone before, or lay ahead. The chasm of time as we know it will have no dominion. Nothing of the finite world is final, only God is final.

Ever since the ancient Hebrew tribes of Abraham, Moses & Isaac our human world has grown exponentially. And is a billion times larger since the ancient times, having far more complexities, and with many diverse races, nationalities & beliefs, including non-beliefs.

The Word of God (God, Creator, Allah, Buddha, Eloheim, God by many Names, Mother Earth, Great Spirit)--- the Word of God will go out everywhere, to everyone, in every condition, even to the homeless lying on the cold cement of the highways of earths huge metropolises, one ragged paper of Scripture in their hand cocooned in a filthy blanket reading it by street lamp, or starlight, or moonlight.

The Spirit. As clarification. Often it is spoken of 'having the spirit'. There are spirits, and there is the Holy Spirit in Her/It's many manifestations. 'Getting the spirit sometimes can be to have high energy, often in conjunction with the carnal. It is in the spirit of high energy & carnality that this earths societies move, that children are conceived, that is the pageant of history upon which life keeps drumming, moving itself foreword thru eons of broken time. The Spirit sent from God, is something different and more--the Holy Spirit (see Infinite Love chapter 37. Page 86, or Proverbs 8:22-36. Holy Bible).) It is a Holy Emanation from God. It's discipline & focus, full of Holiness and cleanliness from which It never departs. An example at a Holiness Church I once attended, guitar, organ, drums, and a soloist were performing holy songs. The drumbeat against the wailing of the congregation in prayer, played impromptu until the Spirit departed. The service soon ended with closing announcements by the pastor. The moment this imposing 6' tall lady minister turned, satin cleric robe floating in her wake, and walked into the back where a meeting was to take place, the musicians decided to hold a short 'jam session' in which the identical instruments were employed. Soon the notes descended into a more carnal pitch, ensued something sleazy and carnal. It is amazing how fast the band degenerated into the common world—with all its pitfalls.

DOC will be a disciplined Order, which will not, itself cause others to fall, nor itself fall nor descend into a decadence, an unholiness, a carnality.

Any one caught partaking of this will be disciplined (including the Founder ((myself, who also has this weakness)). If they are found to have led the Order onto jagged rocks of debauchery, the Order to fall, either in fact or by instigation, the perpetrator(s) will be harshly dealt with.

For obvious reasons no person under 18 years of age will be (a legal minor) will be admitted into the Order.

We will have Islam, Native, Judaism, Wicians, Buddhists, Hindu, former agnostics with no prior religion. It is not necessary to make Jesus Christ your own personal Savior to join the Order, nor to remain in it over a lifetime. All that is necessary is a desire to love & serve God and to seek God & serve Her/Him, which is obvious; the Order being the Holy Order of Mary. Mary was a Jew. Mary, mother of Jesus is a Saint with high honor in heaven, some Marists say reigning along beside the Trinity, (which is God, God's Holy Spirit & Jesus Christ.) Those in the Order will be accepting of the invocations of these deities Mary & Jesus Christ, but do not have to believe in them. Just as, likewise, those Christians must be accepting of the worship practices of other faiths. The name of this Order shall not be changed to any other words to accommodate any other people or concepts. It shall remain an Order of **Mary** a New Order of **Jesus Christ**. God is the Unnamable, Unnamed & to join this Order members must serve this God or concept of God, Creator, Buddha, Allah, Great Spirit, The Almighty, The One. Etc.

Let me repeat: I realize my Order's parameters are to be multi-faith, but for no reason nor at any time should its name 'A New Order of Jesus Christ' be changed or altered. As this is how it was given to me. Also it is a male & female & other Order, tho it is to celebrate the feminine called 'Daughters' of Courage. Something, which is long overdue.

This new Order is a multi-faith organization for all those who call on God/Goddess by many Names. The objective of DOC will not be to convert each other to each other's own religion, but the objective will be to work side by side in the Service & Love of God and in so doing share in each other's tradition. Such as, all may take place in baptism as a holy rite, or simply as a rite of purification. This will be elective. We will meditate in the Buddhist practice.

One should not be above the others in this Order; otherwise we'd be going wrong. But each House must have a head. And all members of a House will take orders from the Prior(ess). What is a Prioress? Who shall be the head of the House? —Each House must have a head in charge. A senior member-in-duration of the Order, irregardless of their chronological age. Experience in some other order will be a part of the determination of actual seniority. How much they know about the running of a cloistered order, and their dedication to Creator.

DOC should be strict enough to lock undesirables out.

    ***

> 5 monastic vows of the Buddhists at Gampe Abbey:
> Abstaining from destruction of life.
> Abstaining from taking what is not given
> Abstaining from lying.
> *Abstaining from sexual activity (celibacy).*
> Abstaining from alcohol or drugs.

Our Order is in agreement of 4 of these 5 vows. But we can do only 4 of them--- we do not include the vow of celibacy. (Although some may chose to do so.)

The Templers were an order set up by the Catholic church during medieval times; 1200, 1300 ACE. They were priests who guarded the roads on which pilgrims traveled to get to Holy Shrines, to protect them from danger; they had a nuns subsidiary order as well. Here are some rules of the Templers:

> 1st, to put aside & leave behind the sins of the world.
> 2nd, to do the work of our Lord.
> 3rd to be poor and do penance in this world, that is for the salvation of the soul.

It can be observed that the rules vary, but not greatly, from order to order.

Allowances; regarding the famous vow of celibacy, those who take an additional vow of celibacy within the Order of DOC, may do so, and may live with others who also take on this vow in a House set aside for them, although it not mandatory for the Order. God told me thru the Spirit, regarding the vow of celibacy to do and set up only what I am able to do myself.

After pursuing the web page of the Benedictine Sisters of Yonkers SD, stumbled across by chance when I was finally able to access some free computer time in a library/gay center around this money-gouging city did I finally realize one must also take the vow of obedience as well. They say, Obedience--- a promise:

> "to listen attentively & respond eagerly to the Will of God as reveled in Spirit, the rule of Benedict, the priories, the community & the events of human history, the call of the church, the cry of the oppressed, and in herself."

Further these sisters ask "Is the religious life a good fit for you?" (Meaning the monastic life) they compare it to a pair of shoes, too large, or too small you will not be happy with either. It must be a perfect fit.

The Benedictian Order vows—obedience, stability, fidelity to the monastic way of life.

From Benedict:
> "Let them prefer nothing whatever to Christ. And may he bring us all together to everlasting life."
>
> Rule of Benedict; chapter 72.

Benedictine rules are the most stringent of most any order, and have been the guidepost of all Christian orders of the monastic life for nearly 2,000 years.

So how would this encompass members of the Order who are religious, devoted to God, but not Christian? First and foremost, they must be devoted to God. This, and this alone will bind us together!

All will take 2 vows. The vow of special service to the poor & unchampioned, in both the human & animal world. Secondly, 'They will delight in the vow of poverty'.

Getting additional information from the vows to service in Mother Teresa's Sisters of Charity let me clarify; the Sisters & Brothers of

DOC will take temporary but renewable vows. But some members of the Order will remain in it; will take on a lifetime commitment to God.

Section 3.
CONTINUATION OF THE EVOLUTION OF THE DAILY DIARY THEME OF JOURNEY

41.
Sunday/Grace Cathedral. The lovely music organ choir is like the opening of a Hollywood movie picture with the latest innovation in vision and most enhanced sound. It's amazing year after year parishioners go to church to hear the dramatic reading. To see at the alter the same pageant unfold week after week, month upon month throughout a entire liturgical seasons revolution from the birth of Jesus to the Crucifixion, resurrection and all the great pageant over their personal human lifespan of 30, 40, 60, years and more, without change the same story, text, and drama, from cradle to grave, and always are fascinated by it.

Sha'ar zahav, Saturday Shabbat, only 6 of us, not a minion—the congregation is off on retreat, also Hebrew school has let out for the summer. This large sanctuary, all its pews empty, one lone presenter stands at the bema perusing Torah, unrolled to a passage, underlined by the silver pointer, a comparative text nearby. I am glad to lend my presence in this small service—like so many small churches before when I added my name to the attendance roles to keep up their necessary charter to remain in their diocese. To uphold their churches, tho I could not put any $ money in the collection plate, as I have none.

Regarding organized religion, if all Jews were to be converted right now would they be converted to Jesus, or to the equal wretchedness of the shallow religion of Christ's corrupted church? ---Prophet Red in personal meditation.

Commentary: "on the state of fanatic Islamic religions on one hand, and the fundamentalists on the other hand with their brain-dead Christians on the other." --Dean Jones @ Grace.

Like a mother cat The Holy Spirit has seized me, taken me and shook me like pray, subdued me, to drag home for her kits. I have been broiled, baked, beaten, stripped and tenderized like a roast for dinner.

My soul then leapt up this much higher. At church had renounced my sins, and was shown that I had formerly stood upon platform shoes of thick, blackened, callous sin upon which I walked, lumbering, uneven and heavy. Stripped of sin I was now barefoot before God (in Spirit). Sitting in flesh in one of the back pews directly on the center aisle of Grace. Not knowing why, I extend first my left foot, then withdrew it, and put out my right. Suddenly there upon my feet was a pair of sandals, sandals! Colored red! Immediately I thought, 'They are small and effeminate, not sturdy strong and able to do battle! Sandals are girlish!' Then I was shown these sandals were neither male nor female in design, but for a child.

"These are a child sandals!" I exclaim.

Is it not said we can only enter paradise of God as a child?

Sandals.

You'll need them. Says God.

Later went to the rest area down bottom of the church, as I raced back up the stairs from the crypt I thought God; I can really make time in these new shoes!

    ***

    Hungry? Come to Me & you will be filled.

Come to God.

I'm hungrier then ever! Said this after coming to God. Hungry for more of God! Hungry for Life in God!

The hunger of a seeker, thirsty and ravenous to know, eat, partake and feel more!

Today there is a solar aurora sitting right over Grace cathedral. Directly above, millions of miles in distance. It is caused by ice crystals in the atmosphere, am told. This kind of atmospheric/cosmic event seldom occurs, can't remember ever seeing one of this magnitude--- a ring around the sun with different shades of light. Far reaching, miles in diameter. I've seen lunar auroras—rings around the moon, remember that ten years ago when we lived in that SRO in downtown Oaktown walking our Great Dane/Shepherd Husky at midnight.

One of Gods solar auroras. Is it a sign from God about my book, which deals with this new Order of Christ?

Is it a sign to Grace and all believers that She hears our voices? And sees our predicaments?

Is it a sign to Grace that we are protected & forgiven by Creators Grace alone?

This solar aurora covered Grace cathedral directly, sending a message from God to Her people. Maybe it covers the entire city of SF--- can it be seen by the whole northern portion of California? I don't know. It is one of God's solar halos. One day it will cover the whole earth.

Back at home, cat in my arms. Mr. Fluffy is a king among cats!

I still have not abandon my plans to re-assume being a fine arts oil painter, maybe I will paint pictures fit for the church:

> Paintings provide very powerful persuasion, greater then that which is taken from writing, as long as they accord with tradition and historical accounts. Because painting stirs and elevates the spirit

more than writing. The reason, as Saint Augustine explained, is that, what we know from writing, we know, as though by hearsay, and this is worth less than painting, which puts it before our eyes.

Las pinturas son un muy fuerte argumentacion y mayor, que el que se oma de la escritura, si van conformes con la tradicion, y con las historias. Porque la pintura mueva y levanta mas el spiritu que la escritura. La razon es, porque como dize san Agustn... Lo que sabemos por la escritura lo sabemos, como de oydas, y esto merece menos, que la pintura, que le pne delante de los ojos.

Salazar de Mendoza, circa 1608 from El Greco & His Patrons by Richard G. Mann.

More Notes:

Regarding an individual who is connected to DOC, who is not in the Order, they may be in the Community. --In clerical terms I guess this is called the laity.

Practically anybody may join the Community of DOC—but many will not be able to join the Order.

Instructions & prohibitions concerning a life of the Community, which surrounds the Order, will occur later in this handbook or in the subsequent midrash, to follow in JOURNEY Vol. 3.

Monastic live out their lives in one monastery. Apostiltics move from community to community doing various works as they are called by God to do. DOC will be both monastic and apostolic.

We will serve God. This must be. And do the things of God. To this we must be dedicated—to actively participate in the stringentness of this Order.

> Every night we laid down with the Shepherd.
> He guarded our flock.

He went with us down the chute.
He was with us
Even at the hour of our death.

We will be His flock in heaven
As white as blossoms of the meadow.
Far as the eye can see.
Living in eternal peace.

Another Sunday service lets out, around 12:20. At this time of day at this point in the sky, the sun stands directly above Grace cathedral. Small children run/dance over the labyrinth. As busily upon a wooden bench, a black clad male figure, older, scribbles on a sheaf of papers. Transman Red is setting up a new Christian & Multifaith Order.

In the angst over this work I am being tortured in the day & tortured into the night by none other then God Almighty. Yet it is unthinkable that I not be tortured—meaning that I not be given the work! Unthinkable!

Regarding religious matters as those reading from the quantum's of info/knowledge they posses which they arrived at thru their studies of text & great profundities, whereas I arrived at it –the knowledge-- thru the Holy Spirit & by continuing to go to church/synagogue services and related Bible & Torah studies over decades; their way was impossible for me. Maybe my way was closed to them.

I'm sure if I could go to debate with this DOC, get up here or there on a podium & after all evidence they bring in, references & counter references, Bible translations, midrash, foot notes & added learning's out of dusty crypts right up to the most modern internet info, all I'd have to fall back on was my faith.

Oh, the Spirit has revealed someone to me here at a Grace, although pleasing to the eye, this person is ugly spiritual sight. Even frightening! A frightening spiritual sight to rival drawings of an archangel of Satan in ascent to power & evil wither they themselves realize this now, or not, I do not yet know. It is probably a primal urgency in them hoping to acquire power. And it is on this note I must chastise myself, and pray God keep me from this horrible pitfall that so many have plunged into before!

More notes on power: Sha'ar zahav, Saturday after Shabbat service, a small workshop. From what I've heard some Jewish women say this afternoon, motherhood and support of family; raising family, keeping family was attributed such a high honor in Hebrew tradition of ancient times, that women were considered exempt from the rituals men had to undergo at Temple--- rituals no doubt to keep them occupied and focused on the straight and narrow way instead of falling into troubles. Of course over generations so much glory was attributed to these males as special spiritually learned people who performed & practiced sacred rituals, it just served to institutionalize sexism of a higher degree of men ruling women then is found in many of the ancient native tribes where there was more equality. In secret some girls and women long to wear the vestments of men, and to do the male rituals—they too want glory, they too want involvement other then mundane domestic tasks, they too want power. DOC like many other evolved religious groups of modern times will empower females just as males have been, and continue to empower deserving males both, also all the sexes, neither male or female, sexes in the service of our Creator and for our Creators Glory.

Maybe God is some Entity that holds all visions in truth; knows & builds with each iota of material available. As human beings we have such a small dedication, so circumscribed by animal ways, acts and pains and needs, but it is to this, our greatest extent, God must work & Things of God be accomplished.

42.
Late night all nature's freaks venture out to do their necessary shopping. Here's a man 8 feet tall, a giant. He suffers from gigantism. Transman shoulders come up to his hips, he is not a normal man, but stooped, and crooked. Sad. Maybe bowed to the gods of beauty to which he is inferior, and the ostracism of the world. He is denied the day's sunshine of disclosure unlike the beautiful people who can be seen in their glamour showing & posing. Is it a god, this worship of the beautiful? What's more, is it real?

Speaking of worship of beauty this reminds me of my gay brothers at one of their most painful failings. Plus I see now all the drag queens and kings of my party youth are all about self & selfishness.

We acknowledge that some forms of homosexuality are a sin—just as are some forms of heterosexuality. ---But that homosexuality is not a sin in itself. We acknowledge that sin is when some behavior causes us not to be Christ's sisters and brothers, incapable of being loving to each other. That is even less beautiful!

If you are ashamed of queerness, of transsexuality or homosexuality in others or ashamed of it in yourself, you don't need to join DOC!

Monday. Another voyage across the bridge, silver span arching blue/white waters. INFINITE LOVE is now ensconced at the Bancroft: "along with St. Ignatius, the Franciscans, a shit load of Franciscans." ---According to archivist Tony Bliss.

Another weekend arrives. Seated in the front pew for the best view of the bema so as not to miss a word and instead was transported on the interior, and saw in Spirit a blue pool of a dark blue cylinder before me, a living well of dark blue--- gift from Creator it was given to me/us. We will drink from this well, Children!

The dresh was a knockout at Sha'ar zahav synagogue Friday Shabbat. The scholar came out of Torah (also Numbers 16, in the Bible.) It tells the story of Korish—how he came to Moses wanting to know why he was putting himself up as the leader of the Hebrew people, accusing him of enriching himself as leader of the 12 tribes. Korash claimed Moses was stealing the tribe's goods and property for himself. Moses said, "I have not even taken 1 donkey from the people." Well the earth swallowed his accusers up! Thus proof from God directly who was right and who was wrong! Praise be to God! Seems that somehow Korish and his cohorts get swallowed alive by the earth opening up---leaving only their incense burners, which the Creator then instructed the Hebrew people to beat this valuable copper into sheets to plate Her/His alter—thus eliminating any suggestion that it would somehow wind up in Moses personal hands. My bud C. had just finished testifying two days ago, about his

Vipashna Buddhist retreat, and how he had many thoughts while in meditation 4 hours per day. And we spoke about a local church minister we both knew—how he was so moved by her great work with the AIDS community and how uplifted he was by her—until he saw her step into a gold Lexus—(a very expensive motor vehicle) which crushed his elevation of her. What a dresh this was Friday! And right to the point! Just when I'm on fire to do the DOC, and realizing that it might bring me $ money--not just donations, but enhancing sales my of books---and here, me having taken the vow of semi poverty/poverty! This stuff is important! The Spirit of the Most High informed me years ago when I first converted that: *to charge for the gifts of God—prophecies, healing etc, is to cheapen the work.* I needed to hear that dresh! We must pay head to the Words of Spirit whenever they come!

Let me get on further about this other of my weaknesses. The Founder (myself) cannot receive any monies nor divert any monies away from the Order for his own personal use, nor so the Prioress/Prior of any of the Houses, other then that which is necessary for the survival, upkeep & security of those Houses, as appropriate given our vow of poverty. Monies, donations etc. will be held and accounted for by a responsible, impartial separate body. If such a time as the Order is dissolved by the Founder since ours is an Order, in part, of Service any funds held in this account, sales of properties acquired by the Order, will be disbursed to various charitable groups within the community of the religious world.

Courage Daughters and Sons! I know it seems hopeless in the face of such overwhelming misogamy and world brutality but we must practice acts of kindness & mercy where we can.

Ever since the beginning of civilization there are cultures who are enriched by exploitation of other peoples, creating underclass slaves, subjugating conquered people, women, criminals, those dreamed by some means to be inferior—perhaps having the 'inferior' label put on them merely so that the stronger ones can steal their labor, appropriate their lands, rob them of their resources, justifying their deeds as 'noble ones, 'over an inferior race.'

It is against all this bulwark of blackened sin we struggle; it is all this corruption of the truth which must be undone!

Further treacheries lay on the internal plane. The devil can give you the world—but there's one step more, after you got the world in your hands, then comes his payment due. I made my pact with God; never let me to fall into this trap! And hope you will pray for me to this end also. I give my life to God of my free will, this is my decision, for Her/Him to keep me from this fate of falling into such major sin! If I ever fall that far, then God must take it all away from me.

In the beginning God created among the list of things---the tree of the fruit of the knowledge of good & evil. —That means that evil is far more powerful then any human being. It is so poisonous that we must not eat of it—at all. Not a bite. If we are touched by evil we must go to the antidote immediately—this is God. Some of us are so hurt we go to evil as a resort. When we are small, very young we go over. Like when as a child I decided to stab my mother with a knife in her heart---even at that young age 7 or younger? I knew it was wrong, rudimentary. To stab ones own mother! But the image of the knife tempted me—what a sweet release. A forbidden pleasure, very satisfying perversion, even to a child, what a sweet release, to avenge ourselves, to avenge our shame. This road when traveled on leads to a life of pain, even more pain then the pain already put on us by others—others who themselves have also embraced evil no matter the reasons for it.

Within days this document will be done. Then it must be sent out of my studio; set out onto the high seas of the public world. I am certainly unsure of just how to go about that!

> "The safest place for a ship is in the harbor, but that's not why ships were built."
>
> --Canon Pastor Rev. Mary Haddad @ Grace, speaking about change; Sunday service.

Furthermore during this service Jesus showed me I shouldn't charge $ money for the handbook—the print on demand company will charge its fee plus printing coast and postal shipping. I will tack on no royalties at all.

FURTHER ADDITIONS: Excerpts from JOURNEY Volume 2, INFINITE LOVE written this year (2007) plus some original text from the novel DAUGHTERS OF COURAGE copyright 1996. And excerpts from JOURNEY Volume 1, which was first published as a subtext to the Science Fiction novels EMPIRE!, Man Gone/Starvax, and Acts Against The Powers of Authority, in my Unity Of Utopia trilogy.

From JOURNAL Vol. 2.

--I will start a work; it will involve the healing of the broken, and housing of the homeless, and other acts, which involve the rising up in stature of a (female's in particular) mind, body, & soul.

--My idea of a religious order would help house the poor, feed the hungry, provide a religious center & discipline for the believers (Christian along with multi faith) which include living together in commune.

--An Order in which we will serve God daily thru prayer, thru deed, and have better lives for ourselves.

--*I'm setting up a new Order—and a new way.* Says Jesus. *You will be married to each other.*

--Rule of the DAUGHTERS OF COURAGE. Uphold the prominence of women in the Order.

--It will be a frugal Order. Account for every penny. Practice good stewardship for God, in careful budget with no extravagance. Pick pennies up off the street. Waste no one, including people.

--Those who truly worship and seek God and are of a spiritual mind, who upholding the goal of good and to carry the Light for humankind will be admitted, not only those who practice Christianity.

--Each house of the Order will have its proper share of cats & dogs, plus other small animals, and no one with compromising allergies to animals shall join this order! Living spaces can accommodate the allergy-prone by removal of all rugs and upholstered furniture (which hold dust, pollutants) and thorough sweeping and wet mopping of floors regularly.

--This Order shall be dedicated for the glory of God & the good of humanity.

---Members of the Order will pray together, and pray often and at regular times! They will frequently be in intercessory prayer for the planet.

--Oh, all who join the Order of the DOC must take this vow:
> Q. Do you renounce Satan and all the spiritual forces of wickedness that rebel against God?
>
> A. I renounce them.

--Those who join the Order will receive basic training in the spiritual, just like a soldier learns maneuvers at boot camp. *Joining a religious order can discipline the immature soul as to those things worthy of life.*

--Our Holy Order Of Mary, the DOC, will not be a business as usual organization! Nor will it be connected to any great extant church!

Notes from DAUGHTERS OF COURAGE the novel.

--Article I. Sex.
Women will be allowed to have sex in the houses. ---If it is the purpose of that house. Some houses will be for celibates and have no sex. Others will be free love among the women. No one should be left out. Sex for everybody-- even the not beautiful, the old. —It will be the duty of those women who choose to live in a sex house that they give all women in need who dwell in that house, sex. (Tho the idea was based loosely on a convent or Christian nunnery, the idea of celibacy was not a feature she chose to continue—unless the members did.)

> Those who wish celibacy, --this can be their calling.
> They'll set up in a separate house within the Order.

But most houses should promote bonding, group bonding, including sex.

        Sex must be done disciplined. —Not wild orgies every day. —Nor dragging in strange women out of the night.

---The Daughters of Courage must uphold the idea that those who truly Seek Gods Face, and cry out to be held in Her arms, will be eligible for membership in the Order, no matter what their religious practices—(of a good nature, but no workers of evil). --- So Christian, Jew, Muslim, those who see God in an entirely Female sense, Buddhist, Hindu, Native Practices, and other worshipers must tolerate each others ways side by side in doing Good, and performing Good Service for Humankind.

--My Order is called Daughters of Courage. Courage. What a hard word. It means we must have it, uphold it, use it as our shield, our energy to maintain our good works, to keep standing in a hostile brutal and bloody world. An Order of People of Courage.

Notes from JOURNAL Volume 1 written as subtext to the Science Fiction trilogy Unity of Utopia; EMPIRE!

--The poor artist must live the monastic life of a saint in self-deprivation. Accept physical hunger deriving from a hunger to know the Divine.

--You must hold to the Way. Yes, isn't The Path putting aside of self? So that one might see more clearly? This self & all its desires needs & fears.

--But make no mistake you believers! God has extended Gods-self into every single nation, every people, in every single time and place and by many different Names!

---Now, for my last exhortation, closing this first volume of JOURNEY, (the Daily Diary); about theology. To remind you that regarding our Holy Bible-- just what it says, it means. – "In My house there are many mansions." All kinds of diverse persons and groups and beliefs are in the huge, universal mansion of Creator! Thus you all are going to be up there dancing in joy!

Notes from JOURNAL Volume 1; Man Gone/Starvax:

--Dear Children; don't be misled—it is only by struggle that a heaven on earth will be achieved. Natural progress of history will not attain these sympathetic goals—nor will its brilliant minds, its brightest analysts and best political theorists—nor will its military arms of great might. There is no Utopia, which comes about thru any of these means, sadly. Not thru its Karl Marx's, not thru its Thomas Jefferson's, not thru its Einstein's. It is thru our daily struggle in a Christ* like mind.
*Fill in your deity, Great Mother, Mohammad, et al.

--Are we working for change—complete change? Or are we just shucking & jiving; going thru the motions of revolutionaries?

--An act we must begin is to found Communities of Spirit. I'm certainly not the first to talk about it!

--3 points would be observed. Spiritual Center. Poverty. Activism.

--A religion-centered home, in which all participants actively prey, worship study the Bible, Koran, Torah, Women's Mysteries, Native Ceremonies, etc; hold regular services, including daily prayer/worship times.

--A base by which the members can do charitable, or activist work.

--In these houses stray dogs and cats saved from being gassed to death by animal control authorities may live out their lives protected, fed, and cared for. Each house will have its minimum/maximum of several dogs, and a small colony of cats. The house collective will do animal love, bonding and care.

--In these houses only foods purchased meat-wise will be free-range cattle, poultry that is humanely slaughtered after a mature lifespan. Some houses may be vegan/vegetarian.

--*God is a terrible truth.*

--Seek the Creator, be aware of self, and you will find your mission, which is Creators intent for you!

--'The will to power, to well being, to wealth triumph over the will to holiness, to genius. The highest spiritual achievements belong to the poor.'
--Peter Maurin, circa 1930.

Note: The will to power. I, the Founder of DOC must be careful of this one! Just as much as the one about money. One way to avoid the pitfalls of taking too much power (absolute power corrupts absolutely) is transparencies. No secrets. Have an organization accountable to the public—from which it ultimately draws its resources both human and monetary. 2. Be allied with some large outside religious body who is within itself accountable by a system of checks & balances. —Other churches check up on their clergy of other parishes within a diocese. DOC must do this—ally herself with a greater body, tho not subservient nor legally bound to it.

--Seems there is, inborn, in all humanbeings, this hunger to know Creator—this itching for the Divine.

--Every penny we stop to pick up along the road of life is a burden in heaven.

Notes from JOURNAL Volume 1, Acts Against The Powers Of Authority:

--Poverty. What a ragged bride she is; whose torn grey garment is made of cobwebs. —She seems mean. A tight mean line for a mouth. Is this the poverty I've embraced? Is this who our Savior has called me to wed?

--In the high theatre of the church on pulpit the minister gesticulates. The masses attending are attentive. I am at my station in the back row.

The preacher is far away, but lifted up over 40 rows of pews which stretch from right to left, a ship full of parishioners, now he preaches: "Jerusalem, Jerusalem, who murders her prophets, I would have gather you up like a hen gathers her brood, but you would not!"

End Notes:

DOC will be reviled in the eyes of some. Those religious fanatics, and bigots, upon seeing gay, lesbian, transsexual & their straight friends in unity together, women empowered, racial mixing, multi-religious organizations under the same roof. ----Just another little kindling to the fire in all the big bonfires they hate.

These types will always bring fear with them, upholding a fire-burning cross, the dagger under a cloke, the malice of discontent blazing in their eyes, but we must persist no matter what!

> 'Dem boys shooten dice. I say boys, what yuh'all doin?
>
> We shooten' craps.
>
> 'Fo a $5 bill, they blowed his brains OUT!
>
> --Old blax street man reminiscing on The Life.

To truly follow God one must remain fluid----listening for Gods voice & direction. Fixed orders get too bogged down in catholic repetitious prayer & form. Jewish rabbis too immersed into the law until can't see past the glasses on the end of their nose.

We are serving God…. Maybe most important, if all my work came to nothing, & just sat somewhere, unnoticed--- & by chance one who WAS suppose to do the work for God just happened to pick up a copy of this handbook and in less then ten seconds glance something caught their eye; caught one simple phrase or WORD of my handbook which triggered the idea of that work which was truly Gods work --- that in just a fraction of a second it became clear to them--- then it would be that the work of my life had come to great fruit! It would be worth it, for after all it is God's purpose we serve and not our own crazy ideas.

Maybe God is something that holds all visions in truth knows & builds with each iota of things. As human beings we have such a small dedication, so circumscribed by animal ways, aches and pains and needs but it is to this fullest extent God must be taken & things of God cherished. And if possible, moved into the 3rd dimension and fulfilled into real Technicolor life!

Sick and tired of seeing wandering black indigents, the criminal (and criminalized) class, remember they have gotten a very short shrift in American society. And that this attitude is the result of an extreme and extended poverty—not by election and with sparse alternative. Poverty must be known and experienced. Even 2 weeks of poverty by choice. Or as the school kids who eat like the rest of the world 1 day a year, a meager half plate of rice. This is good. A way of getting your feet wet. To ease you into the great waters of sharing on a global level.

Those who take the vow of poverty, perhaps voluntarily, for 2 or 3 years is a learning experience but some just live poverty, day after day, year upon year. Being poor dragging on and on for 20, 30, 40 years such a long ordeal time for the despair to sink in and permanently color a life, seeing your future on earth destroyed, and this disillusionment is when you teach rebellion to your children.

In the beginning of his life, Red was a child inspired, sitting next to his/her Colored grandmother on a church pew hearing her sing such a beautiful, mournful soprano the great religious hymns. As an older child he had lost his belief, and had joined that rank of atheism. --- Atheists being the bulldog watchdogs set to guard the rabid born-against Christians to make sure they don't get too far out of line.

Well now I will set up DOC, Holy Order of Mary, A New Order of Jesus Christ, on POD; print-on-demand; then it's back to Sedna! my 4th science fiction book in the Unity of Utopia series & maybe my fines arts oil paintings.

Back when I was young & my vision of art was clearer, and was sure my dedication was only to paint, to write, to live the artistic life. At some point I began to grow out of my art involvement, into the ecumenical world, the religious life. Just as my art, which sustained me for so many years had lifted me above the common world.

Bishop Marc speaks of intentional communities. That's what DOC is meant to be. A community of intent.

God, --(of the church): *I will tear it down & rebuild it, better.*

So the Holy Fire did come to me.

Hide yourself in Me. Says the Lord. These times when cities fall into the sea. World wars. Civil wars. Holocausts, global warming, national disasters, planetary disasters, nuclear annihilation; the rise of chaos.

From Acts Against The Powers Of Authority:

Creator: Don't remember the things of old or the things of the past. I am about to do a new thing.

First this must be wiped away.
Strike bell 2nd time.

Creator: I am God to Whom all pray.
Strike bell 5th time.

They came to me in the desert with 1,000 miles behind them and no returning. & a thousand miles lay ahead, famine, sun baked, drought. They turned to Me then.
Strike bell 6th time.

Turn to Me now.
Strike bell 7th time.

The People: All that is prays to You.

Masses of people bow deeply, bending down deeply, prostrating themselves upon the floor, drinking deeply of the Sprit of the Most High.
Strike bell 8th, 9th, 10th, 11th, 12th, times.

***

Not one of the pages of this book shall be lost, nor any of its words shall be removed, because it has been given to me by God.

Red Jordan Arobateau
June 18, 2007
6:00 AM Pacific Standard Time
San Francisco, CA
USA

Midrash/ Commentary
Journey 4

Midrash: Further Comments on DAUGHTERS OF COURAGE, a Multi-faith Religious Organization's Handbook of Rules, Regulations, and Vows for their Order and Community, plus JOURNEY Vol. 4; my Daily Journal. Continuing its usual Utterance of The Spirit, Poetry, & Other Observations.

You shall obey God.

V' avadta Adonai

Meditations on the Lord

Cleanse yourself of self-pride,
Conceit & envy.
Anger—especially anger.
Vanity.
Greed.
All the shame that you have taken on.

Follow me, I'll bring you joy. Joy ---and Fun!

To follow Me first you must make yourself holy.

Open your heart. Reduce your self.
To be holy you must reduce yourself of self-preoccupation & follow the Path.

The birds in the sky have their purpose. Dropping seeds and fruits from their beaks. They help pollinate earth.
So do you have a reason.
Find your purpose in My Order.

COMMENTARY ON THE DOC HANDBOOK:

In DOC and Community we are Sisters in Christ, Brothers in Christ. For those who cannot take that vow we will be Sisters in the Spirit, Brothers in the Spirit.

> *Your Daughters Of Courage, this Order I am setting up is a Holy Order of Mary. Mary has all power. All power, because she was obedient to Me.*

We must pay special attention to Saint Mary, Mother of God, the namesake of our Order.

Regarding Rule #1, of Belief:
It is not necessary to absolutely believe in God, any who *want to believe* or are *searching* for the Most High are also invited. Tho they may not actually fully believe as of now, they are welcome.

Regarding Rule #11, of Animals:
One of the works the Order is going to do is animal husbandry, care, restoration, preservation. For instance, recently in one of the Buddhist countries there was a national disaster. People were bringing all their unwanted animals to the Buddhist monastery; cats, dogs. They took them in.

Regarding the Rule of Animals, consider page, INFINITE LOVE:
> Each house of the Order will have its proper share of cats & dogs, plus other small animals, and no one with compromising allergies to animals shall join this order! Living spaces can accommodate the allergy-prone by removal of all rugs and upholstered furniture (which hold dust, pollutants) and thorough sweeping and wet mopping of floors regularly.

Regarding Rule #12, of Abstinence:
 Members may drink indulge in spirits outside of their House & outside of the Community and its happenings—which will remain clean & sober events. But if someone returning to their House or

Community is under the influence of alcohol or drugs, they will be disciplined, and if necessary permanently removed. Furthermore they must not become a scandal outside of DOC due to this indulgence, or that privilege will be removed.

Furthermore, regarding abstinence—DOC will have Houses of abstinence of all substances at all times, 24-7. No alcohol or drugs inside or outside the House. Which is a more severe level of the Order. As before stated, members will wisely choose their House of Loyalty upon confirmation.

Regarding Rule #3, of Service:
A friend & wife are caretakers of the poor, the sick, the animal & the crazy. Also of the child and the ancient. Taking many under their wings into their house. (Father Teresa I call him) travels many miles to visit all kinds of suffering individuals in various nursing homes and hospitals. His way is a good role model for what Daughters must do, to do, --- the Work.

Furthermore, here is a quote from JOURNEY Vol. 2., INFINITE LOVE:
> My idea of a religious order would help house the poor, feed the hungry, provide a religious center & discipline for the believers (Christian along with multi faith) which include living together in commune. Many houses set up in areas connected by regular singing and worship services with all the houses come together at a local church, synagogue or ashram which would include their congregations as well. Our religious houses would pray together, eat food together, brothers/sisters, sharing in their mutual vow of poverty which all must take—and provide order.

Regarding Rule #2, of Feminism:
Female born persons will be honored above all in the Order, and will not be subjugated by any male, or male-born persons. God has a special love, a teardrop, a twinkle in Her/His eye, for all the females of the species because they bare young—and extend compassion to their young. Even those who don't give birth have this great capacity for empathy, & what is closer to Gods heart then Love? Men be likewise! Be more like women!

Here is a man, hirsute, tall, masculine structure. He is naked. Here is a man with a scar where his gentiles use to be. Is he a transsexual? Is he one of those who abstains? To his own souls belief, he is better off then what he was before. *So much pain before. So much pain before.*

Regarding Rule #5, of Discipline (Obedience):
The member Sisters & Brothers must be obedient to the prior(ess). If the prioress is a tiny person in physical stature, and those under her are big and physically powerful, she must be assured they are in her control. At the least sign of disrespect, disobedience or rebellion they must be reported and disciplined. This may mean the prior(ess) appealing to DOC hierarchy above her/him. The law of the jungle, the law of man over woman, or young & strong over old & weak will not be followed in the Order nor in the Community, nor in any of it's Communities of Supervision. Any affronts to the prioress/prior will be punished.

Regarding Rule #9, of Corporal Discipline. (Obedience to the House & Head of the House):
Likewise there will be no ganging up on the part of members of a House against the prioress, nor against any single member of that House. If necessary, intermediaries from another House or upper echelon of the hierarchy of DOC must be called in immediately. The House may be disbanded if too many problems are found. Its members barred at worst, or disciplined, and sent off to live in other Houses, and a new House set up at that physical location.

A bad incident involving a difficult person in one of my groups has led me to the realization that corporal discipline is all some people understand. Upon observing this group of mine, and its members, when I see how little respect & loyalty they have for me, I realize that this nascent DOC must be set up in such a fashion with rules, regulations and checks, so to enforce loyalty and discipline for the head prioress, and for the Founder, myself, presiding.

I have seen examples of lawlessness in the church. Drunken men's bellowing voices drives females away from the church. The old or meek would rather stay at home, then be in a pew full of drunken rowdies, or sociopaths. Law must prevail—so that Love can flourish!

Regarding Rule #13, of Fun:
Tonight meeting of the Benedictines shows me how important the rule of fun is. Don't we have joy in Christ? I do! Too much seriousness; grim, sonorous, biblical pronouncements take away joy. Worse, on a spiritual level—for all things begin and end in spirit—on a spiritual level it is a form of power. And isn't it God who is our power, not we ourselves? We have Joy for our deliverance. Fun, in our religiously disciplined freedom!

Additional Commentary:

We will pray in each other's traditions, we will practice each other's disciplines, whenever we can, in accordance with our own beliefs.

--Regarding DOC as a Multi-faith Religious Order. Once you go outside the familiar, you're going to have problems. Some will not want to take that risk, but we must. Having an inclusive Order such as DOC wherein many diverse practices in serving Creator may be shared is a great challenge.

--Regarding Monastic & Apostolic Orders. DOC will be both. —As necessary. Some orders are built by the place—location. This Order will be built by the Word. As often as possible we will secure Housing thru purchase, tho often it may be necessary to rent, and also to squat in living spaces we cannot even rent.

Like so many I am very compassionate. And need a framework to express, handle, control this love—a higher discipline then ordinary friends or ordinary life can provide—what better then the church. And if not the church, then a less traditional Order such as Daughters of Courage? Like so many I wish to do service for Humankind, but seldom feel I have the resources to do this alone. What better way then in community!

--Regarding Emotional Abstinence. A lot of people on this earth have lived lives of enforced hermitage—without being in a monastery. They have few if no friends, go days without speaking to anyone, eat simple meals, are very poor, and have no friend but their Creator—if they know One. And if they don't know Creator, what a sad mess they're in! Such has been the emotional poverty of the insane, the disfranchised, the afraid, the societal misfits. Great and small Artists; from Van Gogh down to unnamed scribblers. Geniuses—with no social skills. And it nearly has been the life of myself, but that I pushed myself out into community settings and made myself known. In Daughters Of Courage, by living communally, praying communally, and by periodic forays to other larger established churches, synagogues, ashrams, mosques, we will enhance the social life of the obedient socially shy Sister or Brother-in-Faith.

--Regarding Fasting. A topic I forgot to mention in the Handbook. Many religions employ fasting. Buddhist, Hindu, Jewish, Islam, Wiccan, Christian, and others I'm sure. To stop eating is the basic human reaction to grief—to no longer be hungry for the world and its things you once craved, or for the items once put in such high esteem. —When faced with a powerful situation such as death, these things are empty & meaningless, and have no power at all to change your situation. It is then to this state of hunger we return when searching the Almighty, or to enforce our intercessory prayer. We must empty ourselves.

--Regarding Rules & Vows of DOC; consider one of the traditional orders, chiefly of the past; an order so severe, that monks rarely talk…lying on their bed of poverty, alone, enduring decade after decade of coldness & hunger. This is how they lived out their days on earth. In stark isolation, possessing nothing, having no families, no loved ones, no warm press of flesh against their own. Meditating on the Lord alone. Finding sustenance in their Divine Creator only. Nourished in the thin wafer of bread, and sip of a cup.

> *We danced together in their visions.*
> --Jesus Christ.

I see a person in a white monks cowl large, bulky made of wool, with a red Maltese style Cross, it is human, not spirit, it is one of the sheep, a member of Daughters of Courage. I think Christ wants to set up a worldly Order. An Order to which many, many more sheep can belong, then the severe disciplines of tradition.

--Regarding removal from the Order of a disruptive member. The process of ousting from the Order will be easy. The Founder can ban an Order member and Community member. The hierarchy can oust or ban a member after a consultation and committee meeting in which all offenses, history of the member etc., are discussed.

--Regarding the Vow of Poverty & Semi-Poverty: now if you see me tomorrow stepping out of a long gold Lexus & observe all kinds of rent girls/boys climbing up the fire escape to my luxury hotel suite, at midnight—you will say I have failed. Failed in my long-standing vow of semi-poverty—but not that of celibacy, which I will not take!

Ordained members have taken the vow of poverty & renounced material wealth. No parents or friends outside the Order can donate food or gifts to those in the Order least we be corrupt.

--Regarding Service. It is strange how awkward are the children of the revolution, who are doing God's work. They have calloused feet from so much work, but they trip, stumble, and fall crashing here & there. Its because they don't have Grace. Or know the Grace of God. It's even more strange when these children who *diligently go about works of Gods directive* to defend poor people and uplift the downtrodden … as the Prophet Isaiah said:

> Is this not the fast that I have chosen?
> To loose the bands of wickedness,
> To undo the heavy burdens,
> And to let the oppressed go free,
> And that you break every yoke?
> Is it not to deal your bread to the hungry,
> And that you bring the poor that are
> Cast out to your house?
> When you see the naked, that you
> Cover them.
> And that you don't hide yourself
> From your own flesh?
> Then will your light break forth
> As the morning, and your health
> `Will spring forth speedily; and your
> Righteousness will go before you.
> The glory of the Lord will be your reward
> Then you will call,
> And the Lord will answer.

You will cry and God will say,
Here I AM.
If you take away the yoke,
The putting forth of the finger
And speaking vanity.
And if you draw out your soul
To the hungry,
And satisfy the afflicted soul,
And your darkness be as the noonday.

Isaiah 58:6-10

…. that these children who right now as I speak are engaged in peaceful marches against war, protection of endangered species, flyering to enlighten the more privileged about the destitution of people in foreign lands; that these children who are self-empowered to set out on great voyages of dynastic upheaval, attempting to change the earth for the better, that these vineyard workers who don't believe anything else society tries to force-feed them, have above all things swallowed societies lie about our Almighty Creator as dictated by those bigoted church leaders who are equally corrupt as the government, and societal mores against whom the children rebel, who they can see right thru. But why won't they see thru the lies of preachers on pulpits, religious doctrinaires of prejudiced one-sided evangelists, why are they so blind they can't see the true Light of God shining, above and beyond everything else? It's too bad they don't because God would empower them. God is already on the side of justice, truth, and love! These children would be ripe for an Order such as Daughters of Courage—they have one foot in the door already!

Furthermore, (Regarding Service) there will be due process in agreement of all members of the House and in the hierarchy of the Order as to what missions of service they are to go on.

--Regarding Housing: Each member will have their own room of adequate size. Once a Catholic service I attended---Dignity, a GLBT service held a community-building workshop at one of its diocese facility—a former nunnery. This building, which had lost its sisters several years back due to atrophy because of age contained a chapel, small, beautiful with alter, statues of Saint Mary, about 4 short pews on each side. A very large kitchen, a meeting area—where our workshop was held. We saw the dormitories where the nuns had stayed; two large rooms with bunk beds. This is the only personal space the sisters had. One narrow bed either below someone else's or above, and surrounded by others—about twelve to a room. In contrast the Benedictian priests have each to themselves a large room with a private shower, toilet, sink—hot running water. Of course they are speechless. Allowed to converse together only in the once-per-week walk thru the woods. Our members will speak, and they will have their own personal room.

--Regarding Silence: DOC does not take the vow of silence, only very special orders do this. But we may as a discipline, practice occasional days, half days or several days of silence, to focus ourselves above worldly matters and concentrate more on Holy ones.

--Regarding Dress. Habits of the member Sisters & Brothers. Dress uncomplicated & simple. If a uniform is desired the cowl in beige, or white for special occasions, emblazoned with the blood red Maltese Cross—symbol of DOC. (Editors note; later addendum: symbol of their particular Faith.)

--Regarding diet; there will be coffee & tea and plenty of this; also poisonness sugar and most anything the members of a house wish, however there will be no meat in vegetarian houses; in addition no dairy in vegan houses. How deep does your empathy extend? How soon will you cut love off? —Your compassion for the weaker, the fallen ones. Will you drink a bowl of carrot soup instead of the turtle? Will you forgo veal, the pâté grais the corpses of tortured beasts? Does your sympatric heart include the lowly animals?

No houses of the Order, nor Community will ever eat veal, pâté grais or other delicacies in which animals are maimed to an even greater degree then usual, simply to entice the human palate. We will try in all instances to eat free-range cattle and poultry all of whom have been allowed to reach a decent middle age, and their byproducts. Pork will be an issue with Islamic members. No House with Islamic members should have pork in it whatsoever, if those members of the house are offended by it. If members must indulge in pork they must do it outside of that House and never bring it into the House if the Islamic members are offended.

--Regarding One Purpose of DOC. God has a great sorrow for this human race S/He has created because its so fucked up. The church/synagogue is all that keeps some people living. But as a young adult I did not know that. Maybe DOC can help introduce a few of the agnostic children of earth to the Heart of the Almighty.

--Regarding the modern-day necessity of communal living. Here is the portrait of a potential member. Caught up in their daily lives. They want to get married, they want to have children, they got to keep working. They want to do acts of mercy but how can they when they can't pay the rent? They want to do more then make donations, they wish to be involved in saving their little portion of this world. By joining together with likeminded souls, all this can transpire—if faith, prayer, belief, and worldly discipline are followed.

Some members will just be happy to have a clean place out of the cold to stay, meaningful work, and group meditations on the Almighty and prayer. Others are more highly motivated. They will go on to be grand devotees and spirited leaders.

--Regarding evolution of the concept of DOC. It is no accident that in the precursor to the Handbook (JOURNEY 2), in JPORNEY 3, INFINITE LOVE, at it's final section heading, Saul on the road to Damascus is quoted. After which INFINITE LOVE ends, and the Handbook begins. It is a fact that I wasn't necessarily planning to set down this Order into print, tho, as witnessed by the quotes in the Handbook, had rudimentary glimpsed it far back in 1996, with DAUGHTERS OF COURAGE—the novel--- in which Prince Valiant and her stalwart dyke wife Serena set up a dyke women's self-help group, with a mildly religious theme. Well like God did to Saul on the Road to Damascus, so S/He did unto me, and the Handbook was birthed shortly after. I hope it and Daughters will bring an epiphany in your lives.

> When Saul had almost reached Damascus, a bright light from heaven suddenly flashed around him. He fell to the ground and heard a voice that said, "Saul! Saul! Why are you so cruel to me?"
> "Who are you?" Saul asked.

"I am Jesus." The Lord answered. "I am the one you are so cruel to. Now get up and go into the city, where you will be told what to do."

Acts 9:1-7, The Holy Bible.

Seems God admonishes. S/He seizes us by the nape of the neck & drags us up to Her holy alter. But in retrospect, this is mild; for others she just sends off on the Titanic—and will deal with them *later*.

--Regarding Obedience: The more intelligent humans are; the more disaffected they are, and the more disobedient they become. They think for themselves. They analyze the faith right out of their souls, so as everything is cut and dried and intellectualized, and they go on in a depressed state—all the while considering this a triumph. It is no coincidence God made the tree of the fruit of knowledge of good and evil, just that—a tree of knowledge-- and not the tree of lust, nor the tree of indolence, or the tree of anything else, but knowledge. On occasion faith too must be exercised! And the headaches of knowledge set aside!

--Regarding the setting up of the Order (WORK), I don't think I, its Founder, Red Jordan Arobateau, Prophet, and Master Author, can fulfill that job! Don't have the physical strength nor stamina & have failed before in interpersonal relationships. And do wish well anyone who does pick up that yoke. I can remain an advisor. God reveled to me that I am a builder. That is my job. An artist. Not an organizer of people! Not a leader of masses!

--Regarding the Rule of Living a Religious Life: In my Sci-Fi series the Unity Of Utopia, all the utopian dreams of humankind have gone astray, and so to the political works of humankind, dear children. I want to stay in the bosom of the Most High, and so should you! @ Grace, snug in his hard wood pew 11am, hungry, stomach grinding from drinking wakeup coffee, Transman Red has a vision of a round red peg screwing into a round blood-red hole, churning & frothing itself in. At last he had found a place where he fit!

43.
By the way, Midrash is written inside my JOURNEY, a journal, (daily diary of sorts) it is a hybrid book. Anything may be found

within its pages! So here's something on a totally different topic then religion, yet baring an important message. In the spirit of archiving my work, the following is a presentation I did for Michelle Tea, on the Beatniks—read aloud in the Koret Auditorium of the SF main library. Since I don't know if the piece will go anywhere else, I'm saving it here for all posterity, plus those readers who may have just begun perusing my work for the first time can find out more about me as well. What follows is, HOW THE BEATNIKS IMPACTED ME:

I was already dropping out in junior high school, being abused at home by my clinically insane mother, as well as suffering with self-consciousness from being biracial, & a transsexual crossdresser in the 1940's. Got the idea to become a Communist—rebelling against the traditional; which was, to me, all those morays of a hypocritical society which was witnessing my abuse but did nothing to defend me. Especially the self-righteous blindness of my patriotic grandparents who hung the American flag out on the front porch every 4th of July. As a 13-year old buying some used Russian textbooks I had the idea to try to learn that language on my own, which was most impractical—seeing I was already flunking out of French in school. Tried to read some Communist literature but it was so boring I soon abandon the idea.

Because of my already disaffected state I would be drawn to them --these beats. Before them, were the bohemians of European literature who had fueled my child imagination as I devoured library books. The concept of one who rebels from traditional society, an artist, a free thinker, the bohemians helped pave the way for my own artistic freedom and personal independence.

In mid-1950's a word was coined, détente. America was in a cold war with The Soviet Socialist Republic, formerly Russia. This was constant major news occupying headlines. Doomsday scenarios haunted the American conscious. Those times of détente Soviet nuclear missiles were aimed at us, and ours at them. Threat of a nuclear attack was ever-present, and every Tuesday at 12 noon air raid sirens wound up and howled for a minute or two. I was ten or eleven, our family still together before it broke apart, living on the black-brown South Side of Chicago, attired in boys clothes, blue jeans and a shirt, oxford shoes, playing in the back yard hearing these air raid sirens & praying to counter-act my worry. I had the unique experience of knowing this atom bomb had been invented in laboratories under the stands in stag field, a football arena at the imposing ivy-covered grey stone University of Chicago, which also housed the special school where my bourgeois parents were scrimping to send me. For the first time the whole school now participated not only in fire drills, but in nuclear air raid preparedness. There was no filing out of the classroom—there was no escape. We learned to cover our heads and hide under our desks en masse.

Not much later in the late '50's; news about these beats had begun to emerge in the ordinary American conscious as well. 'Beat generation'. The idea that these strange individuals considered themselves beaten by the status quo and had dropped out from society, was a shock to traditional white-ruled middleclass mores. Simultaneously this cold war preparedness for possible attack from the Soviets was in every newspaper. In the race between Russian and Americans to dominate space, the Soviets launched spacecraft Sputnik, propelling Russians cosmonauts into outer space before us. This was major news in the US. The foreign sounding name Sputnik was the talk of everyone. Soon, it became popular for people to add a 'nik' to everything. Every word had a 'nik' on the end, hence, in a fortuitous coupling someone tacked on the 'nik' to beat and it became, beatnik. (War resisters later would be called refuse-niks.)

It was in the late 1950's, wisps and ideas of these beats floated to me over the media in magazines, newspapers, radio & TV, one of these first rumors I can recall, was a news report of a beatnik coffee shop all the way at the opposite end of the continent, Venice, California. Reports of a woman folk singer, Barbara Dane in a smoky dim place a seated on small stage; with long hair black leotards, poncho and sandals, strumming a guitar and singing folk songs. This was the first introduction to the beat generation to a mixed up crazy 13-year old teenager. The image media projected was of long-haired women in black leotards and men with sunglasses, sandals, scraggy beards wearing a lot of dark colors as if they were in mourning, who lounged around in coffeehouses listened to guitar singers & poets. I was exploring the outlawed demimonde of gay life. Can't remember how old I was, (born in 1943), when the adult beats were just meeting each other and beginning art. Now could be seen in the streets a few formerly clean-shaven men sporting wicked goatees. Once close cropped hair, crew cut of preference, now letting it grow long, to their shoulders like girls. Hitting bongos with soles of hands until they grew calloused, black clothes, sandals, berets, smoky coffee shops

The beats were officially instituted TV programming in 1958, '59. Presenting beatnik Maynard Krebs on the Dobbie Gillis show. I was still living at home with my dad. The clean cut clean living Gillis has this friend Maynard who had a goatee, long messy hair, dumpy clothes, wore sandals and played the bongo drums. His vocabulary punctuated with beat phrases like 'say man' or, 'I got to get back to the pad & relax Daddy-O.'

The 1950's beatniks were beat. Slouched, walked with a weary look, emaciated, not eating healthy and their protest against society at that point was not portrayed as hardily partaking of their spiritual angst and transforming it into protest politics, just artistic anger. Women wore their hair natural in defiance of beauty parlor permanent hairdos—the beehive was popular in normal society. Hair teased and piled up a foot tall on top of the heads of ordinary women who needed to feel stylish. These beat chicks exchanged proper nylon stockings and prim high heel pumps for black leotards & open toe sandals. Non-conformists. 'Like say, hey, she's a relaxed chick Daddy-O.' Or, 'She's a way-out chick, man.' Holistic is the word we'd use today.

As a teenager I'd started going out to the Near North side, one of Chicago's few integrated areas, which abounded with artists and thinkers, visiting these beatnik coffee shops—now some springing up were commercial places that were owned by non-beat entrepreneurs which featured poetry readings, folk guitar singers and strong espresso a new kind of coffee far different from the 10 cents-a cup-poison I'd first been introduced to in my youth in the small hole-in-the wall eatery's, along with 25-cent hamburgers, coffee which tasted awful but did keep you awake.

I grew up some more, very queer, now running the streets. Then, black jazz world was alive, so was the black blues world, and the beatniks bringing their folk singing and a fascinating new lifestyle become a way of life for many. I was going out to the taverns every night—my flight path carrying me between dangerous gay bars with their ongoing police raids, the safer beatnik hangouts and the mostly straight blues & jazz clubs. Now in my late teens the names of Peter Seger, Woody Guthrie, folk singers, Alan Lomax became common reference points to me & my friends. And other names— like black folk singer Odetta, who I met when she was performing in a nightclub on Chicago's Near North Side, as she took a break between sets, a quiet & moody blue person, seated at the bar, round figure in a colorful dashiki and sandals.

The beatniks were a valve release on the pressure cooker of society for me. A way out of hell of my wrapped up, self conscious, shy, social dysfunction. An alternative, to the prepackaged, tied-up-in-a-knot traditional. Every generation needs one. We need to break away from the accustomed styles, and find new people, new lands---or—begin our own tribe.

In that era the folk guitar was the instrument of choice. Can you think of another genre that has specific musical instruments associated with it—up in heaven it's angels, haloes on their heads, strumming harps. On earth, in the punk rock scene, it's electric guitar & amplified keyboard. For the Beat generation it would be the classic non-electric or steel string guitar and bongo drums. I was about 13 or 14 when I got my dad to buy me a set of bongos, which cost $8 and was always thumping on them, pouring out adolescent energy and frustrations thru my fingertips. Next was a steel-string guitar, which cost in the late 50's, about $13. I went out to smoky coffee shops and art parties with older friends and watched beatnik guitarists, which abounded in those days, if you got close and watched their fingers move you could learn to pick out some cords. As a teen I had to have a guitar and bongos, it was just part of life. And later I was to faithfully cart a guitar at least around to 5 cities in various cases strumming the several chords I'd mastered, which impressed people and they said it sounded nice.

At some point I just assumed this guitar and bongos would just be a normal part of my life, along with my manual typewriter, forever. Periodically I'd either loose or wear out these instruments, and then, lacking this necessity would get a new one, so I could see how the price of bongos and guitars slowly started to rise. Well the manual typewriter morphed into the electric—I wore out about 20 of them—before switching to computer just 2 years ago in 2006. And electronic music has taken over—having been given a boost by Bob Dylan and his Band long ago—at the time considered an affront to the folk singer genre, and a betrayal to hippies everywhere. Time changes things.

The beatniks was a much smaller group then the hippies who arrived later, around 1965 in an earth shaking wave, one hundred thousand flooding the San Francisco streets in 1967's Summer of Love, heralding form all points across the United States and the world. A fiery super nova they swept away the decay of racism and staleness of thought, and regimented style of dress into the freedom modern times. Every city had hippies, building on the traditions of the beatniks. They brought with them strange eastern religion philosophies when I was by now a God-heater. The hippies were only to last in huge numbers around 8 or 9 years.

So, the progression. Bohemians, beats, hippies. In the last days of the hippies of San Francisco I was down on Market street at the congested area of the cable car turnaround; remembered seeing some strange new people— dressed all in black--- a new breed from out of town standing looking around them at unfamiliar 'Frisco. I had heard about them. They were punks. The latest development. Were these punks gong to carry on the tradition? Were they the 1969's modern version of Bohemians dropping out of the conventional life?

A phenomenon you noticed associated with the Beats, as with the hippies later, in 1960, '61, you might be going to hang out in one of these beatnik coffee shops just to find the police had closed the coffee shop down on — some trumped up charge. A 'Closed By Order of the Health Department' sign flapping in the wind. And while it was open police always harassing the place. For instance periodically the police began to come into this hangout and check everybody's ID cards. Over the following weeks they escalated, making more raids on the coffee shop, now certain to take somebody away in the squad car with them. Naturally they lost all but the most defiant, dedicated customers. A few days later, a chain across the front doors, and some infernal paper tacked on from the Fire Department, or some government officialdom of twisted law that police use to do their hatchet job for the sake of social control, when too many neighbors complain about a nuisance, and want to rid themselves of a controversial group. All us disaffected, none of us normal. Us mixing races, a little queer, free-thinkers.

What follows is a scene from a play I wrote around 1961 or '62, carried in manuscript from Chicago to San Francisco. In The Maelstrom, drawn from life, depicts one of these hangouts. A beatnik joint. Not one of the larger, commercial successes where mob pimps pretended to duplicate an authentic hippy den, but a minor one owned by real beats, young people, the usual, which was driven out of business soon.

Scene #5 THE HAVEN. A beatnik coffeeshop. They are drinking tea-the coffee shop has teas of different varieties. And orange, grape and root beer soda pops. Midnight. The voices of Rose, Frank (playing his Obo). Mable, wearing a lampshade orange colored thing with the fringe on it, Fast Sammy, and a witch named Tinkerbell. People dancing to a wild guitar.

Frank: Is it a happening?

Tinkerbell the witch stands on a small stage, musing aloud. Occasionally the witch's voice rises above all of the crowd. This is performance art at its inception. A persistent smile flickers at the corners of her too-thin mouth. Long straggle hair & filthy clothes. Dirty fingernails. She's young. 14, or could be 16.

Mable (noticing the witch): Whose that? Lady Macbeth? Juliette of the Spirits? Julian De Sade?

Tinkerbell begins to shriek from her stage): You want to know futility in one word, not even one word. In a glance—There! (Snaps her fingers.) That gumball machine! It's a waste. The most hopelessly futile thing in this world.

Voice from the Audience: Not if you have pennies to put in it.

2nd Voice: Yeah, not for kids it's not futile. Not in a kids type world.

Tinkerbell: No, it's futile. Nothing should be kept locked up. Not even gumballs. (The witch eyes bright, terribly thin moves around the stage. She stops to stare at different people, and things; pointing a scrawny finger at them in accusation.)

Tinkerbell: Look at this place. THE HAVEN. A sea of faces… the dance of death. Look how ragged and hairy everybody is… Like they were wrapped up in something… Tinkerbell the witch utters a small shriek, then addresses her little audience: And I'm not even high… look into my eyes. Well… (Pause.) Well… Do you see it?

Rose: See what?

Frank: You look frightened.

Tinkerbell (screeching): Look into my eyes tell me what you see! Looking for the truth! Looking for the truth!

The witch climbs off stage and begins to circulate among the audience, no more then ten people at 4 or 5 tables and chairs.

Rose: Everyone's looking for the truth, why don't you look in the mirror?

This and more questions are thrown back at her.

Harassed by her small audience Tinkerbell walks away, steps back up on the stage confronts her audience, shouting: Look at the people here! Hair. All I see is hair. Uncombed hair. Beards. Long hair on girls. Long hair on boys. Grey clothes. Everyone is wearing grey. Prisoners! Bare feet. Feet with straps between the toes, and hair. Long falling hair. And what a name for it. THE HAVEN! Humanity! Linked together—prisoners with handcuffs.

While they are there, the coffee shop is invaded by a gang of bikers; in blackleather jackets, chains, tattoos, emblems, beards. Incredibly filthy. Dirt encrusted skin—grime from the road so thick you can see only red eyes. Boots runover at the heel. Swagger-high on pills and beer. One takes a can of paint, a brush, and sloshes their name, paints it in red on the wall of the coffee shop now reads GYPSY'S HAVEN! Voices of the coffeeshop staff arguing.

Rose: Oh, oh lets get out of here I don't like it one bit! Looks like trouble!

Fast Sammy: We can't call the cops. All they want is an excuse to close another coffee shop. I'm telling you when we had the LOVE DEN over on Larabee street they didn't want us over there. There's some trouble. I call the police. The Captain he says, 'is that the place where guys with beards and sandals and dirty feet go?' Dirty feet he says.

Walking out behind them the staff of the Haven is arguing with the bikers; more and more motorcycles are rolling up on the scene. The quartet is walking "Poor drab kids making a big deal out of their lousy security. Trying to protect a lousy freak-out coffee shop where they don't spend no money because they don't have none. Some lousy HAVEN! Imagine that that gang writing that word Gypsy's up on the coffee shop wall ruining their sign. The HAVEN is a nice place. Those damn gangs.

**

Another view remember glimpse of the Beatniks, when I had finally found my own haven here in San Francisco after fleeing Greenwich Village during an alcoholic breakdown, cleaned up back in Chi-town, then run out of that Windy City by constant police raids on every single gay bar, because it was an election year. You could *live* in the city of Saint Francis. I knew the beats, knew about Ferlenghetti and that bookstore over in North Beach. The hippies had come of age, birthed out of the body of beats, and bohemians before them. Like everybody poor I stayed in the Tenderloin, then later got a room in Chinatown hotel with a small cot, desk and sink a month, facing a grimy airshaft for $30 a month and another slightly larger in a Italian run hotel for $15 per week. All a block or twos walk. I continued my art writing and painting faithfully, still had the guitar tho only strummed it a few minutes several times a week. Had shed the bongos back in Chi-town. Writing on my Smith Corona electric with now several novels under my belt and reams of poetry and a few plays. I can't remember going to City Lights Books but haunted Wild Side West a lesbian owned bar with a diverse clientele on Broadway near Stockton. All though I was an avid artist myself, I had always been more desperate to be around my own kind in the nightlife, the queer life then bother wasting time hanging out around what I thought were straight artists.

This had all been before the Stonewall Riots. Must mention this was a time when we gays were still struggling for our rights, and any positive public step for gays was a victory. This was a decade before the Brigs initiative hit the California state senate and the Anita Bryant Orange juice debacle broiled out of Florida with a vengeance... When 300 marchers swoll what had been back then a much smaller gay pride day celebration, predominately male, and gays and lesbians meshed out of their separate worlds in cooperation, coming together for one of the first times to take a stance against anti-gay bigotry.

1969. Went to the lesbian bars every night—it was my home. By now clean and sober, it was to socialize and not be alone---- and hope of hopes, to find a permanent girlfriend! A popular choice was Maud's Study up in the Height-Ashbury. I remember one evening a dike talking about the beats, and this was not a typical topic of a dike crowd. And she'd mentioned something about poet Allen Ginsburg, and how great it was him winning some award, since he was gay, and remember me being shocked to know that he was gay! I knew his name and had tried to read Kaddish. I'm this big artist but wasn't in the art scene only the street scene and the bar scene. I haunted library's reading avidly, and creating. So naturally had heard Ginsburg's name and remember I was pissed because all these years I never realized the man was gay! Damn! Well what this means, me being uninformed, is that Ginsburg's name just hadn't made it down into the public conscious as a gay man, not in the manner Maynard Krebs had been visually identified as a beatnik, and years later when the truth about Kerouak's at least bisexuality, and Burroughs too, came out presenting such a strong gay influence, it amazing how this wasn't publicly known by the common people. And I was not in the privileged inner circle of this knowledge. So thus their emancipation had not helped me specifically to strengthen my queer identity.

Art can be for better or for worse, and is not always the stellar ideal, which propels the soul to attempt it. Outside of the ambitious art they are able to produce artists aren't so ideal. In fact we are just ordinary people in other ways, not far separated from the common mass at all. There was a dark side to the beats, which I started to learn about only ten years ago. I hadn't known, about William Burroughs killing his wife, either by murder or accident, also the case of one of their group Lucian Car, who threw a too ardent gay stalker over a railing into the East River to drown, in 1944.

That Kerouac refused to acknowledge being the father of his only born child, a daughter, who died not long ago—not attaining even the same short life span he had-- did not endear me to him. Neither did his treatment of 'Mardu', one Aileen Lee a person of mixed-raced heritage like myself, some of whose writings Kerouac may have plagiarized in his piece about her (a great work of art, The Subterraneans). Art so often is done by conflicted people, and its results can be mean. Very mean. For example a companion of mine and myself were involved in a theatre production, which for us was major deal after all the small bookstore and bar shows, which were our world. This was in a legitimate theatre and had a budget of $25,000, which it exceeded by $10,000. During that the 6 months rehearsal and 6 weeks run, as usual for productions the cast knit itself together tightly, having all the subsequent drama & intrigue of interpersonal relationships. Everybody was gay or bisexual or pansexual and most everybody was sleeping with everybody else. Not long after the stage was struck one man had committed suicide, one had dropped out went insane and became homeless, a 23-year old Southern belle debutante had to be airlifted out by medics to recuperate at her family's home taking a year to recover she had so exhausted and depleted herself from all the sexual escapades, drinking, drugs and dancing until dawn. People lost apartments, people lost jobs, they lost their pets, they lost their minds; me and my ex were poisoned by drug laced brownies and were evicted from our warehouse space unable to make the correct rent for 8 months consecutively—coincidently the same months as the duration of the show, because of neglecting advertising to procure housecleaning job contracts. --We were so involved in doing art... It was a wild ride. Some people's art is probably well-ordered, clean cut, this is the ideal, but yes, it has a dark side.

The beats, many in historical retrospect seemed not to have good lives. Early deaths, suicides, life long narcotic addiction. And those murders.

These days of bigoted religion it is embarrassing to discuss morality, to give warnings about morality and struggle for a correct path. I will just say I recall the young Red, 18, battling alcoholism, when he fled the Greenwich Village scene, to come back into the comfort zone of sanity & locate himself.

So my searching not just to make great art, but, to have a decent life, this is something I've learned.

Looking look back over my journey at 63, wonder what my life would have become if I'd stayed in Chi-town—my birth place. Thinking of the factors which got me here... I might have drowned myself in love of the needle; heroin/alcohol my fire burning out amidst the prostitutes, thugs, and criminals of the demi-monde of criminalized gay life in the rummy taverns I wrote about in my classic dike novel Lucy & Mickey and others of the early 1960's, before Stonewall, before Gay Pride. But I took the call of the hippies, my fire ignited by the beats before them and ventured out with just one paycheck in my pocket, my guitar and typewriter, searching for love, searching for art, searching for happiness... I see these San Francisco hills, wrapped in the mysterious San Francisco fog, and think about how I got here, that it was something about the beatniks, the hippies, that legacy of seers, something about freedom.

44.
Mailing Amazon book package. Must fight tourists on Powell Street, Red made his way past Union Square Park carrying his heavy book sack. On route to the post office in Macy's Department Store basement confronts a frantic heedless torrent of wild human animals---animals in proper clothes; sanitized, deodorized, and clean. ---On the surface anyhow. They are madly rushing. In a hurry to go shopping---scary Caucasian block-figures blockading the escalator; won't step aside. Rushing into Macy's front door in an unending stream. They are shopping seriously, deadly, letting nothing stop their consumerism. If Armageddon comes will they be caught with their shopping bags only half full?

This is the way of the world, its imbalance, and unfairness. Some enjoy while so many are in prison. Few of those who enjoy, pause to consider the prisoner. It is a good thing to think about prisoners. Of:
    Mental illness.
    Women under sexual duress.
    Inequity of the wealthy over masses of laborers.
    Political prisoners.
    Animals of a livestock kind brutally penned & slaughtered under horrific conditions of fear & pain.
    Animals of the pet kind, abandon, unwanted, jailed in cages then put to death.

If an individuals wealth is built on a giant pool of all the world's money, then many many more must be lesser off then the funds inside the purses of the rich.

Is God's arm too short to reach out and defend Her children? Is His ear not large enough to hear their cries?

45.

Red approaches Civic Center Gay Pride weekend. Hears a beautiful black drag queen singing Hair, followed by festive Age of Aquarius. Same songs, which were singing when he first got to this hippy-deluged city in 1967. Back then the streets overflowed with people in beads, bangles, colorful costume-clothes.

> How can they be so cold.
> People who care about strangers.
> Who say they care about
> Social injustice.
> How can people be so hopeless.
> It's easy to say no.
> It's easy to say no.
>
> ---From pop hit 1970's.

As a anxious young adult in his 20's recovered during a hospital stay from a bout of Hep C, back in Chicago, Red cleaned up, had left the mafia bar environment and his showgirl stripper who was an abusive alcoholic backstage at the dirty movie theatre --on sin strip, the night life sector-- took his last paycheck, purchased that one-way ticket, got on a train with guitar, suitcase and came out to 'Frisco, trying to save his life. I was drowning in a sea of hopelessness despair, unable to live as a masculine butch lesbian with a happy relationship, job and career… Here in a tenderloin's low cost cheep hotel, moved thru a sea of pain accompanied by beautiful music which floated over the jagged edges, the cheep blinking bar lights, druggies & tricks checking into twenty minute rooms; amid all the chasm broken hearts of cold beautiful naked women who had long ago sold out their souls. I still had my soul and was fighting to keep my mind. *Accompanied by that beautiful music...*

46.
The painful perplexing lack of transmens loyalty to each other again raises it's head. Its been said long ago back in a further removed generation of dyke communities, (disempowered in those days) how the intrusion of a man into a woman only space, into a lesbian relationship or women's centered group could serve to break the whole thing apart.

This is accomplished by two means. One; the super power of born-males who are bigger, stronger; more societal acclimated to being personally forceful, socially aggressive, and being biologically enhanced in these effort as well, with deeper, louder voices, and more imposing bodily structure. Two. *The lack of women or women-born individuals to stand together and fight shoulder to shoulder against any enemy or intruder.* As I have said before any crude, degraded gang member at least knows the meaning of loyalty—but we do not. We, inheritors of middleclass aspirations, have lost the ability to fight to the end for a friend—whether that friend is right or wrong. We try to build family, but it is a loose, informal and not truly dedicated family.

Loyalty is a strange concept, which shifts from class to class. The most lower class uneducated bully in the tavern, knows he must stand by his buddy in a fight no matter if the buddy is right or wrong. Higher up on the social economic ladder, where people are educated and thus highly intellectualize and capable of analyzing situations, loyalty is weaker. The buddy might stop and think; 'my friend is wrong, I should side with the right, and do not back up my friend.' Of course he comes out of the battle having sided with the right—and lost a friend. Or at best having this friendship tested and found wanting.

Time and time again I've seen this happen to myself and others. You wonder what happened to the concept of standing by a friend as we transition out of the criminal past into the new clear light of social inclusion and better jobs and higher community placement. We have turned into white color middleclass dogs, fangs stealthily hidden! Dagger to stab cold to the heart ready, yet never discussed.

God searches the heart.

Several times I have seen this scenario transpire in a group I run. Once in the beginning when our group was harassed by some local bums who hung out there, & this continued for 3 weeks. I stood up to this one man in particular, shouting back at him—others suggested we move our location to get away from him, a few others stopped attending. The result, the man later vaporized into the mists and nevermore troubled me. Again we were tested, when upon the incursion of a homeless bum, one of the malicious variety, who was hated also by other more mild mannered homeless. When this bum refused to leave our table and stopped harassing us, I stood up to him—to be immediately yelled at by some of my dearest and ordinarily most supportive friends in the group! As if the situation was my fault! I was told to sit down! Told I was 'escalating' the whole mess myself! And, did anyone back me up? As he continued to stand there harassing a bio femme woman and her FTM companion plus the rest of us? Out of the table of 15 FTMS and 2 MTFS, it was only one MTF who stood up beside me!

Now on that note let us proceed to the ugly incident, which has just happened.

There is a transsexual woman (MTF) in my group who has had to be removed, because she dominates the group, and I'm sick of it. I will not sit in my ownselfs group and be unhappy, especially because of a non-female born person, for whom this group is not a 'member' but as an invited guest.

I shouted at her when we were all elsewhere, told her not to come back to my group! But all the other transmen at the table are angry at me! Their wives are angry at me—hearing about the whole thing by proxy.

So this is the 3rd time in a row I have caught hell from a male to female transsexual & don't know how the future will go for straight women suddenly thrown together with their trans sisters. I wonder how they are going to deal with some among these new women who are partly still male-acting tho now in female bodies and in female attire. By their bad acting—dominating behavior and sheer steamrolling aggressiveness towards more diminutive bodied biological born females. Sometimes hating them from insane jealousy as well. They are hurting the more female and feminized of their cousins, other male to female transsexuals who have been going out into society making nary a wave, for many years. These misfits are bad news!

They need to get the seams in their stockings straight & have a Big Attitude Change!

This certainly is an ugly and cruel world. It hands me rocks & nobody knows my name. The few that do use it to say evil things about me behind my back This has been a very negative happening in my group. It proves the old lesbian adage that it is unwise to include 'men' in their groups as it has potential to be a threatening energy.

> *Is God's arm too short to reach out and defend her children?*
> *Is her ear not large enough to hear their cries?*

Lay in my bed, drained, sad, my mind having been so jam-packed full of argumentative voices still haranguing at me, that it had now become a blank. Laying on my left side, relaxing into the sheets, eyes focused above me at the ceiling. My right hand wanted to raise itself upward with some gentle urging, so I raised up my right arm. I began to make it move in the gentle motion indicated—and there big scripture letters appeared to me---in Hebrew. 3-feet high, 3 feet wide. I traced these letters in the air making giant motions. Of the few letters the pi predominated. 2 days later at the Gay Day Parade, a rabbi from Los Angeles talked with me. I asked him what are some Hebrew words which start with pi, the first word out of his lips was 'builder'. So I took confidence in this! Am I a builder for God? Great News! The Word is big in our lives. We are saved by the Word! (Some Orthodox Jews wear pieces of scripture hanging on their attire, positioned over the charkas of their body.)

Maybe something great will come of all this snake-like wreathing of angry passions in our tiny ghettoized trans community. As they faced me across the table, in their voices hear the rustle of their demons; scurry of ancient reptiles in the basement of unhappy brains. It takes more then human effort—it takes the intervention of a Higher Power to work some things thru!

Has God chosen me for my passion? It certainly has an angry mean side.

I feel totally unsupported in this---except by God.

Dilemma is all the Transman have no balls. They sit there and listen to her expound silently, as she dominates, maneuvers the conversation.

I hurt their feelings as I dised this girl. Now they have come back at me with rage! I was just screaming inside, 'what a mess.'

I feel tired, overwhelmed, sad. All over the intrusion of a male born person, who is still by in many ways a man inside a woman's body and dress. Falling back on male energy and a deep male voice to dominate all around—including male born men. Disguising it with a coy wink and a pretty hairstyle so her knockout punch effect isn't so obvious. She is a woman filled with misunderstood rage—undealt with. She is a loss as a friend with so much potential, wasted.

She is so different then the femmy new women who do all possible to exemplify their femininity, from voice, to demeanor. Although having this capability, she chooses to project thru a male self—because it carries more authority. Yet she retreats behind the feminine protection society offers to women! She wants it both ways at once!

Women back down to men. They respond to power. They back down to a show of force. They accommodate power. Don't stand up for their rights and their individual voice. Male to female transsexuals don't want to give up their power once granted to them as males. Because nobody gives up power easily, and for almost no reason on earth! And if there is not part of their feminine identity desperately screaming to cut loose the male role altogether, they will continue to be controllers, climbers seeking to maneuver for advantage.

This issue could become a book. A book with the title, Loyalty Among Women. Let me get something clear—I never thought of myself as a woman, tho I might have said so in some of my earlier writings. I was born female, but never been a women—which is a societal construct. But all transmen were once born female and society attempted to socialize us to be women. And we are tested as a group—FTMs—by the worst aspects of society.

Well this is the 3rd time I've had trouble with a transwoman. My play Portraits of a Ghettoized Population ended finally because a single upperclass transwoman refused to go onstage. Trans Space new director refused to let me continue my re-photocopy project. Shortly after, the controllers of the program, a state fund took back 2 million dollar allotment they'd given by the U$ Government & returned it—simply to get rid of all the crazy trannys who were becoming an embarrassment, and closed the place down! Giving 2 million dollars *back* to the government when every social service agency in town is begging for cash? What an insult. Trans can't do anything right. And now trouble in my fairly peaceful group—which is an FTM group---not an MTF group---but this damaged transwoman I brought in is a problem and I can't seem to rid the group of her.

Finally, least I heap all blame on failed transwomen let's spread some of that blame around! I'm going to say something which I'm sure is going to make me very unpopular, but it is I don't think FTM transsexuals have the loyalty to each other that biological born males can have among themselves.

Hate to think this all boils down to such a common denominator as pussy brains & dick brains. And a hard drive mind set fixed before birth when we were all embryos floating in the amneobotic bath.

Later at the Benedictines I view a faded pastel mural on the grey rock wall of Grace. A little small mouth Christ—A selfish, little small mouth Christ motif on an ancient crucifix replica. Horrors!

Group, attacked on one side. No support on another.

I'm mean, stupid. Everybody talking bad about me.

So my poisons hurt has turned and wounded my friends, for this I'm sorry. I only wish we'd become true friends, so they could have withstood my angry desperate broadside attack. I can retreat into a shell pumping out poison inside it until I self-murder, and become like the wandering creature-men/women one encounters in the street sorting thru garbage cans for food, with grim mouths and ragged clothes, no longer caring about personal appearances. I pray God this will not be my fate! That Jesus will intervene in my behalf!

I am a visionary & a prophet. How does anyone expect me to be an armed warrior as well? Which is apparently what is necessary to found & hang onto an organization of human beings on earth. Even, so I've heard (yes), little old ladies tea-parties. Prim little old ladies who in their frustrations put poison in the teapot of their enemies, then invite them to dine!

Well I do take faith in the history of Benedict. (Monastic Rules, 200 ACE. He started his monastic Christian order & was shortly thereafter run out of it by the very brother priests he'd taken in! Because of his severity. They attempted to murder Benedict. —He escaped & went on to establish a new order, even more strict then the first! –It survives to this day in many different groups all over earth. His monastic rules have become the guideposts for most convents and monasteries.

Some of us are weak in the world but strong in heart & spirit. This makes for difficult travel on a material plane. I can only pray to our Savior Jesus Christ & to the Almighty—to whom you all worship, (by different Names), for help. God is the rock of my salvation. The source of my life & strength.

The wonderful thing about God is that God assures me, that She has a purpose for me, and a job. To spread all this poison out into the world—where it came from! Using it to help set things right! To call the shit where I see it in society—where people are dying of it, in ignorance.

God has showed me I have a big heart. Over half the world's people have love in their hearts, but most of them can do nothing about it. Having not even power enough to help their own families. I have been given the power of art, of vision, but don't have the power to do works of this nature---that means to do the work of actually setting up the physical structure of DOC. I can barely get along with friends! I don't have a lover! I drive people away from me! I can't start this thing—only write about it!

Think like all good things DOC was born of pain & suffering & a long time of that.

So the work sits here waiting for someone to do it. To take on its yoke—of love.

Probably its no coincidence just as this process of writing down DOC's Handbook and its accompanying Midrash, this huge upheaval of my group occurs, which shakes my security and threatens some of my social life, and my show *which I've greatly enjoyed.

(*Club Eros, a gay men's sex establishment is the venue for my once per month stand up open mic.)

What was the workings of this group? —It was run on a superficial level, it had a lot of fun, it made connections between people, but it did not have a great amount of support for everybody.

At the GLBT Center overhear a lesbian woman asking "is there any women's coffee shops in the area?" No comes the reply. This, in SF. Gay Mecca. Well it's so hard to collectively do anything for the community –and have it survive backbiting, infighting and processing, no wonder!

People I'm involved say they feel our community (the queer/trans community) has stabbed them with a cold dagger in the back, and when that was done, went around and stabbed them in the heart. Sociologists observe that members of damaged communities wreak more damage upon each other—to the extent of their personal hurt, thereby substantially increasing pain. —When it would be life saving to do the opposite!

Just finished this shit involving my group, so feeling drained. Go on line to look up what bishop Marc has been speaking of--- Intentional Communities. And that's just what DOC is. So hope beats eternal! Setting up one of these babies will be thousands of times more hell then a mere 15-person group! Yes, Hell!

47.
Gay Pride day. You see people who hated you and insulted & argued against you in the public arena ten years ago who rush up pumping your hand a guilty smile twitching on their face, --guilty because what you did then as a radical is now commonplace and they got to admit it, -- filling your ears with 'hellos' & news of the events of their day, but the barbs remain. Opening up the composite shit pit of the past.

Here is a crazy one who was so trying to your political organization, who you had dealt with over & over again, about all kinds of hell so extreme it was ultimately suspected s/he was a CIA plant set down to destroy the group from within! Well after all our discussion, processing, and mediation—to no avail—this crazy soul has finally straightened up, gone to therapy, put herself of psychotropic pills. And is a changed indivdual! Yes, there will be hell, 'till they finally take meds & become new people & ultimately you never get credit for all that work you did with them.

Do not bite off the heads of the children, which includes me!

If you are in this lez, bi, trans, gay, community you realize its huge power of us assembled, but also recognize its just a drop in the full pageant of humanity. As you look from the hill down 5 blocks you see the Gay Day Parade, a long winding colorful snake as it winds along Market street dotted with humans swaying to rumba beats; but up here on the hill people ignore it pouring over their computers at distance out of earshot's of jubilant cries, booming electronic music, and the drum beat rhythm. The straight world is still much more vast then ours.

Striding among giants of the Tenderloin where a bellowing white man built like a refrigerator whose loud voice carries 5 blocks screams "a whole lotta woman, she was a whole lotta woman." He stirs fear into the hearts of females and unnerves all gentlemen nearby. Transman Red intrepidly makes his way towards the parade, with full confidence—tho it's a little scary. For after all, isn't it written? ---

> *All the stomping boots of the soldiers of war on earth's battlefields are like mice feet upon the palm of the hand of the Most High.*

48.
What follows are more instructions & probations concerning the life of the Order & the Community which surrounds the Order, and its works of supervision.

Comment:
We are radical yet conservative. Radical in inclusion; conservative in prayer, and belief in the necessity of a having a belief.

Comment:
(Intended for the ears of the more zealous, radical Children.) Why it is important not to burn the Holy place down: (Holy Place i.e. the traditional church, synagogue, ashram, mosque.) I would not criticize and attempt to bring down the existing Holy Places because despite being outdated they are so valuable & to so many. Also DOC may join with them periodically to worship en masse.

Comment:
Regarding Housing. (Again) Each member will have their own room of adequate size. Our members will speak freely among each other, and they will have their own personal room.

Comment:
Regarding Silence. DOC does not take the vow of silence, only very special orders do this. But we may as a discipline, practice occasional silence, to focus ourselves above worldly matters and concentrate more on Holy meditations.

Comment:
A Service Project for the future. It must be hard for many of the worlds injured people who need so much but never can get the full help they need; even as much as modern science wants to help. We must join hands to create a Compassionate City of Help.

Comment:
The religious family structure of DOC. So perhaps an Order of this nature is different. In that a religious family, is not like a worldly family. You are united by deeper things. It's not just your own human abilities involved in this, but Gods Great Abilities to heal and

mend, to adjust, and to make whole. God's influence drawn into it, because of the religious families prayer and supplication.

Comment:
Earnestness in prayer. You tell God, I want You! I want You! I want more of God! To sit in the pews is not enough! Hungry for miracles! Hungry to see, to feel God's presence. They say God changes things, and I want to move forward!

Comment:
Regarding isolation of non-connected peoples. Today 7 billion people are alive on earth, yet millions are dying of loneliness. DOC & her Communities will bring the isolated ones into closer proximity with their sisters & brothers, as held together by religion, belief, and the Divine Presence.

Comment:
Our helping of people in service must not just be to patronize or maintain, but uplift their status –to that of equals.

Comment:
Its Gods Will that all will be taken in, all people, even the smallest animals. Thus it should be very sad when DOC must not only turn down someone who asks to attach themselves to our spiritual body, from membership in her Order, but her Community, and her Works of Supervision as well! ---Such a Great Sorrow! To cast them back into the sea of life where we found them, unchampioned and alone!

Comment:
Imagine as you will withdraw more from the common world and spend increasingly more time doing religious activities in church groups, ashram's, synagogues, and so forth, the nature of your friends will change. All disputes among you must be ready for this by mediation of peers and/or superiors in the DOC hierarchy.

Comment:
Let me state this in a different way; age or physical condition is no bar to membership in the Order or community/DOC. Although you must be a legal adult over 18 unless your parents or guardians are also dwelling in the same house—to dwell in that house they must be

members. Very aged persons are welcome, and DOC will take them on as a form of Service for the Most High. Regarding Physical disabilities, those who qualify by all other DOC standards will be happily accepted. As usual all potential members must be accepted first for their commitment to discipline and for their mental and emotional states.

Comment:
It will be the goal & prayers of DOC's Order & Community to support and help all local institutes of Holy Worship, of a like mind as herself. (Churches, Mosques, Synagogues, Ashrams, Women's Circles of Divine Mystery.) (Especially small ones floundering, and medium size ones in trouble.) To aid by finances we raise, or by good works. And, to encourage them, by swelling their attendance roles. As stated elsewhere DOC will not itself be a worship institute whose congregants come en masse to us for regular services such as Shabbat, Sabbath Eucharist's, etc! We will worship together, pray together, very very often in small groups but we are not as it were running a religious congregational house of worship! We will meet *very often* in local worship sites of the different religions en mass to worship collectively along with the congregations of those places!

Additional comment: Let me say finally, and again in order for there to be absolutely no doubt—for those of Faiths other then Christianity there will not be an agenda of our Order of conversion to Christianity. And it absolutely will not be expected! Conversion to any particular religion is not the reason for Daughters of Courage! It is Jesus Christ's invitation to all Faiths to work and serve together for good! To do good works together for Creator! —You all call Creator something different—this is fine!

49.
Above in the sky there is a big round full moon...

Sha'ar zahav saved my life tonight. I really needed to have the good Words of Elohim to the people--- after this grim ordeal of my 'group' and its human turmoil. I know I am opposed, I've known it for quite a while—but I will keep on with the work as long as I'm able.

I say this, 'Elohim, Make me better in Your ways you'd have me to be on earth. Because I need to uplift my life and not drift into the gutter of isolation, frozen anger & despair. Because I need a power packed prayer to give on the behalf of so many other people and animals. Because, because, because....'

Also @ Shabbat heard a Martha Graham quote from the Siddur— (Hymn book) read from the bema, which I cannot recall precisely. — How we must do what our path and gifts call for—or the world won't have it. This special gift will not be given to anyone else. If we do not perform the task given us, the world will be a more barren place.

This wisdom certainly justifies the lives of many of us crazy, disfranchised artists who are hard to get along with! We bring to this sad earth an uplifting work—in our own way, and thru our own style—that no one else can do! All the mad divas justified by that beautiful aria only she can sing! The wild Jackson Pollack spattering paints just-so on gigantic canvass panels; who can inspire human hearts! God has given them a place in the profound workings of Her/His mighty universe! I think about women in childbirth, infants torn from their bodies in a blood bath. And the work of art, torn from minds, generated out of angst, pain as a subliminal escape from one world to open up a great vision. The work of art torn out of lives— jobs for pay neglected, evictions subsequently. The work of art torn out of happiness. The loss of wives, husbands, because of no economic stability.

Going down the steps of the ornate stairwell on the shule's third floor sanctuary to oneg, the Spirit of the Most High speaks to me:

> *Make My house your house Red, a lot has been given for it.*
> *Many hundreds of generations, spent in suffering. In having to flee from place to place.*
> *8 million in World War II died in ghettos & concentration camps because of their religion and belief.*
> *4 thousand years of struggle.*

.

I'm being tortured by Christians on one hand, by Jews on the other---thus my spiritual life falls into alignment.

The moon is full in a wild black ocean of drifting white clouds. Wind blows. It's the SF summer. (Coldest winter I've ever known was a summer in San Francisco—Mark Twain.) San Francisco is littered with the corpses of failed transgendered women. One howls from down in the bowels of the subway station; announcing her arrival. S/he is tall, thin—malnourished —clad in a unisex jacket, long black skirt, the proverbial tennis shoes scuffed by much wear. She scurries down Powell Street from Market. She stops howling a moment to lift up her skirt, takes a piss against a newsstand rack without having to squat. Alas Babylon.

San Francisco is littered with the walking corpses of fallen transgender sex workers. Little men with no hope, bottoming for bio guys and bisexual fags. Acquiring AIDS just like any gay man. Having no future, and no past written into their altered ID's presented in their small tough hands to admissions window at the men's sex club; grim expressions on their martyred faces. Their female counterparts, the girls, red lipsticked large mouth; she will perform blowjobs on the cheap, to scrape up money for room rent, and offer her pussybutt in car dates around the corner of Divas TS/TG nightclub, off Larkin street.

FTM transsexuals have it somewhat easier, we are more passable, yes we are invisible. Nobody knows our names, and fewer care. We are indoors, sheltered because of having access to normalcy and stealth. And in this remain divided from one another. We can go all the way transsexual via hormones and be passable as small men. We can disappear and get lost in the straight wide world, carrying our deep dark secret, perpetually afraid to get to close to anyone for fear they'll find out and reject us anyway; while many TS women can't make it all the way down the gender pipeline and get stuck as transgendered half-man/half-woman, with no money for operations, necessary procedures such as facial alteration, beard removal, nor money for housing stability—a decent room, which is so badly necessary in order to be able to dress appropriately; nor time to study voice, posture or grace. FTM passability makes us more safe. It's a good thing because we are smaller stature usually and any physical battles we might lose. On the contrary the battles of a perceived 'male', our sisters, at the hands of angry men are much more severe.

God's been dealing with me a very long time—but that didn't show as much because I maintained a hard, crude surface a la primatif. —I don't know any other manner in which to represent myself & am so accustomed to this. —Bravado.--- By which originally as a young adult I'd managed to crack out of my shyness, self-consciousness. But all the while I was developing spirituality by studies in church & synagogue and hearing Buddhist teachings, & meditations that made inroads as they dripped down into my soul. When I was finally ready to emerge out of this early personality which was a superficial reaction—showing my more 'true self'—everybody was amazed absolutely amazed… Thinking *Red has changed so much*, when actually he had only begun to let shine out the Word of God, which had polished him to more enlightenment on the inside.

50.
Comments:
DOC will remain an essentially urban order and community of intent; where can be found:

1. Diversity racially, and gender-wise.
2. Where oldsters have fast access to medical help.
3. Nearby existing churches, synagogues, ashrams, mosques of many denominations of worship our Order's members & Community can attend.
4. Close to a multitude of libraries, museums, art galleries, bookshops, multiethnic restaurants, for fun, avant-garde movie theatres and other cultural wells.

We will also have lands with rural Houses and communities dwelling in rural areas, implementing food production, animal husbandry, plus animal sanctuary and human retreat from city–madness.

Comment:
This is what a sample intentional community looks like—I've gone online to replicate it, altering the stats and minus it's name for confidentiality:

Population: 230.
Adult members: 200.
Open to new adults: yes.
Open to new children: yes.
Gender balance: 190% m. 40% f.

Government:
Decision-making, by consensus.
Leader: no.
Leadership core group: yes.

Labor and money:
Financial style: members with independent finances contribute.
Labor: expected contribution 4 minimum hours per month.
Fee to join: yes.
Regular fees: yes.

Land and buildings:
Rural.
Land owned by: a landlord.
Number of residences on land: 3.
Co housing: yes.

Food:
Percentage of food grown: 15% to 30%.
Share community meals: 5-6 times per week.
Dietary choice or restriction: common diet.
Dietary practice: vegan.
Alcohol use: prohibited.
Tobacco use: prohibited.

Social factors:
Open to lesbian, gay, bisexual, and or transgender members: no.
Shared spiritual path: yes.
Which spiritual paths: any who actively seek the blessings of their Creator God.
Educational styles: public school or parental home schooling.

Times like this when I really feel diminished as a transsexual and a queer. Feel laden & heavy burden.

Well anyway, for better or for worse, you see by the stats how a Community of Intent is set up!

Comment:
Regarding wine @communion. Thank God for Islam. Who swears off all and any alcohol—no religious wines. @ the Episcopals long ago in a red wooden church on Telegraph avenue I remember after service seeing this alcohol on the table at hospitality and wondering why a civilized church would offer the drink of winos, alcoholics, criminals and fallen saints on its food table!

Comment:
Regarding the state of the Fonder. —My life is a stabilized mess. All my indiscretions which mostly come to nothing, which exist in thought, fantasy, overture, proposition—but all having been spurned; regarding TS women, bio women, gay men, bi women and not simply anything which moves or draws breath as is the joke going around about me.

Of all my sins self-known I stand convicted. I wish to come out of Galatians a minute; 5: 1, 13-25:

> My friends, you were chosen to be free. So don't use your freedom as an excuse to do anything you want. Use it as an opportunity to serve each other with love. All that the Law says can be summed up in the command to love others, as much as you love yourself.
> But if you keep attacking each other like wild animals, you had better watch out or you will destroy yourselves.
> If you are guided by the Spirit, you won't obey your selfish desires. The Spirit and your desires are enemies of each other. They are always fighting each other and keeping you from doing what you feel you should. But if you obey the Spirit, the Law of Moses has no control over you.
> People's desires make them give in to immoral ways, filthy thoughts, and shameful deeds. They worship idols, practice witchcraft, hate others, and are hard to get along with. People become jealous, angry, and selfish. They not only argue and cause trouble, but they are envious. They get drunk carry on at wild parties, and do other evil things as well. I told you before, and am telling you again: No one who does these things will share I the blessings of God's kingdom.
> God's Spirit makes us loving, happy, peaceful, patient, kind, good, faithful, gentle, and self-controlled. There is no law against behaving in any of these ways. And because we belong to Christ

Jesus, we have killed our selfish feelings and desires. God's Spirit has given us life, and so we should follow the spirit. But don't be conceited or make others jealous by claiming to be better than they are.

God please keep me separated from any thing that is connected to the squashing of Your little ones, plants, and animals, anything that would injure the weak and the helpless already so preyed upon by the worlds societies. Already so used as a stepping-stone to greatness for the powerful.

Satan comes to destroy, but I come to uplift—or get out. Yes, that's right. If I cannot uplift and instead come to doing the reverse— becoming a detriment to humanity, I'll get out. Leave it all.

This work is nothing as it stands beside the greatest of works but I pray it will stand among them anyway, & I will not be forgotten --- maybe by humankind--- but not in our Creator's book of Life.

51.
So, this idea for DOC has just been written down. The actual physical structure of it may be set up in a year, or it may never materialize. This depends on the ability, energy and stability of those who get involved.

As previously stated, God has showed me I have a big heart. Yet I drive people away from me! I can't start this thing—only write about it!

Well gosh! Since I don't have balls enough to do the work of beginning DOC I will just go forth & do small works of love & help around the community wherever I go and will itemize them in this on-going Journal, in Volume 5. This plus keep my ever-perpetual vow of poverty/semi-poverty. Here is an example:

>WORKS, Journal Volume 5.
>Today as usual walked and did not consume gasoline in a car or busses. Fed pigeons on route. Held dogs at the shelter. Wrote stuff for people to read in my Journal.

If I can do nothing more I'll just do this & only dream about the Order—and do Gods writing from that Great Mind, poured into my lowly one*, and Its many different offshoots, you yourselves, each doing according to their gifts.

> *Is it not the water jug that fills the pitcher,
> & not visa versa?*

The Lord(ess) Jesus Christ has told me regarding DOC that the heart & soul of these 3 books, are complete (JOURNEY 2, 3, 4) nothing more may be added or subtracted from it & any confusion will be explained by cross-referencing what is already in these works.

If more commentary is necessary it can be found in Addendum to the Midrash—a self-contained volume.

What is one singular purpose of DOC? ----Must repeat:

> --Regarding One Purpose of DOC. God has a great sorrow for this human race S/He has created because its so fucked up. The church/synagogue/mosque is all that keeps some people living. But as a young adult I did not know that. Maybe DOC can help introduce a few of the agnostic children of earth to the Heart of the Almighty.

Remember it is good to attach yourself to a spiritual body of uplifting Light.

There is trouble for those who wander off the Path.

    ***

I don't know if this is true for any one else, but born again Christians coming to Jewish synagogue and perusing God there—seeing the root of the Christian tree, Judaism's strong trunk, the first covenant made by Elohim with humans; see in fulfillment the early pages of the pageant turned back in illumination in Holy Torah scrolls; but personally it drive me wild with inspiration; it sets me on fire to pray!

Well Dear Children, I've not forgot my messianic rants & politics of the earlier chapters of JOURNEY, chiefly found in Volume 1, which first appeared to public light buried by sections in my Sci-Fi Trilogy (those first 3 books from the Unity of Utopia series). I've come thru a lot-- & people did it. You know! —Ordinary people, our brothers & sisters. It's always on the backdrop of the rich—whose vociferous acts of greed we've come to accept for so long as being the root of the source of much of our suffering & pain—our poverty, our insecurity, our powerlessness—upon which that these petty interpersonal DRAMA's are played out---yes, and it's these, these little barbs of rage which we treasure in memory; the grand jealousy and backbiting between us, we, the average powerless/powerful citizens, the axes with which we give WHACKS to each other, overlaid upon the steel fascist framework of societal structure, that wear us down & cause us to exit the battlefield before the battle is even begun.

--Regarding the Compassionate City of Help, it cannot be a business-as-usual city—we cannot import tourist rich who laze about slurping coffee lates, turning business stock/bond dates via cellphone even tho they do try to be polite, carefully driving along in hybrid Suburban non-Utility Vehicle's—all who enter the Compassionate City of Help must relinquish the excess of material goods they have.

2009. Stock Market Crash! All the big corporations start pulling in their horns, the depression is on! Vacant stores up and down thoroughfares, soup lines everywhere, more homeless cocooned in blue blankets then you could ever imagine even at its worst in the first decade of the new millennium. *Babylon is falling!*

So off we go! Eviction right around the corner! Well children I guess I'm on the road. Just like the Beats first indicated to us the Way in the 1950's with dharma bums and new age enlightenment to standard black & white Amerikkka, on the flickering newly popularized TV sets. I guess I'm on the road, in Journey to the most High, Creator of heaven and earth and the universe expanding. I'm on the road, bowing freely, hands uplifted, nose pressed into the dirt of the road to submit myself to the Creators Will, to relinquish all worldly stuff. Jews seek Her/His Holy Torah, they are on the road. Join me, we will travel together to see His/Her face. —On the road, our Allah will come to us. I call upon all you of Islam; worship and bow with me now to the most High Allah. I call upon all you Hebrews to bow down to the One now, your Most High One, unnamable, Elohim, bow down with me. I call upon all you Christians to bow down with me right now, as we travel the road. Call upon the witches & pagans to bow down with me now to the most high Mother Goddess in prayer and supplication to save Her strange & beautiful & rare collection of humans, animals, the environment, the earth/sky and sea. For all its stumbling & failures this is a Holy Book.

I go in the Hebrew house and worship at the root and the trunk of the Great Tree. I go in the church house and worship in its branches thru which God reaches out to re-include all the peoples of earth back into Her Source. I am a saint and very much a sinner. God is alive! God Who is:

Alpha and omega the beginning and the end.

And me? I'm Transman Red, prophet, master author, fine arts oil painter, head-nigga-in-charge, faithful fool, mystic, visionary....and I'm On The Road!

Red Jordan Arobateau
July 2, 2007
4:00 AM Pacific Standard Time
San Francisco, CA
USA

WORKS
Journey 5

You shall serve God.

E' vdu et Hashem Adonai.

Meditations On The Lord

You must pant for God
 Like a wild horse.
You must paw up the earth
In a frantic search,
 For the Most High.
You do realize that don't you
Dear Children?
I have told you so by now,
Great passions for the Almighty
 Will not go unrewarded.
The cool calm collected minds of contemplatives,
Steadfast and good,
Is most pleasing to God.
But the ardent lover whose passions
Do not burn out over time, and in fact
 Renew and increase, must be especially
Cherished in God's Heart.
S/He Who Is passion in power;
 Who Is Love incarnate.

52.
So the Order must begin. The work now is to set it up.

> Well gosh! Since don't have balls enough to do the work of beginning DOC, will just go forth & do small works of love & help around the community wherever I go. & will itemize them in this on-going Journal.

Now, after all the drama of my group & pain of my entire life—still seems I'm marching up The Great Highway. ----Well I guess at some point I'll have to turn in my set of horns & fangs; and only wear my halo around town.

> Today as usual walked and did not consume gasoline by taking cars or busses. Fed pigeons on route. Held dogs. Wrote stuff for people to read.

> Midrash, Journey #4., 2007

Marcus, Native Indian brother speaks of the Red Road. To always seek the higher path in things—there is a great blessing in that. To look upon those who injury you with compassion, even pity—instead of the former hate.

You walk down the Kings Highway taking all disappointments in a stride. Time repairs the hurts. Encouragement from the Great One. So now I'm walking up the Kings Highway, doing Works both small and those larger & maybe great. On my way to visit penned dogs @ the shelter; pink tongues lapping, panting, leaping up vertically in their cells to gain more space---grabbing split seconds of freedom in mid air. All because they have no homes. Attending services @ Synagogue, Church, plus Torah & Bible study, adding my number to the roles of the dedicated flock.

***

Some works are contemplative and many are orders of intercessory prayer. This will be a service Order. DOC. (Daughters Of Courage.) Our, rasion de etre is to serve Jesus Christ (or the Spirit of Love) thru doing service to the weakest humans & animal kind. This is the reason for DOC as a group. And it is the second of our two vows, the other being Poverty. God wastes nothing. I see more about the vow of poverty. —It strengthens you. You see the weakness of those who follow money. So to take on poverty not only makes us one with the poor and oppressed of earth, which is a victory in the political sense, but it does, simultaneously as each day passes in economic struggle, give an enlightened vision. We see the wasteful and mean ways the rich behave, and its futility. And finally, poverty strengthens our inner self—once it is not dependant on any material substance. We grow to spiritual giants, those others remain dwarves, locked into wealth, with artificial money fusing into their physical being so as unreal stuff is fastened to the real, and is a direct pipeline of poison into the higher mind.

Children you are not alone in your poverty! Half the world joins you and greets you with warm affections!

Service is our call, and in addition we are bound together by religious belief, not simply personal or political mandates—we are inclusive, open to all seeking Creator, weather they yet have found Her/Him or not.

An admonishment to the many who may not yet believe, al la Dorothy Day who set up communal living houses across America:

> Saint Dorothy Day—a common day saint (Just Beautified by the Catholic Church—the first step to becoming an official Saint) who set up her socialist communities in Christian houses all across America in the starving post-depression years of the 1930's. She insisted that religious love & stewardship of God, as well as social

programs must go hand in hand. Programs which included unionizing, feeding the poor, day care for children of working mothers, printing & distribution of their radical newspaper the Daily Worker etc. Periodically she'd go storming around the nation disbarring houses that had fallen into spiritual neglect!
Daughters Of Courage—2007, from The Story Of Dorothy Day.

And still am seeking The Path for my life—my higher life. This is a life beyond the plan set down in private mathematical calculations of your Social Security payments plus whatever you can save or earn by some business you can start online, or picking thru trash cans in the street & recycling metal cans et al, to augment your income and continue to rent a room in the high-priced rent mogul controlled fascist metropolises of America waning in it's Last Days; Babylon Falling--- this is life beyond what you had aimed for as a child, then an adult… something more… something even further than your struggle to master the techniques of Great Art so your spirit could soar, and others who read/see this art could also be uplifted…

Am with the rest of us seeking…. seeking… where will I find it?

Unlimited expectations in the great Cathedral of your mind.

***

Stopped by Fields Bookstore on Polk Street, on the way to the Fools this afternoon. It is the last bookstore alive on Polk Strassa, after one went out of business in retirement, and the other, a small crammed bookstore with stacks to the ceiling ceased to be when its owner died unexpectedly at a very young age.

Death is ever with us. Living death of the walking zombies among us, their awful specter urges us desperately to find better ways to live. Picked up one of the Tibetan Buddhist teachings, here's the jest of it remembered: The Path means the path to enlightenment, and transcendence of this world. There are steps. One is to discipline the natural self. The natural self has aversion, anger (and something else I can't remember!) But in the higher self, aversion would be transformed into inclusion. The anger at someone, would be turned into love and compassion for the one making you angry.

To do these things is the first footsteps on The Path.

Later this evening, Alex from Faithful Fools speaks of interdependence, as opposed to independence, at the Fools monthly Round Table potluck. Transman Red testifies that he has learned independence in his life, (thru bitter suffering) but wants to learn interdependence. That is working in community which loners find so difficult.

To live harmoniously in community will be to our great joy.

   ***

Found this searching for something to read at my show; it was written 1967-'77, and is from Champagne, Firecrackers, Gunshots, & The Smoke From The Death Factory; it is a diary of those times, one of the few I ever kept. At the time being 23.

I cannot help but think I have a dream. My mother & father paid for that dream in their blood. I have a paintbrush in my hands, colors flow across canvass. When despair is around me, and the plaster is falling down and no money it means little, because I have a dream. A skill that will put me thru the world. Not everyone has this dream—mine was given to me. Encouraged as a child. Sent to a good school. But my people paid dearly for that dream. They paid in blood and racial segregation. They paid in having doors slammed & insults hurled—from both black & white. They paid in electro-shock treatment, and the infirmities of old age. They paid in being fat, in being week. Some paid by not being pleasing of face. The payment has come due in me, and I'm taking it all! Thru this work of mine! When I see the looks of the faces of my people I get so mad. I know each drop of blood will be exacted in payment. And God will do that, my hands aren't big enough. The brush isn't strong enough, there aren't enough colors—my eyesight is poor—only God knows all the guilty. They are of both sides. God will get the vengeance! When I see pink clouds brushstroked across the sky, I know God is painting the picture. When I see hollowness in the eyes of my people who have lost their souls I know the stones will cry out—because something has silenced our mouths. The stones will cry out! When I hear the silence of seasons turning—can't you hear it? The vast wheel of the universe turning & recording everything; I *know* all things will be righted. All wrongs will be paid back in full & more. Can't you hear it? When the air is very very still? ---That is when the guilty should fear most. When those committing hurt should stop—and listen. Listen in the wind!

53.
Well another trans disaster. Another tranny football fumble. First, that tragedy of the Play—4 months of fun, 5 weeks of sheer hell, then it died. & now my Wednesday social group is falling apart. Split down the middle with me hunkered down in battle on one side & them on the other, howling & pointing the accusatory finger of scorn. —Literally. The small core of the group is going to be meeting across from me at my lonely table! This is why people come to fist fights. They at least could have the decency to meet in a different location! They at least out of respect for me holding my group 4.5 years could meet at a different place! Not right across the room from me! And have told them so pointedly and vociferously, nearly yelling. And I'm going to set up a religious Order? HA! Another big tranny joke!

Way they did it was so shoddy—should have suspected, at first when that evening started off it was a very large, nice group. 2 guys turned up we hardly ever saw, they made their appearance—just to be there when all sided against me, they all got up and met over on the other side of the room. Leaving one stray. The two of us talked briefly, but the minute I went over to the restroom he leaves also.

The backbiting, wreathing pit of snakes—this sad affair of my group will fade away.

> The Prophet: So I have been knocked around by God.
>
> God: Getting you into shape.
>
> Prophet: Aggrrughh.
>
> The Spirit: Spiritual Shape.

After the cold & treacherous way I've been treated by this trans community can only say the TS/TG community Sucks The Big One

Its funny just how life just when think life's getting nearly good to be true— it is. Find your world set on end. —In a matter of days. Of hours! Some fateful event—maybe one prewritten by a mistake you've made long ago—some fateful event with long lasting repercussions strikes.

So the Transman was left to return to his work.

I think about women in childbirth, infants torn from their bodies in a blood bath. And my art, torn from my mind, out of angst, pain, as a subliminal escape from the world. Hours at dawn I'd still be writing. The work torn out of my life—work for pay neglected, evictions subsequent. Torn out of my happiness. No wife, because of no stability of money.

I have an extra purpose. A purpose beyond the natural functions given to humankind. It is to let them know without shadow of any doubt that God wants them back. God wants them back for S/He put breath into all souls. She wants them back! All what She has made & all beings will be reconciled to Her. Any shadow of a doubt, anything in heaven under heaven written, postulated, theorized or explained, is secondary to this knowledge!

All souls are reconciled to God. Even the dragons with their tongues lashing out, and eyes gleaming love God! They rest under Gods Arm, in a beautiful dragon place S/He has built for them. All shall love God.

Maybe I'll just drift away into Gods Arms after I written as much as I've written and said everything I can say.

@ Benedictines tonight we had the following scripture—and this showed me Christ's wish for me, as one of my Works, to go further in the aid of a fallen soul. As the explanation states:

What does Jesus' story tell us about true love for one's neighbor? First, we must be willing to help even if others brought trouble on themselves through their own fault. Second, our love and concern to help others in need must be practical. Good intentions and empathizing with others are not enough. Third, our love for others must be as wide as Gods love. No one is excluded. God's love in unconditional. So we must be ready to do good to others for their sake, just as God is good to us. Are you ready to lay down your life for your neighbor?

> A man was going down from Jerusalem to Jericho, and fell into he hands of robbers, who stripped him, beat him, and went away, leaving him half dead. Now by chance a priest was going down that road; and when he saw him he passed by on the other side. So likewise a Levite, when he came to the place and saw him, passed by on the other side. But a Samaritan while traveling came near him; and when he saw him, he was moved with pity. He went to him and bandaged his wounds, having poured oil and wine on them. Then he put him on his own animal, brought him to an inn, and took care of him. The next day he took out two denari, gave them to the innkeeper, and said, "Take care of him; and when I come back, I will repay you whatever more you spend. Which of these three, do you think, was a neighbor to the man who fell into the hands of the robbers? He said, the one who showed him mercy.' Jesus said to him, 'go and do likewise.'
>
> Luke 10 25-37

There's all kinds of things discovered while working with these Christians, the Benedictines. For instance: (After all things in heaven above or earth beneath; after all is said and done here is the last word, the final call! --- End final to all ends!) Above the niche which holds Our Savior being ministered to by 4 virgins each ensconced in her own small comparatment baring incense, salve, harp and lyre; in gold above the encasing of it all there is a DUCK! Yes! A duck—a fowl! Large breasted, from beneath which peek 3 tiny ducklings! This is the framework—in gold, which houses Jesus Christ! *A Duck niche!* A duck of solid gold and her 3 baby ducklings. QUACK! QUACK!

So I have no idea if the howling banshees will be after me at my little group this coming Wednesday, I've been sickish with stomach upset—maybe a tinge of the incipient cold/flu fought off last week… Plus all this stress.

TS community can say no acts of kindness goes unpunished. Twice I attempted a work, which involved community. The play* (PORTRAITS OF A GHETTOIZED POPULATION) & this group. Most people do the work of their family and that's it. To set ones self into the involvement of setting up a work involving other people—which influences lives— hoping for fun, and to give their labor towards this goal, is an unusual person and not a common one. Both the play and now the group maybe have been cut down at the end with bitterness. Will I go back to the life of a private world, with individual fun on a private basis with a few friends, a lover maybe and involved with events pre set up by some entrepreneur or religious groups, the private life of a writer?

Strange how attacks come from everywhere just when I have concretized this Order into its booklets—at long last, after having envisioned it roughly 11 years ago, plus designed that lovely wooden sign with the Maltese Cross, our emblem and holy words, a photograph of which exists in the Bancroft I'm sure. Well had just finished constructing a very sturdy loft for the end of my kitchen, upon which to store crap, with a den underneath for the computer---- when more hideous disaster strikes----the former owner of Little Mr. Fluffy, my 15 year old cat *wants to take him back!* Why? To show his sister on her stopover this weekend---seems he's been lying to her, claiming my cat is still living with him, and now must prove he still is keeping him as promised! This gay man took care of Fluffy the best possible way—by giving him up to me, realizing that he wasn't a good caretaker because of favoring his dog who chased the cat, and etc. Anyway, cats do not like to be moved! Once they settle into their territory it is a crime to move them unnecessarily, especially a 15-year old cat. And all over a stupid lie he has to tell! The cat's well-being is at stake! Fluffy has already been de-clawed by someone in his past—a murderous procedure for the ease of humans, and to the pain and discomfort and disempowerment of the beast.

I am having to fight this man and the spouse of my ex, who is siding with him. She vows never to help me again if I don't give up the cat. This is terrible news, as they have bought me little coffees before and bestowed on me the egress of their rampant materialism—cast off computers, out of date televisions, bookcases which have fallen out of favor. I don't trust this man with the cat now, he might never return Fluffy—so as to have him ready to show his sister anytime she comes into town! I have called the police department in advance, and been advised what to do. This is shit.

A façade is something for instance extra wood in a lovely design fixed to the front of a building—something that is a frontispiece with empty air behind. —It's made to look nice--& nothing else. Serves no other earthly use but for a show. Façade. This is what many so-called friends prove to be.

Everything is turned into poison.

We are the sheep of His/Her pasture, but all are not treated that-a-way. They been abused by everybody. From anybody who says they were a friend, down to everybody who showed they were an enemy.

We must forgive all who attack us, so one might say it is wise to avoid trouble least it uncover some enemy who offend ourselves. No service is without risk. So we must go out to troublesome places, and I must continue my work no matter what—despite the failures and having to once again dig a new foundation, make a new beginning.

Luckily I have prayed to God for protection in advance @ The Benedictines this evening!

Now these two hate me-for not capitulating to make their lives easier! Transman Red gazed down at the furry white/grey/tan being. And he asked Fluffy if he wanted to go back there—for a few days--- and the cat told Red *"No! I like it here with you!"* And am terrified they would try to keep him, as before stated!!!!!

Am I being opposed spiritually by the dark forces because of my efforts in writing up the handbook for Daughters of Courage, and it's subsequent, explanatory Midrash? Regarding spiritual opposition wise people say, do something great for God & you will be highly opposed. Often this spiritual position can operate thru your personal weakness---my anger and the manner in which I went about dismissing this troubled person from the group, would be a perfect example.

Finally, to wrap up the current episode of all this opposition, I find out in tonight's Benedictines the Maltese Cross was the emblem of the Templers. This Christian Order of soldier-monks was set up to guard the roads pilgrims took on their necessary journeys to visit religious shrines and pray. This Holy Order lasted several hundred years. They came to an end when they were attacked and murdered. Thousands of them killed, all over Europe where they were stationed in all parts of the continent on the Holy roads, and all on the same day! One might marvel how organized were the vandals who slaughtered them! Guess why! The Templers were wiped out with one fell blow—around 1100 ACE—by the clerical higher ups who wanted to end their reign & their power. The king's soldiers were dispatched to ambush the Templers wherever divisions of their Order were, and killed them all!

The true reason? —Politics. The reason given—'they were practicing paganism'. Which was probably not true. Politics, and some one wanting to seize power was the reason! The charge of Practicing Black Magic was a common accusation of the times. — Just as the charge hurled at radicals, or revolutionary minded activists of 'not being patriotic' has been the last several hundred years. An excuse, a construct in the temple of the unreal, built of lumber of evil.

*PS, it is from that mass murder—on a Friday the 13th—purposefully staged in accordance to astrological consultation by the church, that this day bares it's ominous significance.

54.
What have you lost? Asks the Lord.

A place to go on a Wednesday… A place to go & yell on a Wednesday. Was Red's reply.

Just a month earlier had been looking inside self and privately conjecturing was this, the self I preferred to remain? Yelling, banging the table with my fist so the coffee cups shook?

God was ready for me to proceed on with my life…. Cuts out the dead wood. A new broom sweeps clean.

People are rushing here & there going off on long distances, when here I see my sister in a long black coat, hiding her deformities; head bowed, face turned aside so as not to be seen.

Must forgive others & forgive yourself. If we can do one than we can do the other.

  ***

At synagogue helped with oneg and opened doors of the holy scrolls on bema. Carefully kept to diet so can live a longer life—of service.

Freud says that dreams are the royal road to the unconscious. Think back. Back when I was young and unwritten on. Had a powerful dream in which I mobilized a group of young people to begin work on one of my plays (or turned it into a movie script.) Time marches on, with it, healing. New chances for fresh beginnings.

55.
Did I say Faithful Fools leader Carman loaned Alex their van to drive me to the lumberyard, where this young man was invaluable in me selecting wood, by helping pull out the heavy stock beam by beam to select the best pieces. Got materials to construct the loft, as of this writing it stands in the end of my kitchen, giving me essentially a new room. Upon it all the crap I need to keep, plus a space for canvasses, canvass, stretchers, oil paintings etc. Underneath, an eating table with additional computer. My small priests monastic studio has grown another room! Dr. Martinez at the clinic tells the story of a friend who dwelled in one tiny room in this rent-exhausting city. A room in one of the high-ceiling Victorians. How proud he was to have built a loft, now his space has doubled in size!

The members of the Order will have a storage locker of ample size—like a walk in closet about 3 feet across and 3 deep, extending floor to ceiling which will not be used to live in nor sleep in nor for live animals; on the premises of their House, and it will be periodically and regularly visited, unexpectedly by the prior in accompaniment with one other member plus the 'owner' in attendance, as a checkpoint for unwanted contraband, since this storage locker will ordinarily be in an out-of the way place not open to viewing.

There will be no nudity in the houses. At their most unclothed state the members may walk around in proper shorts (not underwear) which are not tight fitting or too short, so as to reveal nor pronounce genitalia, plus a shirt or tee-shirt, and in sandals. No bare feet.

> Oh Master, from the mountain side.
> Make haste to heal these hearts of pain'
> Among these restless throngs abide,
> To tred the city's streets again;
>
> Till all the world shall learn thy love,
> And follow where they feet have trod;
> Till glorious from thy heaven above
> shall come the city of our God.
>
> Hymn 609, Gardiner.

Wrote this down to illustrate more evidence of this city of compassionate help which earth-citizens must attempt to build, even before the Coming of Our Savior, in the End times.

Daughters of Courage is a Holy Order, but we must remember, not offices or institutions—only God, Jesus* is holy. (Mohammad, Buddha, etc.)

    ***

I got to this city 40 years ago; on the human hand, 4 fingers; in November, exactly; it is now July. The timeclock of God moves steady, surely, without a pause. The Almighty knows what came before, what will come. It is all written. Her timing is exact.

Fillmore Street is full of long legged whites. Not a black ghetto anymore. Only 1 black person to be seen walking. This is 2007. The changeover is complete. 1970's it was teeming with blacks laughing, angry, dangerous, musical. Gentrification—a mild form of genocide—that is cultural suicide. In which the former residences of a peoples are razed, and new structures priced way beyond their means to obtain are built and sold off to an alien peoples with far more capital.

1994-95 there was a brief period of time, which I'm one with the gay literary scene heralding my trashy dike novels for sale professionally published. Which could be found at all major bookstores, and minor. They were at A Different Lights bookstore on Castro Street; I also did quite a few readings there. The women's sex clubs (1991-'93) were fresh in memory. Raunchy sex pussy cock dike trashy novels full of emotional angst action, adventure, class, race, profanity, love, spirituality. In them here is all vanished like a castle of the mind its flame extinguished yet still burning perpetually, a history growing more distant. They are kept alive by a used book business which still remains over the internet and at dusty booksellers trader remainders among piles of trade paperback books. The golden Hay Day, we thought it would never end—once finally begun back with women's liberation publishing in the 1970's as we struggled to get a piece in one of the few dike rags, and cut contracts, advances, duefully mailing off submissions to several liberal publishers and the gay press. I was lucky Richard Kasak liked my work and presented 8 of my novels, which still circulate thru the underground market.

So at age 63, this is my greatest and finest Work, beside art and my prophetic writings, it is service.

Ideally one engaged in service is capable of being engaged in a social context, and are not dead to the world, blind, deaf and insensitive to it. So self-absorbed and preoccupied with themselves & their problems so that it renders their service ineffective and everything they do winds up stinking up the place, fouling up everything so it must be redone.

Lot of people are not just brain-dead, but being stuck & belligerently stuck. Stupidly stuck & mean about it. The world has not gone their way want it to, so they sit down & won't lend a helping hand to anybody or for any cause.

For instance a woman asks that the windows might be closed because the bus is cold, but a man sits there, unmoving, unhelpful.

Well I guess I've retired from the world and entered into the Holy Life. My whole weeks are spent between Torah study, Shabbat, and Grace and her various projects—church services, feeding the poor, senior program, bible study; and finally volunteering at the animal shelter and my private art work. One day the Order will be set up on a similar schedule—part of our call & duty is to participate in the religious life of the communities among us; service, and to accomplish those gifts given to us for the betterment of Creators human kingdom.

It does not belong in the human genome to have any ghettos. That is a human construct, of apartheid, of exclusion, of segregation—of making outcasts. We all belong together in a functioning whole. We queers must find our rightful places amid the whole greater community! DOC will go everywhere!

Most of the Torah takes place in the desert. During the Hebrew people's journey it is the primary narrative, recited in the Pentetude.* (Which is also the first 5 books of the Holy Bible.) There are nomadic cultures, such as gypsy's, some Arabic tribes-people, etc., whose whole community forever travel on the road, having stability from being surrounded by their caravans and contained by their own vehicles, but with little connection to the lands thru which they pass. But to hit the road helter-skelter like a divorced troubadour severed from your troupe, not knowing where you are going, with no historic guidance-- your people have never having been there before to have imparted their oral telling in your mind-- having few supplies, nor friends to accompany is not a life to raise a child with, nor one of adult happiness. We will be an apostolic and monastic Order. Those meant for travel will travel inside the apostolic Orders having fun in commune, those meant to work the fields (figuratively) and reap the harvest they've planted therein are monastic, stationary to place.

   ***

   Let them prefer nothing whatever to Christ, and may He bring us altogether to everlasting life.

   Rules of Benedict Chapter 72

Not all in our Order are able to take this wonderful saying, which I embrace as my own. Each religious discipline within the Order will have their own wonderful sayings to share with the others of us. Judaic, Islamic, Wiccian, Buddhist, those of the Red Road—which is wisdom from Native Worship Circles.

There is so much love in the world. Especially in the prayers of children. God uses them to illustrate love, because children still have so much love in them. Our Order is mandated to pray often, & at regular, appointed times. We must learn to pray in the mindset of children at some point of our meditations. Because tho we are equals as adults, we must be as a child before God.

53.
>Kerie eleison.
>Christe eleison.
>Kerie eleison.
>
>*Lord, have mercy.*
>*Christ, have mercy.*
>*Lord, have mercy.*

Music is one of the most powerful ways God engages the human spirit. During this lovely chant of choir/congregation @ Grace I cannot help from almost crying it is so beautiful.

>There is only one art—truth.
>Only one race—human.
>
>Rev. Mary Hadad quoting @ Grace.

I have spoke of my Order and showed the DOC Handbook to several @ Grace—clergy—who are not a bit interested. The Holy Spirit wisely instructs me:

>*Show it to the common people first, then they (*the higher ups*) will listen.*

Here is a computer note from June 2007:

'Sunday bring my books to show XXX'. Sadly this 'XXX' has never remembered to ask about my Order & what I had said. The highest thing shall be the lowest. Mary sits at the feet of Christ, listening to every word! ----While Martha bustles about at the holy alter with holy dishes and chelsers, hymn books and cincture, fussing with cleric collars and robes; all the ecclesiastic traipsing; lip-syncing her sermon in the mirror, preparing for the grand day On Stage before a rapturous congregation!

Tried to engage a priest who spent 25 years in monastery in conversation about his experience, but he would not. Dared not show it (DOC) at Temple—because of the Orders name—although in meaning DOC is for the Hebrews and all other Tribes too, being an egalitarian discipline, it just that Daughters was given to me thru prayer in Christ, henceforth it's title.

54.
Rehash of the first awful meeting of my Wednesday social club, after the Grand Conflagration.

Way they did it—should have suspected, very large, nice group. 2 guys turned up we hardly ever saw, they made their appearance; then all sided against me, they all got up and met over on the other side of the room, just leaving one shy chap. But the minute I went over to the restroom he leaves also.

Regarding one of the 5 or 6 so-called 'brothers' who turned against me in the ex-group; Indian brother Marcus again; *forgive him brother meet him half way. Humility don't come easy.* Flying fuck! So Humility is part of the JOURNEY of walking down the Kings Highway! Taking the Red Road. It's amazing how far a person can go while walking slowly & how fast. Irregardless of sore foot, heavy weight of book bag… plus the great weight of pride & prejudice! Yes, and I'm still walking!

Group night once again. Am ensconced in my familiar spot. None of the old guys show their faces. However one of the T girls and the MTF person in question around whom all this brouhaha has centered do arrive. Alpha Male energy? The one looms over my table, a dark shadow wrapped in a full length coat to mask her male/female persona so questionable in daylight society; informing me why she is dropping out of the group. A highly unnecessary production!

Regarding these two T girls who showed up, just to sit over on the other side of the room. Am advised by friends; do you remember how it was when you had Estrogen in your body? How moody and emotional you were? Well combine this with the energy of an Alpha male and this is the transsexual woman, the former male's—problem. Enough about this group already! Will try to remember what I learned today—to share it with you Dear JOURNEY, *Journal… Diary of days…*

> You can keep going along, day after day, and all you are is a human life with a spirit stuck inside it, or you can live life of the spirit realizing we only inhabit this body for a very short time.
>
> --Marcus, 2007.

So the Work has suddenly grown huge… my work is to release all of these miscreants back into the cosmos. To forgive… yes forgive them & move on with my life. This is a discipline. Must concentrate on forgiveness!

***

The prophetic voice must do both; present the doom & nightmare, and also the good, the reward, the beautiful dream… I will soon present this benevolent face of fate to you, and introduce the Sheep. The higher evolved human who wears from time to time, the white or beige natural fabric cowl of DOC with her red Maltese Cross.* (See later book for adaptations for Multi-Faith members.)

This Sheep will become the unnamed protagonist of JOURNEY in its final chapters.

Fall; winter. I'm exhausted all in the telling but hard-won roses await—just around the next corner I'm sure! Dozens and dozens of red roses! Rich red, with their pungent scent filling the rooms of my life!

Part of life's red roses are your romantic affairs. Regarding my former wife, Jasmin, to remind you readers, in our 16 year marriage for all the dysfunction—chiefly economics---I was happy with her, lying in bed side by side, cozy and warm. Now am alone. For all my spiritual search, high art, busy religious activities and volunteerism, it's still not a life—but it's a survival.

Had I made the leap, into the life of a monastic, I would rule out romance of a personal level, exchanging it for the dance of the divine. IE (From Midrash--Regarding Rules & Vows of DOC;):

> Consider one of the traditional orders, chiefly of the past; an order so severe, that monks rarely talk…lying on their bed of poverty, alone, enduring decade after decade of coldness & hunger. This is how they lived out their days on earth. In stark isolation, possessing nothing, having no families, no loved ones, no warm press of flesh against their own. Meditating on the Lord alone. Finding sustenance in their Divine Creator only. Nourished in the thin wafer of bread, and sip of a cup.
>
> *We danced together in their visions.*
> --Jesus Christ.

But being not this extremely dedicated, nor high-minded, nor I guess as Hungry for Christ… nor as passionate… here I suffer, stuck in the common world. Desiring things of flesh, which will soon pass away. In emotional respects the monastic life is safer… even as it is more severe.

Regarding worship: the Holy Road, the Royal Road, the Red Road. For the care and worries of this world, its just a big step up into the palm of Gods hand—and this road is available instantaneously to us to access, that's the meaning of it—the higher path. To attain this we must first release the old garbage, then take the step! Devotes do this on a minute-to-minute basis, they do it every few days in mediations and spiritual retreats. Mystics, and monastics, cloistered nuns do it over a lifetime—purposely shunted away from common life. The Daughters of Courage will do this in the Houses of the Order, yet while maintaining service for the common world in which we go out into the ordinary realm to do good deeds, and to worship along with various congregations of faith surrounding us in these big falling cities of Babylon—on every continent. American, European, Asian, African, Islander. Worshiping along with Hebrew, Christian, Muslim, Buddhist, Native, and Others.

One more note on the asceticism of priests, tonight at the Benedictian Worship heard the accusation of one radical Christian that churches today are vehicles of ease and comfort, *'they are rose & lily churches, where you get the milk and honey, forgiveness, happiness, peace and everything is fine in the world. But everything in this world isn't ok! How can the church go out on brave acts of justice when it has fallen asleep?'*

Somewhere in the city an ambulance wailing from another sector, fire alarm clangs, death waits behind these noises of alarm in confluence of sounds at the top of cathedral hill. A jetplane, dark, sinister, takes off out of the distant horizon speeding vertically up on powerful wings while a smaller silver plane traverses horizontally over the blue/white sky at a slower pace. The military jet eats up distance much more rapidly like a giant bird with enormous wings compared to a much smaller one with far less wing span. I think of people in foreign lands strafed by jet planes of war, murdered by U$ military might. All the accoutrements people encumber themselves with-- to protect them—yet at the hour of our death, nothing can protect us! And from who? The Hand of our God?

Pronouncing herself the moon stands ½ naked upon a rippled cloud sky like the fur of a wooly sheep ½ half hiding, ½ disclosing, open & pronouncing all this to the world, the universe!

A figure lays on a marble slab nearly naked but for a cloth wrapped about its loins and chest. This marble slab is an alter, it is raised up above the common world. This figure is the priest. This is education, deep waters, solitary, what is needed to find God.

Here is another of life's red roses. To be appreciated by all! In my fantasy I'd sit by a pool in plaid shorts, sandals with friends & people, going in and out of the water and food cooked on an outdoor grill; all kinds of wonderful foods & in the evening we'd go to an auditorium; me in my best suit and tie up on a podium seated/standing & read aloud out of a stack of my books then I'd be heralded for my great works!

***

Well regarding the present state of my life it is going out into greater, wider circles. Finally emerging from the transsexual ghetto. And in so doing, the castle walls grow higher. Let me illustrate:

I have been making friendships with people here & there; my volunteerism, the neighborhood rad bookstore, all kinds of places; @ Grace; thus slowly the noose tightens—it is natural—people come closer to your private life—and the transsexual walls go up. Women of your age group make themselves available---but you don't pick up on their cue. Because it means perhaps physical intimacy will grow out of it—and then you must disclose. "Aw, geeze honey, uh, I don't have a dick." You retreat behind the walls of your non-self disclosure & that's when others back away, finding you strangely cold ….go elsewhere. And you become a Transman locked inside a crystal castle. See them Transman (or Transwoman) working, praying, helping—all behind their crystal walls-- with a sad smile in perpetuity etched on his face, you go about your work & endless duties of earth never touching anyone. Afraid to tell your truth, and its stark reality, the knowledge of which changes your position in people's eyes forever.

Must say—as a duel-sexed person that these problems of transsexuality are elemental ones—dealing specifically with ones genitals, and the state of their physical body---this on a societal scale when people are being murdered in war, and dying of starvation. But Jesus sees my great pain over my condition.

Transsexuality is a medical condition & should be treated as a medical condition not a condition of sin, not one of guilt or shame as it is put upon one. It is something one discovers about ones self usually very early in life and is not one chosen.

It suddenly dawns on me words of my diary JOURNEY may one day be read by those in the monastic life. Those who have kept vows of celibacy, and silence, and denial. Who have severed themselves from human family and human comforts and so to these my words might have greater meaning, in that I too have been alone also, severely so---tho in my case it was not by choice. Because of deprivation of human family in the ordinary world. & I have suffered additional isolation because of my small mental illness which serves to separate me from the average person who finds me strange, and doesn't want to have any contact with me. I want to tell you that the Holy Spirit of God and Jesus both have been a great comfort to me!

For instance: I awoke this morning, Thursday, singing the hymn chosen by the prioress of the Benediction society at last Monday's meeting. Still half-asleep I opened the little curtain between my bed and the window a moment, then shut it. Jesus said to my soul *'am I intruding?'* "Never." I replied. "Never when I'm alone… When *we're* alone, I mean… when we're alone you're never intruding…" Although I don't wish to be exactly found speaking aloud to God in public… People of the world already think I'm strange enough!

One more note on this subject of the stranger, the outsider. My Therapist reminds me that since I have inhabited a queer space since about age, 3 when I demanded to cross-dress in tee shirts trousers and boots, maturing to inhabit a dike/gay ghetto for all of my teen years, twenties and thirties, and now as a poor, Out, public figure Transman—that I have always had freedom. In my poverty with no roles to play, no corporation dress codes to satisfy, no family inheritance to bargain away my freedom for, I have liberty.

55.
This summation probably should have appeared in Midrash (Journey Vol. 4) but didn't get it together until now. So here it is in Works, Journey Vol. 5. The Tattler—tell-all garbage littering my spiritual road; my human path littered with the corpses of more broken 'friendships'.

Summation of the nefarious events of the 'Group' a work, a chore just like writing that Beatniks piece drash was.

All I can say is these so-called 'transmen', they are still dikes, gender queers, processing, taking consensus among them, unable to take a radical individual stance; and the idea of a male figure dominating them as a hierarchal group is abhorrent, yet they will tolerate being dominated by a male alpha dict-atorial behavior when it is disguised in a womanly form. —IE, that fowl Transwoman I threw out!

It is unforgettable, these two male to females sit like large gnomes casting looks at me. Both exuding alpha white male energy. The sad thing is these 2 girls really do have inner women---and they are trompling all over her by their actions!

This whole affair has been pathetic. It serves to illustrate the ancient adage that females run from trouble, males meet it had on. Only in our case the women are suppose to be men and visa versa! And all of them are brats spoiling for a fight. I will not be part of this. Thanks in part to my Red Indian Brother, an Elder's advice to, *let it go brother, just step aside and see how far they catapult themselves, don't give them anymore energy;* and to my conversations with God in the weeks proceeding, and having then given it all over to God, all the sadness about this group which I once loved, had pride in and into which had interjected my love, energy, and prayers. All this now is the Creators to do with it what S/He Wills!

Finally on this subject, wonder what the straight population thinks of our community? Now one more person has seen it in action. The disgusted look on the face of the proprietor, who's watched our group grow with strange colorful genome-manipulated sex changes over the 2 years of his ownership, speaks volumes of disgust. Flitting around the corners of his mouth, where before was a friendly gaze and a curious look. What is he going to say about 'those people' to his friends when they compare shopkeeper notes at the end of a busy week?

At this point I'm sick of trannies. Male To Female Vs. Female to Male! And who is worse, better, and so forth. Its sort of like defending the snake against the cockroach—you don't want either one in your house.

Satan must be whooping & hollering in glee down in Hades, for He thrives on division and hate, God is sad because of our division. But in my heart it is not a lost cause, I still have love in my heart for the girls. These girls...*These girls*....

56.
White male tall, well dressed has a verbal exchange with the black toll taker lady in uniform at the subway booth. He is thanked for his coins deposited. I am not. Ire-regardless of my tie and shirt---I'm a second class citizen being short and colored. I don't want to be a superior alpha male, no, I just don't want to see these little ripples in the social current, in which I am treated differently.

The poor are so down-low they cannot see the overwhelming stark megastructure which looms overhead & beyond them. I was at ground zero today, the epicenter of condo conversion which is wracking the cities poor people and ejecting them generational, and by decades—OUT, until one sorry day the conversion will be complete—there will be no more poor here, and then, then the vans will come to take away all the street dwellers and this will be a perfect city. A perfect Hitler fascist Nazi economically purged metropolis of the first order in the new millennium. This structure Rincon Towers holds 2 million dollar condos for sale, and is one mile tall structure, now steel beams welded, pounded deep into bedrock for earthquake security, now steel beams welded like a scaffold up up up into the blue clouds and white sky, slowly puling up her skirts of glass, and mosaic facing like a prostitute ready to do business for the night ahead. This mile tall structure at lands end guards the foot of the SF peninsula at the Bay beside the blue grey waters, like Cerberus, guarded the portals of HELL.

God came back in the cool of the evening... don't forget Dear Children.

When Adam and Eve ate of the tree of the *knowledge of good and evil* God strolled back to the garden and saw them, nude, —covered in fig leaves—because they suddenly had the idea that they were naked and it was shameful, so Creator knew they had eaten the fruit S/He had instructed them not to touch. And Creator sure was mad. Mad! But holding Her peace She went away... Then came back in the cool of the evening to wreak vengeance. Issuing edicts from Her mouth: henceforth thou shalt work and labor and sweat and strain to bring forth bread out of the soil, etc., ---and thus all the sins, and travail and pain of earth began. So this is a parable to illustrate the calm before the coming storm. The death quiet in the eye of the hurricane...

Lamentations In The Cool Of The Evening, is a good title for this collection of JOURNEY—its first 5 books.

Return home to my family of Parrots and Cat & all my Works. He's a big strong guy. He's the biggest cat in the pack. He's the biggest cat I've had. Mr. Fluffy! One day he will reign in heaven on high like Little Miss Husky my 90 pound giant Dane/Shepherd, a giant among mere dogs. These royal beasts!

Returning to the theme of WORKS, what have I done these last few days? Gave my attendance and added to the necessity of roll calls and numbers to the pews of Shabbat @ Temple, Torah study, and Worship Service @ Grace 11 and 6 pm. Plus Benedictine Society, & Bible Study with Pastor Will. Sat with lonely, bored dogs. Prayed for many animals and people and for our lovely blue/green planet. Counseled a Latina TS acquaintance whom I know from the streets, encouraging her to follow her idea of getting a job. Encouraged two downhearted people @ Grace, and also counseled another woman about her job. Attendant & contributed to a focus group to train future health care providers about TG/TS needs and health issues. Up on the 8th floor of the Fox Plaza overlooking a beautiful view of the City. Wrote Journal, Vol. 5. Prayed & meditated on my slightly sick bed and was given the vision for the procedure for Healing as below described. I know healing exists with the powerful flow of force from God—as I experienced before during fasting and desperate prayer years ago in the late 1970's when I first received religious faith.

Oh, Learned in Torah study today that Deuteronomy (Devarim) was the first Torah the people listened to. It was the original book that Moses recited from to the priests and had it written down for the people—not Genesis. Thus, this Deuteronomy is not just a tacked-on afterthought, which repeats & repeats again all the stuff found in Genesis (Bereishit), Exodus (Shmot), Leviticus (Vayikra), Numbers

(Bamidbar), as it might seem to those pure readers of the Bible who read without instruction.

And listen to what we learned in Bible Study @ Grace: Essenes, a messianic cult was found in archeological digs back in 1954. 72 fragments of the Essenes scrolls were discovered in caves beside the Dead Sea, and it sent the ecumenical world on end! Among these fragments is the Manual of Discipline, rules for an Order just like mine! These messianic Jews lived 200 years before Christ. Scholars believe tho Jesus himself wasn't an Essene, his thinking may have been influenced by them. He may have gleaned his Divine Purpose thru the study of the scrolls of the Essenes.

God is merciful to us thru every dispensation and age, S/He calls to Her/His people in language they can understand, to minister to others as ourselves. S/He calls & human life is enriched by those who hear Her call and participate in Her Holy Celebrations in Her Holy Places.

So I'm marching up the Kings Highway each day is like the first day of my life!

Forgive and reconciled to God, garbage of the Past wiped away; tho continuing to suffer for it in earthly gravity—I must proceed industriously foreword & not lag behind wallowing in gloom!

>Ve a havta eit Adoni.
>*You shall love God.*

I want to be prayer in motion! Feet pounding; feet beating a path onward! A soldier in the army!

>S/He gives strength to the faint. And you will mount up with wings of eagles!

>--Isaiah 50. Holy Bible.

What road do we take upon the Kings Highway? Via media—the middle road?

Well… Journey-- & then we're there…

57.
WORKS continues to embellish upon the DOC Handbook and upon Midrash/ Commentary which followed.

--Regarding Healing:
WOW! Just discovered how the gift of healing works. We have heard of the laying on of hands. Bringing cure of illness both physical and mental to one human body from another humanbeing or group of people, who are gifted by God with this power. At first at least, the human hand should not be used as a channel of Gods healing. The human hand, with its lifelines, fingerprint whorls, veins, creases and calluses is not a pure instrument ready for the Divine; but rather use some article consecrated by God in advance. I was drawn to the vision of the Hebrew prayer shawl in black on white at Temple. Here is the procedure the prayerful use at Shabbat service: The torah scroll is taken out of the arc. Now all Christians know this is the Word of God first come down to human beings about 3,000 some years ago—thus it is a Holy document! The Torah scroll is carried up and down the aisle of the congregation where the parishioners who are all wearing their prayer shawls—TOUCH the Holy Torah with the Fringe & Tassels of the consecrated shawl, then take it to their mouths in a kiss. The fringe of the shawl is the intermediary between the holy and the human, and a blessing is conveyed thru it. During a laying-on-of-'hands' this following procedure shall be used:

> The person who prays shall be wearing her/his holy shawl, and carrying a Bible, Torah, Koran or whatever Holy Book in which they believe. The person praying first in spirit or aloud shall ask the Divine for forgiveness, humbling themselves on a personal level to make themselves 'clean' before the eyes of the Almighty so they can be used as a vehicle thru which Gods' power comes down to heal the supplicant--- that is the person who is sick or troubled. Still gazing upwards at Jesus, or God; whoever your particular type of Religion mandates, you ask aloud, or in spirit for healing and blessing for the supplicant THEN—extending the Fringe, Tassels, etc., of this Holy Shawl up to touch—in spirit—the immaculate heart of

Jesus, or God. The person praying thus establishes a link, or bridge between the Divine from where all power comes, out of heaven. And taking this same Fringe, Tassel of the prayer shawl, they then touch the sick person in the region of their sickness, continuing to pray and invoke the Holy Ones Name (i.e. in the Name of Jesus, or in the name of our Holy & Divine God, etc.). It is thru this consecrated pre-established link that healing shall be done! Perhaps later on in the developing lifestudy of the healer the prayer shawl may be omitted and the person themselves can directly be the link or the bridge from the Divine to the human (or animal) supplicant.

People are laden worries, diseases, crisis—but when they congregate at tabernacle—100rds of them in pews, or on mats praying or beginning their holy songs or chants--- then the Spirit of God begins to dance en masse! The dance of our souls along with the Spirit of God!

--Regarding DOC as a religious institution:
First denial of 3 plus decades of sexual abuse of parishioners by the priests, which includes fondling, groping and rape. On the alter, in the pews, in the counseling rooms, in the classrooms, in the church schoolyard. —anywhere the priests could get their hands on children and woman, the young, and the helpless. Present to you this graphic picture as it was taken in historic photograph, this church, signified by a priest severely chastised for his sins. His right arm and left leg have been hacked off. He stands with bloody stumps in clerical regalia black/white. So now the Christian church stands before you crippled & maimed—but still enjoins you to go follow it to the throne of God. The Catholic Church did not defend the Jews of Nazi occupied Europe and in fact it is suspected even colluded with the Pope to aid in the murderous assault on European Jewry. It is also fact the catholic church for its own survival 'overlooked' Adolph Hitler in his murderous pogroms as he systematically and thoroughly destroyed the Jewish people, and others as the cattle car death trains rolled across the fields of Europe to the death camps. The Catholic Church kept silent. Their Pope kept silent as they continued to distribute wafers and wine on Sunday signifying the body and blood of Christ—

Christ the radical, Christ the upstart, Christ who was murdered himself for his revolutionary stance some 2,000 years previously; a Christ who calls us of the modern day also to step forward and do justice, protect the innocent, and give our lives for our neighbor! Why was the Catholic Church sleeping? How could its parishioners have gone on and on in blindness from 1939 almost to the end of the war in 1945 seeing nothing, hearing nothing and saying nothing?

The DOC shall not be a complacent and complicit Order seeking to camouflage itself for survival into docility, ignoring the anguish of other people's lives during its life and times! If DOC's stand for justice causes the end of DOC, all the better! We shall die knowing we have followed Christ to the last possible ends of this earth, martyrdom! This is our purpose! To Serve Justice and Truth in God!

Somewhere between heaven & hell, situated in ordinary time sits earth. It is traversed by many paths & walks of life. On it is a Golden Road, a Royal Road, the Red Road, The Path, The Kings Highway— all being one and the same, that Way above the billions of common ways. And I'm marching along this Kings Highway.

This Way is a road of Wisdom. Wisdom! This Way is a road of Truth! And Justice!

Every day every step of our lives is a choice between good & evil. Better and worst---and *best*. The shining Golden Path.

Saw a vision of Gods fleshy Hand. A hand about as big as I am— meaning my entire body. It is the hand of God by Who these Words come, not from me myself. I am simply a scribe—like my grandfather in Belize Honduras on the streets of that South America city writing and reading aloud letters to the illiterate common people back at the turn of the century, 1890's. Today the literacy rate has improved in South America and in this country. Within the borders of the U$A almost all can read or write on the rudimentary level at least. Yet I am speaking to a spiritually illiterate nation… perhaps dumber about the ways of God Almighty then they were back into those distant 1890's and 1900$_{rds}$!

I remember 1976 when I had nobody and nothing. My father had just died. My friends were false friends—bar cronies who shouted familiar 'hellos' to each other upon entering the dreary beer hops stinking tavern from out of a foggy cold night. I was back in the bottle, a drunk alcoholic with unknown blood sugar disorders making me sick; robbing my energy. I prayed & fasted to the salvation of my soul. A change came about in my life, and I was lifted up. My situation today is not as bad. Did a whole lot of praying then, and it is to this people must return for a breakthrough in their personal situations, as all good things come down from the Eternal One.

At Grace approaching the Communion table:
>Christ is a voice crying out in the wilderness; along with whores, the sick, the wild; those restless for God. Uplift your voice! Call out to God!

Thereupon was shown me the vision of a large red heart, as large as the whole end of the Cathedral, 8 floors high uninterrupted, from the ceiling along its length of stained glass windows down to the concrete grey concrete floor. The beautiful cantor lady sings; *My heart is restless until it finds its rest in You.*

Wild songs of the brokenhearted who have nothing to loose.

The preacher informs the congregation we must be transformed by God. The desires of our hearts must be transformed to Gods Will. We must transform our purpose according to the vision of God

A much closer walk with You irregardless of any other human being.

58.
--Minor clarifications:
Reason for the title of my Order being Jesus Christ, if I were a Buddhist and got the inspired idea for this Order thru meditation it would have been called Daughters of Courage a New Order of Buddha or the like. All are included in my Order on the behalf of Jesus. It does not mean all must believe in nor worship Jesus at any point in their membership or association with the Order and or Community.

--Addendum:
To be a Daughter of Courage might incur some embarrassment—as a son who is a Daughter! A Jew, Muslim or Wiccian who is in an Order named after 'Jesus Christ'. It takes a strong hearty soul to be a Daughter of Courage. We shall be bold, brave & proud! —Proud as Children of the Most High!

--Minor clarifications:
I say 'My Order' referring to the Daughters of Courage, after this sad experience of my group—the Wednesday night group—in the common world. It is a sad legacy. Nearly a year ago I saw a lagging on part of regular members for it not to be referred to as My group—but Their group collectively tho this was never stated. Although among the assembly none of them had begun it, nor continued on from beginning to end constantly, missing no days (I missed 4 days in 4.5 years) there was a silent hanger-on who was there often but who never started it and said little. He was valuable in e-mailing regularly and subsequently some new people arrived but nothing to the extent I did in person by going out into the streets and announcing it by word of mouth constenly, and having put up the original notice which went into the gay papers done by myself which continued. As many of the people I wanted to reach did not have e-mail access (like myself) the group I reached out to was more working class (if they were working at all). Worse these people have aligned themselves with a much larger FTM group and have begun to suck my group into that! It is a case of outsiders attempting to appropriate a smaller group, which they did not begin! Now I see why when Benedict (300 ACE) was driven out of his first order after an attempted assassination, and why he went on to found the most rigorous order with at least 72 rules and laws! So there would be no room for doubt! The discipline, empowering himself, the Prior(ess). Rules, which must be followed, etc. So it is for this reason to call DOC *my Order,* because I desire that no Johnny-come-latelys nor extraneous persons hog in or push me aside as they did Benedict in his order 1,800 years ago, even attempting his murder as they are doing in my group today 2007. Thus my claim. However in truth, I cannot claim anything but being the Daughters of Courage's sole earthly founder beside no other mortals! And cannot claim that I 'invented it' or created it thru personal cogitation, research etc., for as it came to me—in Spirit--

truly it is Jesus Christ's Order—for it is thru the Holy Spirit it was dictated to me, it's prophet and founder!

If the Word about my Order ever gets out I hope Buddhists won't try to arm-wrestle Christians & Jews or any other body over it, nor Jews arm-wrestle Christians as to who should be the 'boss', nor Christians demand to be first in the line of hierarchy, since they in fact are the sole group who can take the Christ part of our vows, in full; each & all of them because of their life-long investiture in their old methodology & ways, for it would be a battle royal. The idea is that all the main religions & practices which uphold one true God/Goddess come together in Service to the Planet, plus worship of the Divine, and live communally, growing their own fruits & vegetables whenever possible.

--More instruction:
Sylvia Brown psyche says severally damaged persons on earth go to a transitory place before heaven, a place in which they are healed with great love and made whole. It is after this they pass thru the pearly gates. DOC would provide this healing to those who need it, here on earth.

Severely damaged people. Do you know how many times they've cried themselves to sleep during the night?

The Daughters of Courage will attempt to house the insane. Yes. In a lovely house with common gardens, private small 'apartments' self-contained, with bathrooms & small kitchens. Shared will be courtyards and vegetable and flower gardens well policed by gentle priest/peacekeepers to make sure the insane don't hurt each other or themselves. We would be able to perform this Work because of our large population of Service workers. Godly person power. Only manageable insane would be welcome. Those perhaps severe in behavior, but non-violent, such as the woman who wears black and never shows her face to anyone. Who stands for hours in one place gazing silently at what we do not know. She will have a safe house, pleasant surroundings, and gentle caretakers about to help with food, laundry, medical aid, etc. The man who never speaks who pushes a shopping cart laden with nothing, writing, writing, illegible gibberish in tiny letters on scraps of paper. Driven by some steady, unseen demand to constantly push squiggly lines out of his fingertips moving ever-flowing across the surface of some found paper notepad. He can move his shopping cart silently among the trees of the grounds at peace, well housed and fed—and like all of the insane guests free to come and go at any time. Pushing his shopping cart out of our doors into the dirty cruel fast-moving city anytime he chooses.

All you can do is the work God has set out for you & then sit back and see what God does with it. And see how far God carries your work upon Her wings.

So you see I have slowly come to realize that this gift from God shall return to Her, that all the riches of it are Hers! How lucky I am to have been chosen to be caretaker to it!

Joy –Joy unspeakable. Joy. Joy so great it is palatable—you can taste it on the tongue, in the mouth, in every fiber of your body.

> *The quick victory is enjoyable*
> *but the long conquest is preferable.*

The Red Road, or The Path as Buddhists have it, is littered with little acts of good. Which serve to put more good out into the universe & inwardly keep us going focused on God; God within us, God within each other. Keeps us going right & not retrograde (backwards).

59.
Well—like I said before when going down Fillmore Street, at my age and by my generation, I've seen dynasties upheaval. In a long, extenuated process the once all-blax Fillmore turned like an hourglass upside down become all white—40 years. This witnessed from 1968 to 2008. A people displaced. Slowly, slowly, ever encroaching the city moves against its poor—glacier-like, taking decades, generations—in 50 years the changeover is complete. No poor left. Nobody who earns under $30,000 per year can possibly live here. All ways & means being sealed up by the withering circle of rent control disarming the poor, and stronger condo conversion rights empowering the relatively wealthy. All I can do is hope to hang in here—in this City of resources, food banks, elder services, medical clinics,

religious community, gay/lez/trans freedom; and live as long as possible in its Graces.

> *Those who walk around with a heart split in two.*

> Another high-rise building going up.
> How high will it go?
> Another black man damn disgusted gets on the damn bus
> cussing out the driver.
> Should I call 911 police emergency?
> Another high-rise going up;
> pushing out the people
> who cuss with their mouths
> and fight back with their fists
> in impotent solutions.

Friday nite Shabbat service. I got my holy hat on my head & am ready to rumble!

I see one group member who throughout the life of it actually only attended sporadically who now rushes up and attempts to engage me in conversation about the matter—on the Sabbath! He wants to do business on a Holy Day! He has his opinion about it—to add to all the pile of the others. And I do not wish to ever engage any of these people in conversation about this Dead Matter again!

***

Another blow. Jasmin wants me to take her name off the lease!

It's on the behind-the-scenes urging of her partner who has grown fowl-tempered about the possibility they may loose their condo due to overspending. In a frenzy she tries to snatch Jasmin's name off of the lease! The cruel rent management corporation tells me I have to prove sufficient income to be able to stay here by myself! According to a lawyer at temple they cannot force me to disclose my income—since I'm already in the unit, having previously qualified! So the rent management corporation is calling my bluff! It's a tug of war and my spirits suffer because of it. Life is nervous and trepidations.

And all these people attacking me are higher placed then I am. They seem not to be happy until they take away the last shred you have—because anything you have makes them nervous. They worry it might be used as power against them!

About this Dead Group Matter again! —The Final Word: Dear Lord please take all this fear out of my heart, all the fear that I'm going to loose my studio apartment because Jasmin wants to take her name off the lease and I can't qualify the credit check of income by myself. All fear & worry about the now-dead-to–me-group. Please help me on with my life. In the Name of the Lamb, Jesus Christ. Please bring me peace! Peace in my life!

Oh, by the way, God has showed me that worry accompanied by love is not 'worrying too much' if worry causes you to pray and in praying summoning up love out of deep regions of your heart. Thus it is not too much worry in that it is bringing forth Love. Amein.

***

I think here its so much rich & poor. Too much rich you know?

--German Tourist SF 2007

***

Citizens! Each leaving from or returning too free housing of a good order which they, themselves personally own for life—tax-free. In each house, sufficient food. Walk along the avenue, different shapes of people wearing diverse colors of cloths. Every face a smiling face.

--Living in The city Of Compassionate Help.

--Works (continued).
Day:
Reached out to people in the street I knew from Grace about Benedictian society.

Early in my morning (12 noon) a word came to me from the Lord: *Honest.* 'Honest' says the Lord--& me a petty thief. Stole ¼ roll toilet paper from men's room @ Grace Cathedral. Why? Asks the Spirit---the answer is also given—Why? Because I need it. Must constantly offset expenditures against the time of Rent. Which means draconian thrift, eating in food banks, using found transfers or walking to get around in lieu of throwing away precious cash on bus fare, and buying nothing extra. Anyway, after this small crime, was in a hurry to get across the plaza to the Cathedral first before any others of the Benedictines, to set out the hymnbooks. It is a good thing when the children of God are racing to be first to do Gods work. Deep solemn immense cathedral, grey, who by the light in stained glass windows reflects time passing, now turns blue as the sun sets, no longer striking the reds & yellows of the biblical tableau in glass. This cathedral arches up higher then the 6th floor where Jasmin moved us in desperation, back in 1998, to downtown Oakland, headless of the fact that I am afraid of heights, and where she threatened to throw her tan warm body attired in a dancers long colorful skirts out of the window she was so dismayed at our poverty. Cathedral is 6 floors up and from there reaches beyond, ---maybe 8 stories, the first leap towards heaven! Red moves down the aisles framed by solemn deep rich mahogany wood pews picking up the blue hymn books; as he progresses down the rows the stack in his arms grows heavy & heavier & in the last row, a copper penny sits right on top of one of the books! God has well seen how, to pick up pennies in the streets of this falling Babylon has become the poor Transman passion! But solemnly he takes this penny and sets it down on the red cushioned pew, adding the blue hymnbook to his stack. He doesn't even steal the penny! *Honest.*

Do you realize how far a penny goes in heaven? One copper penny---to infinity!

Night: Out shopping in the streets—spy a chair perfect for his table under the recently constructed breakfast area. Ask and volia! It appears! Backless, only thing wrong is its broken silver stem, and stained seat cushion. After rolling it home, he does a few repairs—removes the stem with monkey wrench; puts found crimson towel on seat, now it sits under his storage loft in the food/computer nook. WORKS—recycling junk, saving money, rebelling against consumerism & materialism.

Evening:
They were hurt & they armed themselves well. Seated in group around table in the upper room of the TG/TS clinic Transman Red listens to problems primarily of the women, his sisters, —male to female. They are in varying states of dissatisfaction from resignation, anger, rage, to despair. Hears the story off one who accompanying another in a store felt everybody in the place was staring at her and had a panic attack ad before she could be called upon by the store clerk to answer some question and thus reveal the timbre of her baritone voice, ran out in a mad dash rather then speak and then everybody would know what and who she was. Another girl underage fresh off the bus from out-of-state escaped from foster care where her gender was disrespected. Not addressed as she but he, made to try to be straight and all the hatred and completely stupid lack of understanding of TG/TS people. They all get on the Greyhound bus and head out here, to this small peninsula city, directly to its Tenderloin TG/TS epicenter. Red sits listening, while he eats 3 bowls of clam chowder free, courtesy of Walden House, a drug rehab facility. WORKS. (To listen empathetically.)

Day:
In Shaun's revolutionary bookstore Babylon Falling read about the inhumane poultry industry; how female chicks beaks are ripped off at birth without anesthetic to keep them from pecking each other. Permanent disease sets in after that, painful in their short abused lives. Their brothers, male chicks are ground up and fed back to them in a hellish device of cannibalism, to enrich the capitalist chicken farmers. How sad the world is, the center of caring for the lower animals is small, a ring of peace. Activist peace. And actions as elsewhere stated fall all along the range of passive to aggressive. At store Transman Red is faced with two brands of eggs, the cheapest a box of a dozen, $2 are from the above kind of place, where murderous violence is committed upon the lowest of Gods creatures. The free-range chicken eggs are $3.30. Being so poor the first one is tempting. After a thought, he purchases the expensive—and loving brand… WORKS. (Of a compassionate nature.)

Inside the animal shelter, the elderly Transman goes to sit with one of his several favorite inmates, a large, elderly German Shepherd. Notice the edge of his door the paint is gone; wood gouged from where he's eaten it off, in boredom or desperate need to escape. Red's hour and fifteen minute visit brings comfort. WORKS. (To visit the prisoner.)

Further acts of mercy visited to me: Brother B. who is employed in a garbage disposal facility brings me a wad of senior and disabled subway tickets he, being young can't use. Hundreds of dollars of free red & green tickets have been given to me over the years!
by B. and other conspirators against fascist kapitalism!

Acts of good are like flowers blue, violet, pink, yellow, golden, red, orange, scattered along the Kings Highway.

Works--Act of compassion:
Lou one of the owners of the men's sex club where our show is held, scoops the tiny twisted body of a disabled woman up and carries her inside, seats her in a chair her aid/helper-friend follows caring the manual wheelchair. She and her friend provide the necessary extra 2 people, which make it a decent show. Yes, am back to counting. With support of the former group withdrawn (thankfully I won't have to see them in the audience, thus less tension and stress, at least they aren't trying to take over my show!) we still had an audience of 5, plus 4 performers (a decent number) 9 all told. We've done worse in the past.

The whole thing is ugly. Just ugly. Thought & memory of a particular woman—a partner--- enticing her FTM boyfriend away from my table by holding a plate of cake under his nose—with no regard for me sitting right there, and how I might feel. The original group meeting table I'd held down for 4.5 years & him getting up & scooting away after I went to the restroom. It was all so childish and obnoxious. I am glad to move on from them. Our show went well & I hope to have many more. For Jasmin's sake and for my practice in public reading on an ongoing basis, not to mention the handful of much-needed dollars I collect every time.

My shrink tells me, I don't want conflict in my life, she sees me drawing away from this mess fast—while others might have stayed around bickering and growling and fighting. I told her it was most observant of her. I hadn't put it into words myself. I had enough conflict being a tiny child in my abused home. Yes, I run from conflict, which makes it difficult being a firebrand and voicing my opinion and making a strong stance so often against the current culture so that conflict is bound to arise.

Well, little barbs & snares keep jolting my memory of the whole sorry mess, but they are lessening! Am moving on, having let it go. Sometimes see a sad deflated red balloon in the gutter and it briefly hurts me. There is no good can come of this stealing my group away from me!

Ah Benedict!

***

So he followed the Hebrew service around the turning of the year, the month of Av, destruction of the temple, 3,000 years ago; ---when disaster struck twice, wiping out my group of 4.5 years in 2 weeks, then the affair about my cat and then Jasmin desiring to remove her name from the lease on my home! The time of comfort is soon to come. How the people wait and long for this!

1945.
I remember around 1 or 2 in the after noon the oil stench hung on the air from the days kill at the slaughter house all that misery pouring out into the hot Chicago summer air. Evidence of barbaric treatment of animals. Reminded that penned terrified cows and bulls pushed down a chute where their frantic flailing legs are broken by the fall and are bludgeoned to death by a huge powerful man wielding a sledge hammer to their cranium.

The animal gives of itself so that the human race might dine. Some poor families can't get enough food. Each dying being gives off the stink of itself—this writing is my scent! Learn from it! HOWL!

60.
Works:
Grazing mentally in the Buddhist section of Fields Spiritual Bookstore on Polk Street. Am struck by an odd fact. That Maha beads are the Buddhist rosary beads! Similarities.

Further reading raises embarrassing questions for DOC such as is Buddhism is essentially atheistic---and is Wicca polytheistic? Where as we all agree the first vow of the Order is to serve God (the One God) by many names, each in our all tradition…

Worship service is important---service is a soul cleansing sight to the congregants. It separates them from being totally earth-bound and flesh bound—a state from which there is no escape only decay and death. Even the most primitive tribes who assemble before the elders; who hear the drumming, see the mystics chanting under the stars must be helped by this! This ritual cleanses the spirit. Washes thru a human soul. Services the soul in such a fashion as to relieve it of its burden. Thus attending worship service en masse at some tabernacle with other faiths once per week (at least) will be mandatory for DOC. If none in the neighborhood allow us or ban us from their places then we will have to resort to doing our own service—and this should not be confined to the Order's single houses separately by themselves, but in the true tradition of a gathering of community in worship we would combine with other local houses and worship en masse.

As I said Muslim, Christian, Hebrew, Hindu may worship in their own unique traditions, all are praying to the same God I think—using different Names and traditions—as if God was divided up like a big pie! Maybe in the confluence of several 'parts' of God united together we will receive miracles, however all parts of God are all the same God, the Almighty and Unnamable!

Works:
Busy processing my biggest order from Amazon.com—STREET OF DREAMS. 5 copies. Plus another trickle-in of JAILHOUSE STUD, & DOING IT FOR THE MISTRESS, 1 each. About this time realized while glimpsing thru the pages of the books I was assembling, that I was sitting on a gold mine—because I had revealed my soul. Found a cheap 5 cents-a-sheet copy place. Lugging heavy sheets around town. Up to the cutter, (a different place of course) $2 to cut the whole thing. Will make a profit of $7 approximately per book. If I charged minimum wage for my labor the profit would shrink down to about ten cents per book!

Works:
To be attentive to dreams & visions sent by Creator. To be wise. To be Mindful—as the Buddhists tell us in their discipline.

There is a grey building rising just beyond the fog; it appears down at the end of every street, no matter which way one turns. It appears looming, brick, walled up, secret, and has, at its pinnacle a single eye by which it can observe each & everything about us while revealing nothing of itself. It is power incarnate on earth. A building, to which every other thing pays homage.

In this mysterious and sinister scenario the Voice of the Eternal seems distant and not relevant; God has spoken: *I'm setting up a new world.* But these words are of little comfort. Much more important is the pressing reality. Right now 3 false gods stand on the human horizon, masked, in dull red cylinders. Gigantically tall, and broad. One of them is Kommunism. One of them is Kapitalism. A state more powerful then the church. The third is oil. Power derived from oil, which runs all nations.

What must come? A spiritual revolution. A changing of dynasties of earth.

Listen!
I look down the corridors of memory. You can hear/see one approaching. One of God. Before God, comes God's Prophets. God the Eternal for Whom there is no Name.

Sat in Babylon Falling, Shaun's revolutionary bookstore browsing among the stacks. Owner Shaun expresses admiration for those old 1920's words for the rich back in the days of the Wobbles—the 'Plutes' being one. Which stands for Plutocrats. As I have said, Korporate Kapitalism Kills us. —Us poor anyhow. We are informed in Babylon Falling that a rent increase of $200 in a non-rent control unit on the part of the Rent Management Corporation has evicted another young female tenant. Skyscrapers silver and glass are so high & mighty seems they are rooted in the sky.

Pay attention plutocrats; regarding the nations—least they be as:

> The corpses of Empires, they stink as nothing else.
> ---Rebecca West

When time itself comes to an end!

Sukat:
Dear God, I want to feel safe, I want to be at peace, not worried about housing, backstabbers, friends turning into enemies but the most serious of these is housing! Security in this futile dusty rent mogul city turning into the whirlwind devouring peoples homes and scattering their loved ones, belongings, pets into all 4 directions of the winds dropping them onto the plane lands of the nations here and there, no longer connected to anything.

Works:
Contemplate the following,(from Journey 3 Midrash):

> Reduce yourself of self-preoccupation
> I am not greater then the sum total of the parts.

Works:
Attend Sunday Services @ Grace. The outgoing pastor of Glide Memorial church—that Tenderloin social action church who feeds thousands of poor people 3 meals daily--- has climbed up the long cement blocks today to speak from the pulpit at this cathedral atop the hill.

> We Welcome Everybody: You will see in our pews every Sunday, Christians, Jews, Muslims, Hindus, Buddhists, side by side. They are all the same in our eyes, we welcome them all with love.
>
> --Pastor Fitch.

So you see I'm not the only one on this track. A la, the concept of Multi-Faith Order, DOC worshiping in concert, living in harmonious community together, and performing acts of Service, and Justice, soldiers in the trenches of our Creator.

Let me repeat myself for the sake of worrying minds of both future & present. —Buddha, Muhammad, Jesus, all are sent from God and are part of God, so in this way they are all one in God, yet they are all different entities & we a greater mass are all made in Gods image & in this way we are all one, but as you know we are different. But even tho we call God the Eternal by different names God is still One God, so in the Order we are serving together this one God (each using their own sacred name for God, and their own traditions and rituals in service) & it will not be necessary for each side—Muslim, Jew, Buddhist, Hindu, Christian to steal sheep from the other nor to convert the other to itself.

We must always remember we are bound together in service of the Most High God. This is why such diverse religious practices can serve together under one roof and perform Services arm linked in arm with their sisters & brothers.

I have spoken of a City of Compassionate Help, here it is—straight out of the hymn book, one of it's more powerful social action song. The whole 1,000 strong congregation stands and together; we sing the following:

> Oh holy city, seen of John, where Christ, the Lamb doth reign,
> Within whose four-square walls shall come no night, nor need, nor pain,
> And where the tears are wiped from eyes that shall not weep again!
>
> Oh shame to us who rest content while lust and greed for gain
> In street and shop and tenement wring gold from human pain,
> And bitter lips in blind despair cry, "Christ has died in vain!"
>
> Give us, Oh God, the strength to build the city that has stood
> Too long a dream, whose laws are love, whose crown is servant hood,
> And where the sun that shines is God's grace for human good.
>
> Already In the mind of God that city rises fair;
> Lo, how its spender challenges the soul that greatly dare—
> Yes, bids us seize the whole of life and build its glory there.
>
> --Hymn 583

Dear Lord(ess) Jesus and by all my understanding of the divine Torah (the Word of the Eternal One) please let me be generous when my ship comes in—in other words, when I get rich according to a dresh @ Shabbat service I am considering a prospective list of places to which I could donate—those engaged not in business alone but in Service.

Works:
Sit over coffee debating this same subject with Doctor S. "Tell them, I'm both. A Christian and a Jew. I don't feel they're mutually exclusive." He is a Christian, his fiancé is Jewish. Then our meandering conversation turns to Meditation. "Buddhism is a discipline. A healthy thing to do. It is a way of life."

Can look at this world of its blackened sin & you are doing your good deeds in some particular part of the world—so that it changes into grey—for there you are making a difference.

Works:
Visited Dogs, one of my charges has been adopted. She's "gone home". Complete Joy! For both staff & animal. A Loving Person has found her here in the shelter and she's trotted off at the Persons heels. Another dog sees her on leash gaily prancing away out doors to freedom and barks uncontrollably, scratching on the glass door of its pen; then bites the head off of one of its toys. White stuffing lays in puffs over the floor.

Frantic, confined dogs. One sets his forepaws on his blue blanket and begins to tear it up. Sharp teeth rip, rend, followed by a squat urination at the other end of his cage. They too want to Go Home!

Works:
(Attend revolutionary functions & lend support by personal presence.) Faithful Fools monthly potluck. This is the 62nd anniversary of the bombing of Hiroshima, August 6th 1945. We spoke of Sadako, the little girl who died of radiation poisoning after her city where she lived with her family, Nagasaki was bombed by the U$A's warplane Enola Gay. And how, 62 years later Japanese school children still make paper cranes with their tiny child hands to decorate their schoolrooms and send garlands of cranes to the Japanese Holocaust museum in honor of her. There are at least 2 reasons God keeps people alive on this earth, beyond a natural time of reproduction

replenishing earth with its future generation—this is one: a person who is not repentant & has not reconciled themselves to God so S/He gives them ample time to discover Her Might & Her Love---before the person goes on. Two: those who have found God and now are industriously employed in Her service doing religious charitable works, setting alter cloths, leading worship services, being apostles of the Lord in this latter day. Some, like little Sadako are taken up to heaven early. Thus remain fixed statues in our memory. A bittersweet reminder to us still earth-bound. Sadako died 10 years after the atom bomb was dropped on her city—of radiation poisoning. We spoke of war. Of soldiers having to melt humans with flame-throwers to dispose of their bodies washing this human debris down the sewers of Dresden. How it took 2 weeks to finish the job. Spraying with forced water flow the last pieces of flesh down the drain. We sat around the Fools roundtable making Peace Cranes and spoke of bombing. Soon all the Peace Cranes red, blue, silver, gold, white, purple, green, orange, sat in a flock on the table. I put mine on top of a little tree in the middle. With my big ego, proclaiming de facto that my bird was the boss, but M. tells me that's where Cranes like to be-- on top of the tallest tree, so it was in the right place.

Works:
(Self discipline. Regarding forgiveness.) Sad sight of a red balloon, deflated, in gutter amid trash. I am sad. At the betrayal. My sad ex-group! I forgive them all & move on!

It was a very hard thing for Transman Red to do—and he knew they no longer had his prayers.

Anger over this whole affair is one of those soul turds you got to get rid of because they constipate your being—soul restrictions harbored in the deep dark recesses of our minds. A dark fire forever burning. The very worst thing we can do is to hide our sins from God. (Who already sees everything.) That is diabolical & evil. Best is to reveal all of our human mistakes to God readily & willingly & fully; i.e.: my lust for power! My Machiavellian plans for what I will do to save the world once I become famous (and hence rich).

61.

Thursday @ Grace. The following scripture was read, which gave rise to remembrances, regarding the day of my adult baptism, when these Words came to me in a dream; *'Many are called few are chosen.'* And, how you must ask God to be born again—totally in Spirit. (John 3: 3, 5.)

> Truly I say to you, except a person be born again, s/he cannot see the kingdom of God.
> Except a person be born of water and of the Spirit, they cannot enter into the kingdom of God.
>
> That which is born of the flesh and flesh; and that which is born of the spirit is spirit.
>
> --Jesus Christ

Thursday morning. Mind blank. Before the machinery of the mind starts up. More as it is in childhood. He came out of his body like an envelope—then he was covered head to toe in the world. Attended Cannon Lampen's Bible study 10 am—a time at which he was not awake. Came in right after the bell chimed and was greeted by the elderly gentlemen, a war hero who defended Britain at the English Channel against the Nazis in World War 2. He is 96. Being that Red was half asleep, as the woman who reads the commentary after each bible verse advised the Transman later, his mind was too groggy to focus on a lot of peripheral crap, so that it zeroed in entirely upon the scripture, which he then seemed to take to a high spiritual level immediately. "It is the powers of concentration which made it more meaningful to you and gave you that divine breakthrough." She said.

My Dream. As you recall, I reported shortly after becoming a Christian at age 33 or 34, upon the death of my father, of receiving a heavenly dream-vision-premonition of my second (adult, and self-chosen baptism) which happened a month or so later. I was walking down an incline of rocks towards a sandy/rocky beach, a frail human, headpiece full of straw—as TS Eliot has it. Sun blazing overhead. In this scenario, booming from out of the heavens, the Voice of God declared: *Many are called but few are chosen.*

Well today's scripture states that if we are transfigured by Gods Holy Spirit we throw off depression, mortal worry, for we are living for God. However as God seldom intrudes upon a persons life, we must ask God to be reborn. To walk wrapped in Her Spirit. We must realize that after this, life will change. We will no longer be focused upon all those wants and desires which motivated us for a lifetime. For dreams of fame & glory. For fantasies of a lover and a happy, mortal home. We may just have to throw away everything and follow the Savior. Are we ready for such a drastic switch in our life path? Or do we wish to follow a more familiar course, one tried, trodden and true ---right up until our death? So I am delaying asking fervently for the Spirit—knowing all this. I figure our merciful God said this to me long ago in that dream, (1975 or 76?) Nearly 31 years past, by saying 'few are chosen'. My theory has it that it isn't from us blindly struggling to please God down here in our lives on this earth, by service, prayer fasting etc., that --'then we will be chosen'-- no, the deciding factor is *us*. It is within us! It is we who present ourselves to God with full commitment, turning our complete selves over to God's Will; our dreams for the future, our wants in the present and give this up to God surrendering our souls and saying I give my life to You, I will follow You! It is only when we completely do this that we will be chosen! So the secret is not some mystic performance record –how many totaled up Sunday Services attended, or prayerbooks distributed ---that we must attain for God to reach down and appoint us the chosen persons. No, but our own decision to lay down our lives, give up everything, and follow where ever the Hand of God will lead.

Strong stuff.

Am I ready to do this? Are you ready to do this?

The rabbi calls it Our Jewish Journey. To Native American Elders it is The Red Road. Buddhist meditations say it is The Path. The Way. As I said... *I'm marching up the Kings Highway; each day is like the first day of my life!*

Works:
Animal shelter. To his delight Red found of his charges, the two crazy loveable penned up lonely German Shepherds, the younger of

the two, the female is ADOPTION PENDING! --- What a joyous Day when an animal goes home!

Works:
Of attendance. @ Temple. Saw another conversion to Judaism in a colorful ceremony. The male partner of a Jewish man. Great oneg downstairs after. Munch to my hearts delight—the reward of the faithful!

Works:
Of preparation thru prayer. During service I asked for God to set the time and place for me to finally begin painting again. —After procrastination of a year (See PASSAGE).

Works:
Following day—Shabbat Saturday--@ service right before the Barchu when the congregation rises and God is greeted with a demand to 'bless me', bowed to and prayers of thanksgiving are made, I saw again the now familiar dream-like vision of the Holy Smoke in its corkscrew extended out to me thru space from above the ark in which are kept the Holy Scroles—in a vision just out of the periphery of the conscious mind. Immediately after, up in the air to the right, again in vision I perceived a dim sense of a huge figure and then saw grain of mustard seed larger-then life hung in space before me; this vision vanished quickly 2 or 3 seconds—like the one, which had proceeded it. I knew God had spoke to me, reaching out and showed me that I have faith even as small as a mustard seed (which is the seed of the Mustard plant, so tiny it can barely be seen by the human eye). As it says in Scriptures if we have faith even as small as this seed, miracles will be accomplished. The miracles that move mountains.

Ural the Hebrew month begins over the body of the dead Av, passed. Month of change—after destruction has wiped out the old. So spookily foreshadowing my life. Big destruction/changes, now free space to move on into something far better I hope!

Both in synagogue and church periodically cast my romance antenna about me. I am so choicy in looking for a lover. This woman seems too weak, too frail, too vulnerable. That man, too powerful, and the next one too strong and tall. —I wander thru this world alone.

@ Grace the drash was to choose life. @ Grace saw myself gazing out at the world, icy, analytical, from the cold calculating part of my brain—there is no compassion inside that part. Jesus I want you to look out from behind my eyes and show me how to see as you do. I have been shown there is certainly an evil—and a good. I chose life. So there we are come around, full circle. If we must be perfect before we can go to the alter and meet with God—there's not one of us can make that journey. We must come just as we are no matter what condition; sinner, unbeliever, wicked in thought, impure in deed--- there at the alter of the Most High God, heads bowed, we begin our transformation.

Back @ temple, seated in a front pew gazing at the bema, and ark, its ornate doors shut, behind which is housed the Holy Scrolls, my mind thinks back to a nursing home which was my employment years ago—and the broken body of a fairly young man, 30's—who'd had a stroke. He was paralyzed, stiff, laying on his right side. He had been a salesman, dressed in a natty suit, just weeks ago. Another patient pushed him out of his bed; there he lay on the floor, amid his twisted bedclothes stained with human excrement. Did I try to help? No, because my shift was ended. Did not want to grapple with the heavy body of this man, the mess made over everything, his twisted bedclothes wrapped around him during his fall, the unchanged soiled bed. I threw off my uniform and headed home, leaving him for the oncoming shift.

Where was your compassion? Asks the Lord.

I was in a hurry to get out, hated to pick up this heavy man, put him back in the bed, after having change sheets & mopped the floor after an already exhausting shift. I was over-laden and overworked.

> *Sit with me. Say a prayer for me. Kaddish.*
> *Kaddish.*

***

Works:

Attendance. Monday. 6pm Grace. Blue/red bearded, robed patriarchal figures upholding the faith in stained glass. I been with God a long time—30 years. Yet not a *very* long time which would be a lifetime—a continuous 60 devout years. Years lessened by my break for 25 years of atheism.

Approaching the small chapel inside the huge cathedral the pious Transman, small black-clothed figure stops in amazement. Gazes at a mural of faded pastel, which rises the 20-foot height of the stone niche.

O'mah Gawd! Another surprise! Just now saw it! All comes clear to me! Over time my eyes have grown accustomed to this chapel. Before, where the only thing noticeable was male patriarchs of great importance—as dominant as the absence of females was obvious--- for those who thought of them at all. Just now saw a Mary above everything! A poignant figure; Mary, with a big golden halo holding her Christ Child. Yes, this same painting where the black man, depicted as a slavish savage is a supplicant bended knees, half naked before a clothed Caucasian knight. Also to the right hand side (where I sit) again a newly seen revelation, a painting, this one small 24" by 20" Mary holds Jesus! This after months of seeing nothing but the male-dominated art!

God: This is My house

Red: I feel at home here, safe, I like being here, lofty arches, surrounded by religious icons with deep symbolisitic meaning.

God: *My House is in the human heart.*

I was here yesterday amid 1,000 people, now I'm comparatively alone. Maybe 5 other people in this huge gigantic vault of stone. So quiet, distant footfalls echo half a block away—inside the entrance, away in front. 6:20. Some fellow Benedictines arrive amid much thumping & bumping & conversation. Grace's grey stone reminds me of the private school I was sent to as a child, it was housed in the imposing ivy league style University of Chicago which is made of grey brick, with green ivy vines/leaves climbing, adorning its walls. A place of quietude, study, libraries, respect for intelligence. Unlike the teaming lower-class black/brown ghetto where our family home was situated. So much ignorance in the African-American community. When one realizes that this ignorance was engineered, 300 years ago by the rich class of slave owners to suppress its working force of slaves, by refusing to educate them, the indicting finger of guilt is suddenly spread in a much wider arc then just pointed at its victims themselves. The more kindly plantation owners were forced by severe penalties of law not to allow their slaves to learn to read or write. The rich slave owning class spread myths about those black in skin color that they were 4 tenths animal, and only 6 tenths human—all to use humanbeings for profit. These things must be said. Told and retold, least the future forgets!

Well regarding society & change, specifically the black community; often a stale dead cycle needs to be interrupted. We have so many tools. We have tools of mental therapy, of early intervention, of mediation between warring parties; all this to make human interactions and human lives better—but we can't institute them, thus our world is lousy, mired in human predicaments. Unchanging, from generation to generation.

    ***

Works:
Tuesday. Today, what did I do? Talked to other humans, comforted animals, gave of my artistic talents to schul, withstood despair, took care of home & pets, asked God to uplift my soul; 'hold me until times get better'. Amen. *And let the people say, Amein.*

Works:
Wednesday. Talked to a friend on phone—counseled & listened & was counseled in return & reassured & in this process connected to humanity. 1 hour.

Later attended the young visiting Rabbis study—this one on queer prayers & Torah. Am getting deeper into religious study here & am known by more of the congregation. —Just as @ Grace, up on Holy Hill.

62.
In the beginning God gave very little of Her Words to humans. Cities were really small. Villages. People's brains had only recently developed in size to fully human about several tens of thousands of years ago, out of our slow progress from the animal stages. God kept noticing a leakage of human values in putting Her/Himself first, which is Her righteous place being the Creator of us, and of our world, our universe, our galaxy and time & space! So Creator had to keep stating and restating over and over and over one most important law ----*thou shall have no other Gods before Me.* God repeating self over & overin each subsequent book of Torah (& later the Bible) *Serve me! Serve me!* As it says in scripture that we should imitate God and be like God, so I too will repeat myself again---this Order, Daughters of Courage shall have two very important rules:

> To serve God—known by many different names. Each according to their religious tradition and faith.
>
> To serve humanity.

On this rest all the law and prophets, Jesus said. We must put ourselves wholly in the hands of the Almighty and ask for her Will to be done. The result is that we may do works small or great, or both. Only S/He will make that decision, of where to set us down into fate and locate us in time and history. We must ask only for Her Glory! Won't life be simpler then, more pure, and much, much happier.

Works:
Thursday. Walked everywhere, for health, & to save 50 cents carfare. This results in no air pollution. Visited wogs. One 3-legged pit bull—Reverend Lovejoy—who was found injured in an abandon junkyard. Animals are much higher then people. They talk to God everyday. They see their family members who have gone on—over into heaven—what do you think they're doing all day with all that sleeping, or gazing into space? They are conversing with their dead animal relatives. They will be glad to go home. But will wait here on earth long enough to be companions to us, To be food for us, to help us run our race, to do their earthly jobs. Humans on the other hand,

we are insane. They are terrified of dying. Can't see heaven. Don't believe in God—are non-holistic.

Works:
Went grocery shopping. Found the beef so exhorbient for such a small parcel, so turned to the pork which was cheaper substantially, but knowing the nastiness pork can be and previous experience with it spoiling sooner, and me getting sick, I decided upon a cheep parcel of beef—which was very small. So this is the solution. Just get smaller amounts. Eat less meat, filling up on more vegetables. Appetites. How we stumble over it. It has caused us pain.

Eat less meat. Meat turns into shit—a shit pile teeming with microorganisms of disease. However, biologically some must eat meat and cannot forgo it totally. So fix a clear plate—of vegetables and only trace amounts of meat. Instructs the Lord(ess). Save the planet.

There's an old song, *how long has this been going on?* Stated before, back in antiquity kings were appointed by divine right—supposedly they were sent from, and kin to the gods. When one king died, the next in lineage to former king became the new ruler, no matter if the person was mentally incompetent and their reigns wreaked havoc on the poor masses below with erratic taxes, failure to protect, or provide nor plan for its people.

Works:
Part of a good Samaritans Works is to have brilliant ideas and inform the world of them. Here's one. No one person can govern a mass of citizens, of people increasingly diverse, the world grows smaller, needs become greater, it takes many different heads to govern the whole. Yet officials who get elected are often the most popular in the eyes of the people, for instance movie stars or sports heroes, or the richest who can employ the gargantuan publicity needed to barrage the media and woo votes to the polling booths. In the future each 'elected official' should be a champion who swears inside their heart to do justice, and do the best for the people. Each champion who is elected by popular vote because they are already famous, or popular may know little about the matters of the position to which they are applying—i.e. mayor of a town, governor of a state, senator or

representatives of a district, so each champion going into the ring in battle in the contest for election should be the head of a board or panel or group of advisors, each advisor appointed not by blood relation, nepotism, fellow kaptialist interest, but *by their ability and proficiency in their field.* Itt is to each advisor in each various department that the champion—the newly elected official---turns to find out the correct manner of governing in that instance, not by their ideas alone, which may be stupid, or prove to be faulty. Just because they have the charisma or money to be elected doesn't give them the ability to be a legislator and make wise decisions! Then a small expert on any given field who cannot hope to be elected, could provide the information and resources to inform the elected official in that position and it would be their ideas, and plans which would be carried out on the governing level. This, in positions like inspectors, department water, health, fire, police garbage collector, mayor, governor representative; even, president. This is what the governments of the future should involve. Not one elected officials alone per office, but officials necessary to fill the empty positions, complete with their personal cabinet of highly informed consultants, to back each one of them up with facts.

Works:
Counseled Shaun @ Babylon Falling bookstore about security cameras, surveillance anti-theft devices.

Works:
Made contemplations with the Spirit:

>I'd just have joy. Joy & peace.
>
>*Harmony.* Says the Lord.
>
>*Harmony.*

I wish I was dead, I blurted out this thought—(but not like in the suicidal days, of depression; so unhappy). --- Simply had been visioning myself gone over to the other side. All the fun up there, comfort; joy. —I meant to say, *I wish I was in heaven.* Had memories. I was 12, 13? Living at my birth home @ 6540 St. Lawrence Avenue on Chicago's black south side. An old women was walking down the street across from me—the type of blue haired old middle class lady, her African tight curls straightened in high Negro bourgeoisie fashion. Suddenly she fell down on the pavement. Did I go over to help? No. I kept walking, ignoring her.

Of course this got back to my mother. Who told me that this lady saw me there across the street and I'd just kept walking and did nothing to come to her aid.

What did they expect? Me to give of myself? When I was nearly dying emotionally, and mentally from the abuse at my schizophrenic mothers hands?

I've learned since those days. Now I'd rush over and give help, a comforting word. I'd be the Good Samaritan Jesus speaks of. Honoring the second of Jesus' commandments.

Works:
Of confession. Here is a topic I must dig up out of my soul. It takes a lot of guts to say this. It is a confession I hate to even read or think about. It must go into this work, as a testimony to the ability of a human being to change. From a time when I was poor, 16, an alcoholic. It hurts my soul. It's already available in my collection STORIES FROM THE DANCE OF LIFE Vol. III in the autobiographical story 'Round Belden Corner:

> Belden is getting feeble. Her feet slew out, legs bending. They were week. No protein. Rickets. It's happening gradually. And I punished her. She had shitted in a pile by the door and urinated on top of it, into a puddle. This putrescence soaks into the rug. A shabby brown-no rug. I kicked her in both ends once each and punched her face, bending a small lower tooth loose inward in the gum. (Baby teeth.) Threw, in anger, the metal stool I use to sit on when I paint, across the room, which caught the radiator, clanging, reverberating out into the hallways, up thru the house, marrying with communal sound.
>
> It breaks my heart now, but they are only animals. That's all. I am putting too much into this affair. She is not my relative,

nor relative conscious even. Yet I am still sad. Sad, sad, sad. Saddened by it all. I cry even. She is a force with a face. That face—fun, body, that she is being slowly mutilated in, is a poor blink in her 'recall'. In heaven do dogs have long have long noses, just big old round mouths, squareish heads and no floppy ears? Colorless, furless of course. They feel pain. They get sad. How the Creator hates for them to be mistreated! No, actually, it's only me who HATES. Hates and gets full of rage… The Creator just gets Sad. Weeps. I am frustrated. I fly out of control at anything. How I regret. Now, -the whole thing.

--Red Jordan Arobateau, 1959, Chicago.

***

I am doing this book, Works, from the heart—and as a writer, I'm taking notes, thus I have prepared a book for the world.

63.
On the avenue Transman Red continues his observation of the human species, to write down later at his desk at midnight.

> *It's nice to identify accounts of foreign tourists, 4 I-talians in the park, 1 female, nice young people.*

Next into his sight comes a loose street woman.

> *In red boots she strolled, laughing, screeching down the avenue a wine bottle disguised by a brown paper bag in one hand, with the foolhardy craziness of the recently freed from a situation of life-long imprisonment under abuse.*

Next, a transsexual.

> *See her on the street strolling along 6'2" clad in elegant pants suit and pausing to look at self-reflection in storefront windows.*

> *A man tells a woman "I never see you eat."*

Red & Turnip. They appeal to the perverse in each other. Sit negatively dissecting the world and agreeing most of earth could be thrown into the garbage. Unnecessary kings, rich plutes, both of us believing that social change is necessary.

After having a vision of non-professor Turnip in the fashionable district walking down Dimitroff-Strasse. --- A pipestem figure nattily dressed, hat with colorful band, tight trousers strolling with an effeminate gait & realized she is the transmale incarnation of Lady Una Trowbridge complete with molecule, then Red dreamed it was Gods mission for him to humanity *to bring them to the light.*

To remind the human race that it has sold out—badly. Not only the U$A, all nations, in all times. In my country, Amerikkka, 400 years of genocide towards native populations, of black slaves, of women suppressed to second-class pay starvation wages, while male counterparts earned more with which they could, at their discretion, squander on tobacco & liquor, or feed their families. Other nations from their historic roots 2,000 years badly injured its lesser peoples, its nations of less magnitudes & its afflicted, ragged—any of which might be Mohammad, Jesus or Buddha revisiting earth in human disguise!

There is no waste, for all things return to Me; says the Lord:
>   1. Flowerpots crushed in gutter; earth with half dead plants spilling out.
>   2. Unwanted animals in the Kill-shelter put to sleep because of lack of human support.
>   3. Humanbeings who can no longer trust each other so live out their days without friends, without community.

The old Transman, clad in black shuffled along the avenue carrying his heavy pack of books. As usual he took notes:
>   *Our world is sitting on the edge of a precipice—which way will it go?*

Made sketchy sentences on a small pad of paper he carried in his pocket, on the human drama surrounding. Observed 2 serious punks:

The female, silver studded clothing over her scant frame, a vest, shit-kicking knee-high lace-up brogans, punk hair, tattoos, piercings, with a pet rat riding on one shoulder; white fur with pink feet gripped into the material of her vest.
People. The world. SF, a metropolis. Every flavor is here.

This jungle of screaming, hollering clawing monkeys, who must make peace with their sisters & brothers.

64.
People are better off if they follow a religion. This is a very basic crude and material world. Religion keeps the mind fastened on the higher ways. It has specific rules for behavior and tenets of redemption.

So this is the final Work, the societal Work. This group possibility of Creators people to achieve a higher planet.

Torah's 10 commandments says nothing of rights—it is commandments. We have the free will to obey them or not too. We being of a higher mind, and seeking a higher path and having learned thru previous sad experience how it is to live otherwise—in darkness, stumbling upon the lower paths--- have given ourselves to God to obey. —Then all else is granted to us. And we live in a perfect world. Perfect meaning humanly perfect, upon an earth-plane, which is not heaven, which is full of errors, mistakes and compressed by the pressure of dark forces. Our world is however made far better by obedience to God. In a case presented by Torah a body is found outside the city limits. The elders of the two closest towns go and measure the distance of that body from the edge of their towns—and the one, which is closest must take the situation in hand. The religious leaders of that town assemble. A blood sacrifice is made and prayers are said to please God. From that point on that particular parcel of land is cursed. Until the murderer is found the owner of it cannot plant nor work its earth, but propitiation to God has taken place. The prayers of the elders during this sacrifice, are the swearing they have done all they could for the dead person while he/she was still living. Fed them during their stay, and upon their departure have provided then an escort out of town. Further interpretations from the

Talmud say this includes to have given the person a way to earn a livelihood while in the town. Ultimately what rabbis ascertain, it means they had done a reasonable job of social responsibility for a stranger in their midst.

Our world has grown from the days of ancients, it is becoming one planet interrelated thru jurisdictions, treaties, trade agreements, international law. The blood of all victims of social inequity is on everybody's hands. So that's why Amerikkka and the rest of the world has to wake up!

More about Social Justice, in regards to the Utah miners. 6 coal miners in Utah recently died underground. While hope for life still existed, 3 more men were sent to rescue them—who were also killed by the treacherous shifting weight of the unstable mountain. All simultaneous rescuers tunneling from different directions in to save them were then withdrawn. Sheer greed and corporate kapitalism was the cause of this loss of life! Highly unsafe mining being done inside this weakened and compromised mountain, where no one should ever have ventured to begin with. Human greed of the owners to try to pull out the last million dollars in coal—with no regard for the lives of workers. This same week 2,000 miners have lost their lives in China, due to flooding. Their desperate and hysterical relatives then stormed the mining company headquarters tearing it apart. The Chinese now see what imitating U$ Kapitalism brings upon them! We have a human responsibility to each other. Says Deuteronomy 23. Social responsibility & justice!

This is a good way to wrap up JOURNEY—the end as it was in the beginning. Bereshiet. I talked about justice in the beginning during my rants in Lamentations, wrapping this up with the final work, I will speak again about the Work of Justice.

> *24 hours a fucken' day I slept down under the underpass.*
> --Homeless tramp, 2007.

People with no homes are sleeping everywhere in unsafe and unhealthy conditions. The human body must lay down to rest. The human body needs shelter, safety, peace, food, medicine, education, and jobs. Why aren't we providing for the least among us? ---An increasingly growing number. Those who can't work must be cared for. Those who are able must work some kind of job. This is individual responsibility first and foremost, reinforced by community responsibility equally.

Justice—for coal miners & others engaged in hazardous employment, including sex workers.
Justice—for victims of murder & assault; assuming responsibility both domestic and international, as global responsibility.

Spoke @ Grace with A, a young woman whose first hand testimony provides more evidence that Korprate Kapitalism slowly is killing the planet. She lives in the town of Arcadia in Humboldt county. Their economy is depressed, because a large rich corporate family bought up forestland previously held under strict ecological mandates, and then began illegally clear cutting. This corrupt, vile family business leveled the ground to thousands of acres of tree stumps; took all this profit out of it, putting nothing back, and now business has come to a standstill. They are killing the planet.

Works, Dear Children. To defend the forests whose tree leaves oxygenate our planet, whose roots hold the soil from erosion!

Works:
Thinking, studying, feeling, becoming informed of world issues— then acting. In the ancient Hebrew tradition, the spirit of Tikkun Olam.

Justice for all Human & Animal life that started out of a sperm & egg; Gods fine machinery set in motion by breath of a soul spoken--- Mipi Eil--- out of God's mouth into existence.

As previously stated in the DOC Handbook (Book 3.) our goal will be to work to end human & animal suffering on earth.

Ideals of justice. Justice for nations, for individuals, justice for rights of native American tribes, justice for all native peoples of earth, tribal people in South America, Aborigines in Australia, the Maoris in New Zealand; native peoples of Tahiti, Hawaii; justice for Chinese and Korean female victims 'comfort women' of Japans soldiers in World

War 2, justice for women, children, men, of Hiroshima and Nagasaki, Japan Atom bomb survivors of World War 2.

We must turn our planetary knowledge to raise the quality of life—no more cats all the time hiding from dogs. People hiding from each other. Women hiding from men.

Dear Mohammad, Most Compassionate, please bless the animals 3 legged thru human neglect.

Dear Jesus, please heal & make whole this entire planet.

My last injunctions Dear Children: stick to the Rule. —The Golden Rule. Let your feet stay on The Path. Never discount anybody. Avoid your enemy. Be ever cognizant of that Mortal enemy to the human race, who has been previously discussed. Pray always for protection from It. Be Positive!

I would be heard.

I give God the credit for this book because lets face it, I did not invent myself, and did not create the circumstances of my birth, which shaped me, which 'grew me'. Do give myself credit for:
    1. Answering the Call at a young age when there was no encouragement to be a writer—a most nebulous subject.
    2. Remaining sensitive.

All I know is not by study but by intuition & revelation.

To assure you God made me with all my desire for acquisition, for power, for sex lust & for love both human-earth bound, and agape and for the divine uplifted.

Please excuse my battered Hebrew, and misspellings of the Kings English.

    ***

Another year heading our way, the liturgical process both Hebrew and Christian gone round laboriously amid infinite increments of drash, sermons, Amidah's & so forth. So the great Mandela turns, in it all people, creatures, sea monsters, land and earth and sky. Another year passes, processing our souls. —Dear Mohammad, may our souls be rinsed clean and not get more blackened with sin and crimson with spilled blood.

> Meditations; Visualize this:
> *The whole world is a snail, which must shit.*

Works:
To see visions. The Pieta, carved of marble by Michelangelo. Painted by numerous renaissance painters, and early artesian. The Madonna holds the infinite Jesus at her naked breast—our Savior calling for his Mama!

> Jesus: *Mama! Mama!*

So today we are babies, barely clothed with a small cloth, naked, held in Jesus' arms; we are each individually held to Her/His breast. We are ordained to come into the world, maturing, learning, and to do the Work!

> The Work of Tikkun Olam! Justice.
> The Work of Love! Agape, far reaching!
> The Work of Building.
> The Work of Teaching.
> The Work of championing those animals, plants, prisoners of human kind who can do no more then plead in silence for peace.

Remember God knows all. Ask why S/He created dinosaurs, knowing they would 2 billion year later become thru process of time wearing down and metamorphose, oil for human use. And God replies, *it's not how I did it but that I did it.*

And now to think nations are murdering each other over this oil, 2 billion years later! Instead of using the oozy black stuff wisely for human comfort for all!

Luke 12: 49-56:
> I am come to send fire on the earth; how I wish it was already kindled. I have a baptism to be baptized and how I am pained until it is accomplished. Do you think I came to bring peace to the earth? I tell you no, I came to bring division.

Isaiah 5:1-7:
> The Lord said;
> I will sing a song
> About my friends vineyard
> That was on the side
> Of a fertile hill.
> My friend dug the ground,
> Removed the stones,
> And planted the best vines.
> He built a watchtower
> And dug a pit in rocky ground
> For pressing the grapes.
> He hoped they would be sweet,
> But bitter grapes were all it produced.
>
> Listen people of Jerusalem
> And of Judah!
> You be the judge of me
> And my vineyard,
> What more could I have done
> For my vineyard?
> I hoped for sweet grapes
> But bitter grapes
> Were all that grew.
>
> Now I will tell you
> What I am gong to do with my vineyard.
> I will cut down the hedge
> And tear down the wall.
> My vineyard will be trampled,
> And left in ruins.
> It will turn into a desert,
> Neither pruned nor hoed;

It will be covered
With thorns and briars.
I will command the clouds
Not to send rain.

I am the Lord all-Powerful!
Israel is the vineyard,
And Judah is the garden
I tended with care.
I had hoped for honesty
And for justice.
But dishonesty
And cries for mercy
Were all I found.

I want to remind you in this, our country that the eyes of the world are on us & we've been shitting all over the globe like a baby not even in diapers; us, U$, the world foremost super-power, an infant. In it's fist nuclear weapons. In its head a demented ideology that is nihilistic having no thought, nor practicality behind it; a baby, staggering drunken, greedily and bloodthirsty possessed with a selfish heart not yet mature.

65.
Works:
Community Thrift Store on Valencia. Recycling by making old junk useful. Turnip and I go shopping for pennies. He finds an old Mayan calendar engraved on a bronze platter & a battered wooden cassette tape holder. Cassettes are a past & gone technology so they are everywhere! Free, and better sounding then the modern new discs. Here an old Remington Rand typewriter sits in state a mirror to those of the future from the past. You see in memory mother's crystal chandeliers dangling from her living & dining room ceilings decorated in bourgeois materialism which we had to take down and clean yearly dipping each diadem in a bath of ammonia & sudsy water; things of the stale, stifled memories fresh as if they had happened yesterday—of the childhood torture which refined my perversity, and under whose depression I labor today. Pick up the following volume, dusty of curious forgotten lore:

'I never had a mother."
-- Honre de Balzac.

This was a cruel exaggeration, written in a moment of anger. But a child's feelings are nonetheless acute for being in part unwarranted. There are bastards of the imagination born in wedlock who nevertheless feel themselves to be rejected by their parents, without knowing why. These more then others long for worldly triumphs to compensate for their deep-rooted sense of loss.

--Andre Maurois 1965.

65.
I hope this book will open the doors of your perception. High art is a gift from the most Illustrious God & anybody who uses it under the sway of demigods influence for a mass sweep of humanity with infectious ideas, is evil and dishonest. Don't underestimate the power of high art used as propaganda. I prey for the protection of the people around me that I don't lead them into sin—nor corrupt them, nor that anything might be written or said by me might make them fall. I prey that if this does happen that God Almighty will shield them and be their protection withier or not they are capable of believing in Him/Her. And if they must fall that it is a Felix Culpa. A lucky fall during which the robes of ignorance are stripped off their eyes and tho they are snatched bare and naked, they are also become sighted and free.

> Oh Lord of hosts,
> How long will you be angered despite the prayers of your people?
> You have fed them with the bread of tears;
> You have given them bowls of tears to drink.
> You have made us the derision of our neighbors,
> And our enemies laugh us at us in scorn.
>
> ---Holy Bible.

***

The human race has proven time and time again it cannot be trusted. It cannot be trusted with the keeping of farm animals in a humane fashion, like a small child who begs for a pet, later neglects and starves his/her charge. It has proven it is incompetent as long as personal greed goes unfettered!

We are in a day, fast approaching, the last days of earth—of the human spirits thereon. S/he will be calling Her children home.

66.
From Buddhist nun Pema Chodron:

> "Tho our lives may seem far from perfect we have excellent circumstances. We have intelligence. The availability of teachers… ibid… study and meditation. But some of us will die before the year is up. The next 5 years some of us might be in too much pain to concentrate on Buddhist teachings much less live by it."

Bodichitta in Buddhism means "the Awakened Heart." From it we gather that each birth is precious. There is enough pain, enough contentment within each life to stimulate, yet pacify the individual to allow them to work each day. There is a fleeting window of opportunity rapidly fading—in which to do great works.

> "We can't tell what tomorrow will bring. Moreover many of us will become more distracted by worldly pursuits—for two, ten, twenty years or the rest of our lives--& no longer have the leisure to free ourselves from the rigidity of self absorption…
> …The Buddha's point is not to squander our good fortune."

Buddhists call revelation, or enlightenment, the spirit of awakening. The Path to Enlightenment, is the most important part of our Journey.

Again from Buddhist nun Pema Chodron:
> "We can't overestimate the power of commitment until we resolve unequivocally to undertake a task and see it thru to the end. There is always hesitation & vacillation. Therefore Shantideva calls on an egoless courage that is not easily threatened & goes foreword."

Well this is to tell you Dear Children, in closing, that it necessary for you to awake! And then to go industriously on your Works of Peace, Liberty, Justice & Love, to aid human evolution.

Many religious doctrines I disagree with most of it. Some students just take the bad with the good. I disagree. —We can choose electively what principals and disciplines to keep or throw away, for ourselves—but the ideal end result will be still a condition of holy poverty, forgiveness, social action in the spirit of Tikkun Olam, sharing with those walking The Path along side of us. The 'ideal life' is not to resemble a lazy student who by taking all the easiest courses at university graduates in gymnasium, bowling, and thinking they will graduate with honors.

As you see I have presented several different religious disciplines to you, for you to choose among them in your spiritual journey, or to adapt parts of each for yourself. To keep all, or some, of any. There is no law against this! We are free! Now let us begin! Each day is the first day of your life! Begin your Journey!

Works:
Found tie in a pile of discarded clothes on the street coming home at night—giveaways. It's blue, sufficiently long. Clean and *free!*

Let your step be lightened. Says the Most High God, to him, and the old Transman, a figure in black; black hat and heavy backpack who had been shuffling on donated shoes, began to jiggle and then fairly dance up the street.

The human body is a perfect body I have given you. Says the Lord. I see the nuns clothed in white garments practicing smart dietary control. The yoga's practice breath and diet. The monks dine simply and do scheduled work every day, throughout their lives. Know the monastic monks are among the world's most longed lived individuals often attaining years into the 90's.

67.

--Further Commentary: Buddhism is not a God worship so even better to fit in with the divine plan! It is a discipline, which all DOC members must undertake.

Awhile ago I spoke to the Lord regarding my painting—neglected for 30 years & the Spirit told me;

Do it while you can.

I now offer you the following—a collaboration in Spirit over time/space—inspired by the gurus I read in stand-up poverty @ Fields bookstore on Polk Strassa; specifically from Buddhists, especially nun Pema Chodron:

The great Buddhist teachers says we are blessed—there's time; tho we are far from happy we are housed, we can get food without too much difficulty, we have the tools to create, the power to assemble, the mind to understand, the use of limbs and senses to perform tasks. "this brief fleeing window of opportunity" might never come again. Now is the time to act—while we can.

I want to tell you that I am not a rabbi, nor a minister, nor a mullah. Having not gone to rabbinical school nor spent years in a religious university. I am a prophet and an artist and a builder.

Further I have not extensively studied the holy Bible nor Torah; much less Koran and Buddhist teachings. Having learned little outside of bible, and torah studies, and things overheard in intellectual discourse among my peers. And all this, in separate places, not together. The Jewish in one place. the Christian in another. The Buddhist mostly among Agnostics who seem able to tolerate that one the easiest.

What I have, has been given to me, by the most High God, according to my pre-existing interests. Which means that I was already a seeker. Already furious, and hungry, for social justice & liberation for all people, including myself, from worldly enslavements. Carrying the banner and marching in liberation demonstrations thru many decades in several cities. I marched in the second row behind

Martin Luther King and other dignitaries in the Chicago SNCC demonstration of the early 60's.

I have been educated on the streets, and by reading free socialist literature and Maoist handouts and communist propaganda, more readily available then the right wing conservative propaganda published by plutocrats.

Also those passages copied in quotes, which I attributed to their authors may be less then accurate because of doing this in bookstores pen in hand, backpack slung over my shoulder—since I could afford to buy none of them.

I've said it before—people are not made to live in ghettos. Black people aren't made to live in them, transpeople are not made to live in them, gay & lesbian people are not made to be set outside the common mass—because ours is a sorry world. We belong to the greater world. Its fine to get together with others like yourselves but not to live your life there exclusively 24-7! Transsexuals eat their young. We are a thankless people. Its not life, it's a ghetto, it's a prison.

Some of the sorriest people alive today are the lower caste of the worlds black people & black Africans. Could it be because they are the world's oldest people---it is a fact our whole human species has arisen from Africa. This is the place from which all tribes of humans evolved from a single family, moving out across the globe in millennial migrations. From 7 women the microchrodial DNA of our human race is traced. Could it be because the original sins of mankind were committed there, in the deeps of Africa, the first murders, betrayals, corruptions? My African American roots have given me strength. And endurance, and patience—and the will to overcome. As a child in the early 1950's closer to the reports of the very last slaves just then dying out; slaves, who were part of my ancestry, I was inspired to get back what they had lost. Inspired to determination because I was given my freedom by their past struggles and endurances and sufferings so that I could arise and do great things---things they were suppressed from doing. On the counterpart of the lower caste example, there is the evolved black person who can be higher then many of their contemporaries of different races because of them knowing those struggles, having those strengths, having been exposed to those trials directly themselves and also thru seeing their relatives and neighbors around them undergoing pain and thus developing a higher insight, a deeper compassion, a greater experience from which to draw as they entire the theatre of the world. As a Higher, more evolved person.

I'm sure my ideas will be insulting to many—I would feel like a failure if they were not! I am sick of this stupid world and its copouts and side-steppings. A great change is needed. A great change is in order. And a great change is coming.

Works:
Attend Benedictine Society. Grace is alive & bustling with people like bees in a giant beehive.

They all come to me. Says God. I hear their footfalls. Heavy. Or shuffling. Light as a feather. Those silent. Those who must be carried—infants, the sick; the very old. *Mine.* Says God. *All are Mine. Out of My hands they come and into My hands they will return.* Even as everything turns to dust all our great works, going into ruins like mighty cities.

I would bring fire to the earth—oh that it was already kindled.

Suddenly given the understanding upon leaving Grace while high in the Spirit, to step aside for the children of this world who go pushing upon their way; their time is short. They act out their impatience, selfishness, even cruelty because they don't know what they are doing. This has happened repeatedly while leaving Grace; i.e. some woman yakking on cellphone driving fast, cutting the corner too close behind me, and me cursing her at top of my lungs. Or some male asshole the bumper of his car coming too close up upon me at the crosswalk. Tonight as I descend the hill at the corner a man, intent on his way is charging along and I stepped back, unlike my usual self who would have ploughed on ahead. It is like the understanding has come on me at least this evening, *the understanding come into me* in a way that I can be obedient. The way of this world is short. People will live on this simple death-bound plane in an unconscious reality until their last moment, or they will transcend, mature.

Regarding---'given the understanding'. This phrase means, for instance a scripture of holy text one may already know, in fact may have committed to memory, but all this still captured in the mind alone, and 'known' only on the intellectual level. Suddenly a transformation occurs inside the seekers heart—they are 'given the understanding.' Their heart is enlightened. Now the message of the meaning becomes incorporate into their entire being, enabling them far more to obey the lesson. This lesson which formerly was an impossible discipline.

Regarding:
> And all this... study, done... in separate places, not together. The Jewish in one place. the Christian in another.

Another idea to be done in the City of Compassionate Help would be the simultaneous study of Torah, Koran, Holy Bible, Buddhist Teachings, all together. Along with service to the Most High.

68.
Well WORKS, the final volume, is closing. I give it to you, in love & discipline.

I must tell you there are probably numerous mistakes in this. That these are the words directly from the hand of God who wrote them thru me, but that I transposed some first on paper then again onto disc. Transposed them sometimes half asleep. Others times walking, other times while standing up on lurching busses with a backpack on my shoulders. Whenever the Spirit hit me. And couldn't always decipher my handwriting later when copying them. And that I have tried to make apparent that strong language the Spirit has given me directly thru use of italics, indentations, or other variance in font, while afterward returning to a normal font for the continuation on of the thought which, tho inspired, was not directly spoken to me by God, but is the intellectual reasoning's of myself following the first brilliant flash of idea.

Remember:

The glorification of beauty in our society is a false god. Not just because it belittles and creates a caste system of the beautiful alpha person and all secondary less-thens; how about deformed people? People who have been in terrible accidents? God want us to see what real love is, and how it must be shared between all the human species! We've got to get back to the basics! What a terrible love this other is! What a superficial love!

Remember:
To love them because you love their soul.

Remember:
Divine justice is just that—divine. Vengeance is not for humans to carry out, out of their own minds, but for God, and the workings God has set up for that purpose from above. It is our job to let go, to forgive, to move on; stepping aside as the instigator is swept on to their fate.

In the name of God the Compassionate, the Merciful here is my Work.

I am blessed, having been 'given time adequate, quietude necessary for reflection'.

I am doing this from the heart—as a writer, I'm taking notes, thus I have prepared a book for the world.

I could say prophets are a dime a dozen. God speaks, the prophet hears the message and takes it, by some means and reveals it to others. God created us, and reveals Gods Self to Her/His creation with pleasure, yet few are listening.

I'm a soldier in the army of the Lord...

The sheep is everybody. This one, that one. One of the multitude. The protaganist of the story. On their Journey. No longer an individual named Red, no longer named anybody in particular. This special sheep is different from the herd. For He/she is traveling up the Red Road. Taking earthly salvation quite serious.

A figure lays on a marble slab nearly naked but for a cloth wrapped abut loins and chest. This marble slab is an alter, it is raised up above the common world. This figure is the priest. This is education, deep waters, solitary, what is needed to find God.

--WORKS, 2007

A spiritual revolution. A changing of dynasties of earth.

Listen!
I look down the corridors of memory. You can hear/see one approaching. One, of God. God's Prophet. God the Eternal for Whom there is no Name.

I'm marching up the Kings Highway.

69.
Somewhere between heaven & hell, situated in ordinary time sits the earth. It is traversed by many paths & walks of life. On it is a Golden Road, a Royal Road, the Red Road, The Path, The Kings Highway— all being one and the same, that Way above the billions of common ways. And I'm marching along this Kings Highway.

Wisdom. This Way is a road of Wisdom.

This Way is a road of revolution, change, love, and building. Of community, companionship, prayer, worship, sacrifice and sharing. Of all good things Creator shall give to us, as we go along.

Well… Journey-- & then we're there…

Red Jordan Arobateau
August 22, 2007
3:00 AM Pacific Standard Time
San Francisco, CA
USA

www.ingramcontent.com/pod-product-compliance
Lightning Source LLC
Chambersburg PA
CBHW021913180426
43198CB00034B/166